Mometrix
TEST PREPARATION

GACE

Spanish
Secrets Study Guide

Dear Future Exam Success Story

First of all, **THANK YOU** for purchasing Mometrix study materials!

Second, congratulations! You are one of the few determined test-takers who are committed to doing whatever it takes to excel on your exam. **You have come to the right place.** We developed these study materials with one goal in mind: to deliver you the information you need in a format that's concise and easy to use.

In addition to optimizing your guide for the content of the test, we've outlined our recommended steps for breaking down the preparation process into small, attainable goals so you can make sure you stay on track.

We've also analyzed the entire test-taking process, identifying the most common pitfalls and showing how you can overcome them and be ready for any curveball the test throws you.

Standardized testing is one of the biggest obstacles on your road to success, which only increases the importance of doing well in the high-pressure, high-stakes environment of test day. Your results on this test could have a significant impact on your future, and this guide provides the information and practical advice to help you achieve your full potential on test day.

Your success is our success

We would love to hear from you! If you would like to share the story of your exam success or if you have any questions or comments in regard to our products, please contact us at **800-673-8175** or **support@mometrix.com**.

Thanks again for your business and we wish you continued success!

Sincerely,
The Mometrix Test Preparation Team

Need more help? Check out our flashcards at:
http://mometrixflashcards.com/GACE

Written and edited by the Mometrix Exam Secrets Test Prep Team
Printed in the United States of America

TABLE OF CONTENTS

INTRODUCTION 1

SECRET KEY #1 – PLAN BIG, STUDY SMALL 2

SECRET KEY #2 – MAKE YOUR STUDYING COUNT 3

SECRET KEY #3 – PRACTICE THE RIGHT WAY 4

SECRET KEY #4 – PACE YOURSELF 6

SECRET KEY #5 – HAVE A PLAN FOR GUESSING 7

TEST-TAKING STRATEGIES 10

LINGUISTICS, COMPARISONS, AND CULTURES/CROSS-DISCIPLINARY 15

- ELEMENTS OF LANGUAGE STRUCTURE 15
- PERSPECTIVES ON THE STUDY OF LANGUAGE 18
- LANGUAGE USE 20
- THEORIES OF FIRST- AND SECOND-LANGUAGE LEARNING 21
- FIRST CAMP: LANGUAGE LEARNING IS LIKE ALL OTHER HUMAN LEARNING 21
- SECOND CAMP: LANGUAGE LEARNING IS UNIQUELY SUPPORTED BY THE BRAIN 23
- SIMILARITIES AND DIFFERENCES IN LEARNING FIRST AND SECOND LANGUAGES 25
- STAGES AND PATTERNS IN SECOND-LANGUAGE LEARNING 27
- COMMUNICATING WITH STUDENTS 28
- INSTRUCTIONAL STRATEGIES 30
- ASSESSMENT STRATEGIES 32
- PHONOLOGY 35
- MORPHOLOGY 39
- ORTHOGRAPHY 44
- SYNTAX 47
- SEMANTICS AND PRAGMATICS 76
- LAWS REGARDING BILINGUAL EDUCATION 80
- MODELS OF BILINGUAL EDUCATION 83
- DEVELOPMENTAL PROCESSES IN BILINGUALISM AND BILITERACY 85
- ROLE OF CULTURE 86
- TARGET LANGUAGE INSTRUCTION IN THE BILINGUAL CLASSROOM 88
- CONTENT INSTRUCTION IN THE BILINGUAL CLASSROOM 90
- SPANISH GEOGRAPHY 91
- SPANISH HISTORY: 700-1492 91
- SPANISH LITERATURE AND ART DURING THE MIDDLE AGES 92
- SPANISH HISTORY: 1492-1807 92
- SPANISH LITERATURE AND ART: 1492-1807 93
- SPANISH HISTORY: 1808-1935 95
- SPANISH LITERATURE AND ART: 1808-1935 96
- SPANISH HISTORY: 1936-PRESENT 98
- SPANISH LITERATURE AND ART: 1936-PRESENT 99
- SPANISH CULTURAL PRACTICES AND PERSPECTIVES 100
- LATIN AMERICAN GEOGRAPHY 101

Pre-*Conquista* Latin American Civilizations to the 1500s ____ 106
Conquista and Colonial Periods in Latin America: 1500s-1750 ____ 107
Movements and Modernism in Latin America: 1750-1900 ____ 108
Latin American Revolutions and Post-Modernism: ~1900-1960 ____ 110
The "Boom" and "Post-Boom" in Latin American Literature: 1960-1980s ____ 114
Latin American Cultural Practices and Perspectives ____ 115

Listening, Reading, Writing, Speaking ____ 117
General Test-Taking Strategies ____ 117
Listening ____ 117
Reading ____ 118
Speaking ____ 120
Writing ____ 121

GACE Practice Test ____ 127
Listening ____ 127
Reading Comprehension ____ 134
Cultural Knowledge and History ____ 143
Writing–Response to a Personal Letter ____ 149
Writing–Opinion/Position Essay ____ 149
Writing–Respond to a Passage ____ 149
Speaking–Respond to a Passage ____ 151
Speaking–Oral Presentation ____ 152
Speaking–Conversation Topic ____ 152

Answer Key and Explanations ____ 153
Listening ____ 153
Reading Comprehension ____ 154
Cultural Knowledge and History ____ 156
Writing–Response to a Personal Letter ____ 157
Writing–Opinion/Position Essay ____ 158
Writing–Respond to a Passage ____ 159
Speaking–Respond to a Passage ____ 160
Speaking–Oral Presentation ____ 160
Speaking–Conversation Topic ____ 161

How to Overcome Test Anxiety ____ 163

Online Resources ____ 169

Introduction

Thank you for purchasing this resource! You have made the choice to prepare yourself for a test that could have a huge impact on your future, and this guide is designed to help you be fully ready for test day. Obviously, it's important to have a solid understanding of the test material, but you also need to be prepared for the unique environment and stressors of the test, so that you can perform to the best of your abilities.

For this purpose, the first section that appears in this guide is the **Secret Keys**. We've devoted countless hours to meticulously researching what works and what doesn't, and we've boiled down our findings to the five most impactful steps you can take to improve your performance on the test. We start at the beginning with study planning and move through the preparation process, all the way to the testing strategies that will help you get the most out of what you know when you're finally sitting in front of the test.

We recommend that you start preparing for your test as far in advance as possible. However, if you've bought this guide as a last-minute study resource and only have a few days before your test, we recommend that you skip over the first two Secret Keys since they address a long-term study plan.

If you struggle with **test anxiety**, we strongly encourage you to check out our recommendations for how you can overcome it. Test anxiety is a formidable foe, but it can be beaten, and we want to make sure you have the tools you need to defeat it.

Secret Key #1 – Plan Big, Study Small

There's a lot riding on your performance. If you want to ace this test, you're going to need to keep your skills sharp and the material fresh in your mind. You need a plan that lets you review everything you need to know while still fitting in your schedule. We'll break this strategy down into three categories.

Information Organization

Start with the information you already have: the official test outline. From this, you can make a complete list of all the concepts you need to cover before the test. Organize these concepts into groups that can be studied together, and create a list of any related vocabulary you need to learn so you can brush up on any difficult terms. You'll want to keep this vocabulary list handy once you actually start studying since you may need to add to it along the way.

Time Management

Once you have your set of study concepts, decide how to spread them out over the time you have left before the test. Break your study plan into small, clear goals so you have a manageable task for each day and know exactly what you're doing. Then just focus on one small step at a time. When you manage your time this way, you don't need to spend hours at a time studying. Studying a small block of content for a short period each day helps you retain information better and avoid stressing over how much you have left to do. You can relax knowing that you have a plan to cover everything in time. In order for this strategy to be effective though, you have to start studying early and stick to your schedule. Avoid the exhaustion and futility that comes from last-minute cramming!

Study Environment

The environment you study in has a big impact on your learning. Studying in a coffee shop, while probably more enjoyable, is not likely to be as fruitful as studying in a quiet room. It's important to keep distractions to a minimum. You're only planning to study for a short block of time, so make the most of it. Don't pause to check your phone or get up to find a snack. It's also important to **avoid multitasking**. Research has consistently shown that multitasking will make your studying dramatically less effective. Your study area should also be comfortable and well-lit so you don't have the distraction of straining your eyes or sitting on an uncomfortable chair.

The time of day you study is also important. You want to be rested and alert. Don't wait until just before bedtime. Study when you'll be most likely to comprehend and remember. Even better, if you know what time of day your test will be, set that time aside for study. That way your brain will be used to working on that subject at that specific time and you'll have a better chance of recalling information.

Finally, it can be helpful to team up with others who are studying for the same test. Your actual studying should be done in as isolated an environment as possible, but the work of organizing the information and setting up the study plan can be divided up. In between study sessions, you can discuss with your teammates the concepts that you're all studying and quiz each other on the details. Just be sure that your teammates are as serious about the test as you are. If you find that your study time is being replaced with social time, you might need to find a new team.

Secret Key #2 – Make Your Studying Count

You're devoting a lot of time and effort to preparing for this test, so you want to be absolutely certain it will pay off. This means doing more than just reading the content and hoping you can remember it on test day. It's important to make every minute of study count. There are two main areas you can focus on to make your studying count.

Retention

It doesn't matter how much time you study if you can't remember the material. You need to make sure you are retaining the concepts. To check your retention of the information you're learning, try recalling it at later times with minimal prompting. Try carrying around flashcards and glance at one or two from time to time or ask a friend who's also studying for the test to quiz you.

To enhance your retention, look for ways to put the information into practice so that you can apply it rather than simply recalling it. If you're using the information in practical ways, it will be much easier to remember. Similarly, it helps to solidify a concept in your mind if you're not only reading it to yourself but also explaining it to someone else. Ask a friend to let you teach them about a concept you're a little shaky on (or speak aloud to an imaginary audience if necessary). As you try to summarize, define, give examples, and answer your friend's questions, you'll understand the concepts better and they will stay with you longer. Finally, step back for a big picture view and ask yourself how each piece of information fits with the whole subject. When you link the different concepts together and see them working together as a whole, it's easier to remember the individual components.

Finally, practice showing your work on any multi-step problems, even if you're just studying. Writing out each step you take to solve a problem will help solidify the process in your mind, and you'll be more likely to remember it during the test.

Modality

Modality simply refers to the means or method by which you study. Choosing a study modality that fits your own individual learning style is crucial. No two people learn best in exactly the same way, so it's important to know your strengths and use them to your advantage.

For example, if you learn best by visualization, focus on visualizing a concept in your mind and draw an image or a diagram. Try color-coding your notes, illustrating them, or creating symbols that will trigger your mind to recall a learned concept. If you learn best by hearing or discussing information, find a study partner who learns the same way or read aloud to yourself. Think about how to put the information in your own words. Imagine that you are giving a lecture on the topic and record yourself so you can listen to it later.

For any learning style, flashcards can be helpful. Organize the information so you can take advantage of spare moments to review. Underline key words or phrases. Use different colors for different categories. Mnemonic devices (such as creating a short list in which every item starts with the same letter) can also help with retention. Find what works best for you and use it to store the information in your mind most effectively and easily.

Secret Key #3 – Practice the Right Way

Your success on test day depends not only on how many hours you put into preparing, but also on whether you prepared the right way. It's good to check along the way to see if your studying is paying off. One of the most effective ways to do this is by taking practice tests to evaluate your progress. Practice tests are useful because they show exactly where you need to improve. Every time you take a practice test, pay special attention to these three groups of questions:

- The questions you got wrong
- The questions you had to guess on, even if you guessed right
- The questions you found difficult or slow to work through

This will show you exactly what your weak areas are, and where you need to devote more study time. Ask yourself why each of these questions gave you trouble. Was it because you didn't understand the material? Was it because you didn't remember the vocabulary? Do you need more repetitions on this type of question to build speed and confidence? Dig into those questions and figure out how you can strengthen your weak areas as you go back to review the material.

Additionally, many practice tests have a section explaining the answer choices. It can be tempting to read the explanation and think that you now have a good understanding of the concept. However, an explanation likely only covers part of the question's broader context. Even if the explanation makes perfect sense, **go back and investigate** every concept related to the question until you're positive you have a thorough understanding.

As you go along, keep in mind that the practice test is just that: practice. Memorizing these questions and answers will not be very helpful on the actual test because it is unlikely to have any of the same exact questions. If you only know the right answers to the sample questions, you won't be prepared for the real thing. **Study the concepts** until you understand them fully, and then you'll be able to answer any question that shows up on the test.

It's important to wait on the practice tests until you're ready. If you take a test on your first day of study, you may be overwhelmed by the amount of material covered and how much you need to learn. Work up to it gradually.

On test day, you'll need to be prepared for answering questions, managing your time, and using the test-taking strategies you've learned. It's a lot to balance, like a mental marathon that will have a big impact on your future. Like training for a marathon, you'll need to start slowly and work your way up. When test day arrives, you'll be ready.

Start with the strategies you've read in the first two Secret Keys—plan your course and study in the way that works best for you. If you have time, consider using multiple study resources to get different approaches to the same concepts. It can be helpful to see difficult concepts from more than one angle. Then find a good source for practice tests. Many times, the test website will suggest potential study resources or provide sample tests.

Practice Test Strategy

If you're able to find at least three practice tests, we recommend this strategy:

UNTIMED AND OPEN-BOOK PRACTICE

Take the first test with no time constraints and with your notes and study guide handy. Take your time and focus on applying the strategies you've learned.

TIMED AND OPEN-BOOK PRACTICE

Take the second practice test open-book as well, but set a timer and practice pacing yourself to finish in time.

TIMED AND CLOSED-BOOK PRACTICE

Take any other practice tests as if it were test day. Set a timer and put away your study materials. Sit at a table or desk in a quiet room, imagine yourself at the testing center, and answer questions as quickly and accurately as possible.

Keep repeating timed and closed-book tests on a regular basis until you run out of practice tests or it's time for the actual test. Your mind will be ready for the schedule and stress of test day, and you'll be able to focus on recalling the material you've learned.

Secret Key #4 – Pace Yourself

Once you're fully prepared for the material on the test, your biggest challenge on test day will be managing your time. Just knowing that the clock is ticking can make you panic even if you have plenty of time left. Work on pacing yourself so you can build confidence against the time constraints of the exam. Pacing is a difficult skill to master, especially in a high-pressure environment, so **practice is vital**.

Set time expectations for your pace based on how much time is available. For example, if a section has 60 questions and the time limit is 30 minutes, you know you have to average 30 seconds or less per question in order to answer them all. Although 30 seconds is the hard limit, set 25 seconds per question as your goal, so you reserve extra time to spend on harder questions. When you budget extra time for the harder questions, you no longer have any reason to stress when those questions take longer to answer.

Don't let this time expectation distract you from working through the test at a calm, steady pace, but keep it in mind so you don't spend too much time on any one question. Recognize that taking extra time on one question you don't understand may keep you from answering two that you do understand later in the test. If your time limit for a question is up and you're still not sure of the answer, mark it and move on, and come back to it later if the time and the test format allow. If the testing format doesn't allow you to return to earlier questions, just make an educated guess; then put it out of your mind and move on.

On the easier questions, be careful not to rush. It may seem wise to hurry through them so you have more time for the challenging ones, but it's not worth missing one if you know the concept and just didn't take the time to read the question fully. Work efficiently but make sure you understand the question and have looked at all of the answer choices, since more than one may seem right at first.

Even if you're paying attention to the time, you may find yourself a little behind at some point. You should speed up to get back on track, but do so wisely. Don't panic; just take a few seconds less on each question until you're caught up. Don't guess without thinking, but do look through the answer choices and eliminate any you know are wrong. If you can get down to two choices, it is often worthwhile to guess from those. Once you've chosen an answer, move on and don't dwell on any that you skipped or had to hurry through. If a question was taking too long, chances are it was one of the harder ones, so you weren't as likely to get it right anyway.

On the other hand, if you find yourself getting ahead of schedule, it may be beneficial to slow down a little. The more quickly you work, the more likely you are to make a careless mistake that will affect your score. You've budgeted time for each question, so don't be afraid to spend that time. Practice an efficient but careful pace to get the most out of the time you have.

Secret Key #5 – Have a Plan for Guessing

When you're taking the test, you may find yourself stuck on a question. Some of the answer choices seem better than others, but you don't see the one answer choice that is obviously correct. What do you do?

The scenario described above is very common, yet most test takers have not effectively prepared for it. Developing and practicing a plan for guessing may be one of the single most effective uses of your time as you get ready for the exam.

In developing your plan for guessing, there are three questions to address:

- When should you start the guessing process?
- How should you narrow down the choices?
- Which answer should you choose?

When to Start the Guessing Process

Unless your plan for guessing is to select C every time (which, despite its merits, is not what we recommend), you need to leave yourself enough time to apply your answer elimination strategies. Since you have a limited amount of time for each question, that means that if you're going to give yourself the best shot at guessing correctly, you have to decide quickly whether or not you will guess.

Of course, the best-case scenario is that you don't have to guess at all, so first, see if you can answer the question based on your knowledge of the subject and basic reasoning skills. Focus on the key words in the question and try to jog your memory of related topics. Give yourself a chance to bring the knowledge to mind, but once you realize that you don't have (or you can't access) the knowledge you need to answer the question, it's time to start the guessing process.

It's almost always better to start the guessing process too early than too late. It only takes a few seconds to remember something and answer the question from knowledge. Carefully eliminating wrong answer choices takes longer. Plus, going through the process of eliminating answer choices can actually help jog your memory.

Summary: Start the guessing process as soon as you decide that you can't answer the question based on your knowledge.

How to Narrow Down the Choices

The next chapter in this book (**Test-Taking Strategies**) includes a wide range of strategies for how to approach questions and how to look for answer choices to eliminate. You will definitely want to read those carefully, practice them, and figure out which ones work best for you. Here though, we're going to address a mindset rather than a particular strategy.

Your odds of guessing an answer correctly depend on how many options you are choosing from.

Number of options left	5	4	3	2	1
Odds of guessing correctly	20%	25%	33%	50%	100%

You can see from this chart just how valuable it is to be able to eliminate incorrect answers and make an educated guess, but there are two things that many test takers do that cause them to miss out on the benefits of guessing:

- Accidentally eliminating the correct answer
- Selecting an answer based on an impression

We'll look at the first one here, and the second one in the next section.

To avoid accidentally eliminating the correct answer, we recommend a thought exercise called **the $5 challenge**. In this challenge, you only eliminate an answer choice from contention if you are willing to bet $5 on it being wrong. Why $5? Five dollars is a small but not insignificant amount of money. It's an amount you could afford to lose but wouldn't want to throw away. And while losing $5 once might not hurt too much, doing it twenty times will set you back $100. In the same way, each small decision you make—eliminating a choice here, guessing on a question there—won't by itself impact your score very much, but when you put them all together, they can make a big difference. By holding each answer choice elimination decision to a higher standard, you can reduce the risk of accidentally eliminating the correct answer.

The $5 challenge can also be applied in a positive sense: If you are willing to bet $5 that an answer choice *is* correct, go ahead and mark it as correct.

Summary: Only eliminate an answer choice if you are willing to bet $5 that it is wrong.

Which Answer to Choose

You're taking the test. You've run into a hard question and decided you'll have to guess. You've eliminated all the answer choices you're willing to bet $5 on. Now you have to pick an answer. Why do we even need to talk about this? Why can't you just pick whichever one you feel like when the time comes?

The answer to these questions is that if you don't come into the test with a plan, you'll rely on your impression to select an answer choice, and if you do that, you risk falling into a trap. The test writers know that everyone who takes their test will be guessing on some of the questions, so they intentionally write wrong answer choices to seem plausible. You still have to pick an answer though, and if the wrong answer choices are designed to look right, how can you ever be sure that you're not falling for their trap? The best solution we've found to this dilemma is to take the decision out of your hands entirely. Here is the process we recommend:

Once you've eliminated any choices that you are confident (willing to bet $5) are wrong, select the first remaining choice as your answer.

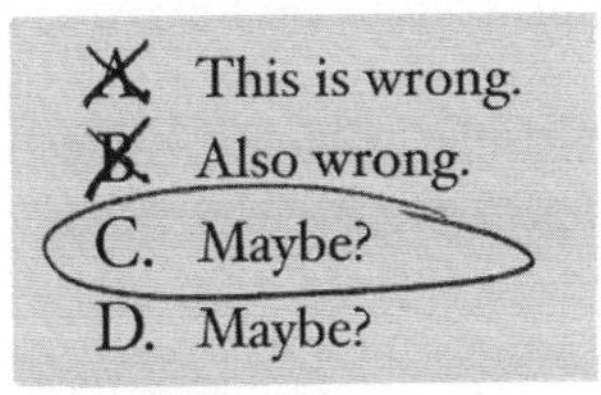

Whether you choose to select the first remaining choice, the second, or the last, the important thing is that you use some preselected standard. Using this approach guarantees that you will not be enticed into selecting an answer choice that looks right, because you are not basing your decision on how the answer choices look.

This is not meant to make you question your knowledge. Instead, it is to help you recognize the difference between your knowledge and your impressions. There's a huge difference between thinking an answer is right because of what you know, and thinking an answer is right because it looks or sounds like it should be right.

Summary: To ensure that your selection is appropriately random, make a predetermined selection from among all answer choices you have not eliminated.

Test-Taking Strategies

This section contains a list of test-taking strategies that you may find helpful as you work through the test. By taking what you know and applying logical thought, you can maximize your chances of answering any question correctly!

It is very important to realize that every question is different and every person is different: no single strategy will work on every question, and no single strategy will work for every person. That's why we've included all of them here, so you can try them out and determine which ones work best for different types of questions and which ones work best for you.

Question Strategies

☑ Read Carefully

Read the question and the answer choices carefully. Don't miss the question because you misread the terms. You have plenty of time to read each question thoroughly and make sure you understand what is being asked. Yet a happy medium must be attained, so don't waste too much time. You must read carefully and efficiently.

☑ Contextual Clues

Look for contextual clues. If the question includes a word you are not familiar with, look at the immediate context for some indication of what the word might mean. Contextual clues can often give you all the information you need to decipher the meaning of an unfamiliar word. Even if you can't determine the meaning, you may be able to narrow down the possibilities enough to make a solid guess at the answer to the question.

☑ Prefixes

If you're having trouble with a word in the question or answer choices, try dissecting it. Take advantage of every clue that the word might include. Prefixes can be a huge help. Usually, they allow you to determine a basic meaning. *Pre-* means before, *post-* means after, *pro-* is positive, *de-* is negative. From prefixes, you can get an idea of the general meaning of the word and try to put it into context.

☑ Hedge Words

Watch out for critical hedge words, such as *likely, may, can, often, almost, mostly, usually, generally, rarely,* and *sometimes.* Question writers insert these hedge phrases to cover every possibility. Often an answer choice will be wrong simply because it leaves no room for exception. Be on guard for answer choices that have definitive words such as *exactly* and *always.*

☑ Switchback Words

Stay alert for *switchbacks.* These are the words and phrases frequently used to alert you to shifts in thought. The most common switchback words are *but, although,* and *however.* Others include *nevertheless, on the other hand, even though, while, in spite of, despite,* and *regardless of.* Switchback words are important to catch because they can change the direction of the question or an answer choice.

⊘ Face Value

When in doubt, use common sense. Accept the situation in the problem at face value. Don't read too much into it. These problems will not require you to make wild assumptions. If you have to go beyond creativity and warp time or space in order to have an answer choice fit the question, then you should move on and consider the other answer choices. These are normal problems rooted in reality. The applicable relationship or explanation may not be readily apparent, but it is there for you to figure out. Use your common sense to interpret anything that isn't clear.

Answer Choice Strategies

⊘ Answer Selection

The most thorough way to pick an answer choice is to identify and eliminate wrong answers until only one is left, then confirm it is the correct answer. Sometimes an answer choice may immediately seem right, but be careful. The test writers will usually put more than one reasonable answer choice on each question, so take a second to read all of them and make sure that the other choices are not equally obvious. As long as you have time left, it is better to read every answer choice than to pick the first one that looks right without checking the others.

⊘ Answer Choice Families

An answer choice family consists of two (in rare cases, three) answer choices that are very similar in construction and cannot all be true at the same time. If you see two answer choices that are direct opposites or parallels, one of them is usually the correct answer. For instance, if one answer choice says that quantity *x* increases and another either says that quantity *x* decreases (opposite) or says that quantity *y* increases (parallel), then those answer choices would fall into the same family. An answer choice that doesn't match the construction of the answer choice family is more likely to be incorrect. Most questions will not have answer choice families, but when they do appear, you should be prepared to recognize them.

⊘ Eliminate Answers

Eliminate answer choices as soon as you realize they are wrong, but make sure you consider all possibilities. If you are eliminating answer choices and realize that the last one you are left with is also wrong, don't panic. Start over and consider each choice again. There may be something you missed the first time that you will realize on the second pass.

⊘ Avoid Fact Traps

Don't be distracted by an answer choice that is factually true but doesn't answer the question. You are looking for the choice that answers the question. Stay focused on what the question is asking for so you don't accidentally pick an answer that is true but incorrect. Always go back to the question and make sure the answer choice you've selected actually answers the question and is not merely a true statement.

⊘ Extreme Statements

In general, you should avoid answers that put forth extreme actions as standard practice or proclaim controversial ideas as established fact. An answer choice that states the "process should be used in certain situations, if..." is much more likely to be correct than one that states the "process should be discontinued completely." The first is a calm rational statement and doesn't even make a definitive, uncompromising stance, using a hedge word *if* to provide wiggle room, whereas the second choice is far more extreme.

✓ Benchmark

As you read through the answer choices and you come across one that seems to answer the question well, mentally select that answer choice. This is not your final answer, but it's the one that will help you evaluate the other answer choices. The one that you selected is your benchmark or standard for judging each of the other answer choices. Every other answer choice must be compared to your benchmark. That choice is correct until proven otherwise by another answer choice beating it. If you find a better answer, then that one becomes your new benchmark. Once you've decided that no other choice answers the question as well as your benchmark, you have your final answer.

✓ Predict the Answer

Before you even start looking at the answer choices, it is often best to try to predict the answer. When you come up with the answer on your own, it is easier to avoid distractions and traps because you will know exactly what to look for. The right answer choice is unlikely to be word-for-word what you came up with, but it should be a close match. Even if you are confident that you have the right answer, you should still take the time to read each option before moving on.

General Strategies

✓ Tough Questions

If you are stumped on a problem or it appears too hard or too difficult, don't waste time. Move on! Remember though, if you can quickly check for obviously incorrect answer choices, your chances of guessing correctly are greatly improved. Before you completely give up, at least try to knock out a couple of possible answers. Eliminate what you can and then guess at the remaining answer choices before moving on.

✓ Check Your Work

Since you will probably not know every term listed and the answer to every question, it is important that you get credit for the ones that you do know. Don't miss any questions through careless mistakes. If at all possible, try to take a second to look back over your answer selection and make sure you've selected the correct answer choice and haven't made a costly careless mistake (such as marking an answer choice that you didn't mean to mark). This quick double check should more than pay for itself in caught mistakes for the time it costs.

✓ Pace Yourself

It's easy to be overwhelmed when you're looking at a page full of questions; your mind is confused and full of random thoughts, and the clock is ticking down faster than you would like. Calm down and maintain the pace that you have set for yourself. Especially as you get down to the last few minutes of the test, don't let the small numbers on the clock make you panic. As long as you are on track by monitoring your pace, you are guaranteed to have time for each question.

✓ Don't Rush

It is very easy to make errors when you are in a hurry. Maintaining a fast pace in answering questions is pointless if it makes you miss questions that you would have gotten right otherwise. Test writers like to include distracting information and wrong answers that seem right. Taking a little extra time to avoid careless mistakes can make all the difference in your test score. Find a pace that allows you to be confident in the answers that you select.

✓ Keep Moving

Panicking will not help you pass the test, so do your best to stay calm and keep moving. Taking deep breaths and going through the answer elimination steps you practiced can help to break through a stress barrier and keep your pace.

Final Notes

The combination of a solid foundation of content knowledge and the confidence that comes from practicing your plan for applying that knowledge is the key to maximizing your performance on test day. As your foundation of content knowledge is built up and strengthened, you'll find that the strategies included in this chapter become more and more effective in helping you quickly sift through the distractions and traps of the test to isolate the correct answer.

Now that you're preparing to move forward into the test content chapters of this book, be sure to keep your goal in mind. As you read, think about how you will be able to apply this information on the test. If you've already seen sample questions for the test and you have an idea of the question format and style, try to come up with questions of your own that you can answer based on what you're reading. This will give you valuable practice applying your knowledge in the same ways you can expect to on test day.

Good luck and good studying!

Linguistics, Comparisons, and Cultures/Cross-Disciplinary

Elements of Language Structure

Phonology

Phonology is the study of the sound patterns of a language. Some important concepts in phonology include the following:

Phonemes

Phonemes are meaning-distinguishing sounds in a language. Adding the sound */r/* to the word **bat** creates a word with a new and totally distinct meaning: **brat**. Changing */b/* to */r/* in the word **bat** creates a word with a new and totally distinct meaning: **rat**. Therefore */b/* and */r/* are phonemes in English. Different languages have different sets of phonemes.

Allophones

Allophones are the physical sounds used to produce speech. One phoneme may have several allophones. For example, in Spanish, the phoneme */v/* may be pronounced */v/* or it may also be pronounced */b/*. Pronouncing */v/* as */b/* does not create a word with a new and totally distinct meaning: **bienvenidos** may be pronounced **bien*b*enidos** and still carry the same meaning.

Segmentals vs. Suprasegmentals

Segmentals are the phonemes used to create utterances in a language. Suprasegmentals are the non-phonemic factors used in speaking a language. Stress, intonation, and word juncture are examples of suprasegmentals. Suprasegmentals can be functional (creating different meaning) or non-functional (not creating different meaning). For example, in Spanish, syllabic stress can be a functional suprasegmental. (**H*á*blo** = *I talk*, **habl*ó*** = *he talked*.) The syllabic stress changes the meaning of the word.

Minimal Pairs and Sets

Minimal pairs and sets are pairs or groups of words that vary by only one phoneme. **Bat** and **rat** are a minimal pair in English, and **bat**, **cat**, **hat**, **mat**, **gnat**, **pat**, **rat**, **sat**, **tat**, and **vat** are a minimal set. Since phonemes differ from language to language, minimal pairs vary as well. For example, **caro** and **carro** are a minimal pair in Spanish but would not be in English.

Syllables and Clusters

Syllables must contain a vowel or a vowel-like sound. They may have a consonant or a consonant cluster before and/or after the vowel. Syllable structure can be denoted with C for a consonant and V for a vowel. For example, the syllable **at** is VC, the syllable **bat** is CVC, the syllable **brat** is CCVC, and the syllable **bank** is CVCC. Different languages have different allowable consonant clusters.

Coarticulation

Co-articulation is when one sound is made at almost the same time as a second sound because of our speed of speech. This can occur as <u>assimilation</u> (for example: say "**I can go**" quickly. The */n/* at the end of **can** and the */g/* at the beginning of **go** are pronounced almost together as the sound */ng/*). It can also occur as <u>elision</u>, when one sound is just left out (for example: say "**She opened the door**" quickly. The */d/* at the end of **opened** is not heard.)

Morphology

Morphology is the study of the basic meaning-carrying forms of language, or what words and other meaningful "chunks" of language are and how they are formed. Some important concepts in morphology include the following:

Morpheme

A morpheme is a "minimal unit of meaning or grammatical function". A basic word is a morpheme: for example, **play**. However, in the forms **play*ing***, **play*er***, and **play*ed***, the units ***-ing***, ***-er***, and ***-ed*** are also morphemes, units that carries meaning or grammatical function. **Play** is considered a free morpheme – it can exist and carry meaning on its own. ***-ing***, ***-er***, and ***-ed*** are examples of bound morphemes – they typically must be affixed to a free morpheme.

Affix

An affix is a "chunk" or a bound morpheme that is attached to a free morpheme in order to produce a new word. They can be prefixes (attached to the beginning of a word: ***dis*obey/*des*obedecer**), suffixes (attached to the end of a word: **talk*ing*/hablar*é***) or infixes (placed in the middle of a word: not typically used in English or in Spanish).

Derivational vs. Inflectional Morphology

Derivational morphology is the process by which a new word is created or a word is changed to be another part of speech by adding bound morphemes. **-er** is a derivational suffix, changing the verb **play** into a noun meaning "a person who plays": **play*er***. In Spanish, **-dor** is a similar derivational suffix, changing the verb **jugar** into a noun meaning "a person who plays": **juga*dor***. Derivational prefixes also exist in both languages (e.g. **dis-** in English and **des-** in Spanish)

Inflectional morphology is the process by which a word is modified to indicate grammatical function such as singular or plural, present tense or past tense. English has very few inflectional morphemes (**-s**, **-ing**, **-ed**, **-en**, **-er**, **-est**, **-'s**). Spanish has a much wider variety of inflectional morphemes. For example, to mark person in the present tense alone, the inflectional morphemes **-o**, **-as**, **-a**, **-amos**, **-áis**, and **-an** are all employed.

Roots and Stems

A root is a morpheme without any affixes, either derivational or inflectional. You may have heard it called a "base word". In the example above, **play** is a root. A stem is any word that has been inflected, minus the inflection. A stem may contain derivational morphemes. So, for example, in the word **players**, **play** is the root, **play*er*** is the stem, and ***-s*** is the inflection. In the word **desobedecimos**, **obedecer** is the root, ***des*obedecer** is the stem, and ***-imos*** is the inflection.

Allomorphs

Allomorphs are a set of morphs that communicate the same inflectional information. For example, in English, to communicate the idea of "plural", we can employ the morphs **-s** (**cat** – **cat*s***) and **-es** (**couch** – **couch*es***), as well as some irregular forms such as no change (**fish** - **fish**) and middle vowel change (**man** – **men**). This group of morphs that pluralize a word are called allomorphs. In Spanish, the morphs **-o** (**hablar** – **habl*o***) **-oy** (**estar** – **est*oy***) and **-go** (**tener** - **ten*go***) all communicate the inflectional information that the first person (I/yo) is completing the action in the present tense.

Syntax

Syntax is the study of the structure and order of components within phrases and sentences. Traditionally, the term "grammar" has been associated with syntax. Some important concepts in the field of syntax include the following:

Generative Grammar

Generative grammar is the set of rules for a given language from which all well-formed sentences can be generated. Additionally, only well-formed sentences will be generated if these rules are applied. This set of rules is finite, but can result in an infinite number of grammatically correct sentences.

Deep and Surface Structure

It is possible for two sentences to look different but still contain the same basic syntactic structure. "**I wrote the book/*Yo escribí el libro***" and "**The book was written by me/*El libro fue escrito por mí***" have different surface structure. However, on an underlying level (called deep structure), they are both formed with the same syntactic components – a first-person pronoun, a verb, and the noun phrase "**the book**". This same deep structure would be shared by even more sentences with different surface structure (e.g. **Did I write the book?/*¿Yo escribí el libro?***).

Structural Ambiguity

Sometimes two distinct deep structures can be expressed by the same surface structure. For example, the sentence "**Pedro hit the intruder with a baseball bat/*Pedro golpeó al intruso con el bate de béisbol.***" could come from the deep structure "**Pedro used a baseball bat to hit the intruder/*Pedro utilicó un bate para golpear al intruso***" or it could come from the deep structure "**Pedro hit the intruder who carried a baseball bat/*Pedro golpeó al intruso que llevó un bate***". This surface structure is an example of structural ambiguity – the sentence itself does not tell us which deep structure's meaning was intended.

Transformation

Transformation describes how the individual parts of a deep structure sentence can be arranged and rearranged into different surface structures. For example, in English, "**Juan gave Mary a gift yesterday**." can be rearranged with the adverb first:" "**Yesterday Juan gave Mary a gift**" or to be an interrogative "**Did Juan give Mary a gift yesterday?**" In Spanish, these transformations would be similar, although the interrogative transformation does not require as much: "***Juan le dio un regalo a Mary ayer.***" "***Ayer Juan le dio un regalo a Mary.***" "***¿Juan le dio un regalo a Mary ayer?***"

Recursion

Recursion is the ability to be repeated an infinite number of times. Generative grammar must be recursive. For example, a generative grammar rule states that a sentence may have a prepositional phrase describing an object's location (**The flowers are *on the table*/Las flores están *en la mesa***), and it may have a prepositional phrase describing the location of the object in the first prepositional phrase (**The flowers are on the table *in the kitchen*/Las flores están en la mesa *en la cocina***), and so on. Children's games and songs often take advantage of recursion ("The tree in the hole and the hole in the ground…").

Semantics

Semantics is the study of the meaning of words, phrases, and sentences. This is considered distinct from syntax, because an utterance can be syntactically correct but semantically "odd" (e.g. **The cake ate the children**). Some important concepts in the field of semantics include the following:

Semantic Roles

Words and phrases can be thought of and classified in terms of the role they play in a sentence. Verbs typically play the role of **action** Nouns and noun phrases can be the **agent** (doing the action), the **theme** (affected by the action), and, when used with prepositions, the **instrument** (the means of doing the action), the **location**, the **source**, or the **destination**.

Lexical Relations

The meanings of words can be thought of in relationship to each other. Words can be **synonyms** (start/begin, *empezar/comenzar*), **antonyms** (tall/short, *alto/bajo*), and **hyponyms** (dog/animal, *perro/animal*).

Homophones

Homophones are words with different written forms and different meanings but the same pronunciation. Some common English homophones are **two/to/too** and **bare/bear**. Because of its letter-sound correspondence, Spanish has fewer homophones than English. One example is ***ola/hola.***

Homonyms

Homonyms are words with the same written form and same pronunciation but two or more unrelated meanings. Some common English homonyms are **bat** (sports equipment, flying mammal) and **bank** (financial institution, side of a river). Most Spanish homonyms involve a form of a verb (e.g. ***calle***: street, subjunctive of verb *callar*).

Polysemy

Polysemy, in contrast to homonymy is when two or more words have the same form and different but related meanings. One English example is **bright** (more than sufficient amount of light, more than sufficient amount of intelligence). One Spanish example is ***cuello*** (neck of an individual, collar of a shirt).

Homophones, Homonyms, Polysemy, and Language Learning

Each language has its own set of homophones, homonyms and polysemes, and this can cause confusion and difficulty for language learners. For example, an English speaker learning Spanish may think that he can use ***banco*** to refer both to a financial institution and the edge of a river as he can use **bank** in English. However, in Spanish, ***banco*** only refers to the first, and ***orilla*** is used for the second.

Perspectives on the Study of Language

Classifications of Languages

Languages are often classified into "families" or organized in a "tree" with "branches", similarly to how we might chart our family tree. This is possible because our modern languages developed from a smaller number of older languages. For example, French, Italian, Portuguese, and Spanish all share a similar linguistic heritage, developing primarily from Latin. Therefore, they share many features with each other and with their common "parent" language and are considered a branch of a language "family". Linguists recognize approximately 30 distinct language families that at least 4000 of the world's more than 6000 languages can be categorized as belonging to.

Language Change

Language change has been occurring for as long as human language has existed and will continue to change as long as language is in use. Language change can occur at any and all levels of language – phonetics, morphology, syntax, and semantics.

Synchronic vs. Diachronic Change

Diachronic change is the change in language that happens over time, for example, how modern English has developed from the Middle English spoken 1000 years ago. Synchronic change is the change in language that happens at the same time but in different locations or among different groups of speakers. This can be easily seen in regional accents and word choices. An example of synchronic change in Spanish is how the *vosotros* pronoun is rarely used in Latin America but continues to be used in Spain.

Mechanisms of Language Change

- Phonemic splits and mergers: Phonemes can be divided, merged, or switched to create new pronunciations of words. For example, in most of the Spanish-speaking world, the phonemes pronounced */s/*and */th/* are no longer distinguishable. Therefore, the words **casa** and **caza** will be pronounced the same. However, in other regions, these two phonemes have not merged, and therefore **casa** is pronounced *CAH-sa*, and **caza** is pronounced somewhat like *CAH-tha*.
- Borrowing or loan words: A language can borrow a word from another language when there is no existing word for that concept. For example, the word **jeans** is commonly used as a loan word in Spanish-speaking countries.
- Euphemisms, taboos, and metaphors: Words can take on new meanings when used to avoid saying something unpleasant or unacceptable. For example, **passed away** is commonly used to mean **died** and **neurologically atypical** replaces **idiot** or **mentally retarded**. When words are used as a metaphor, they may also eventually gain that new meaning – many English and Spanish words come from Latin words that are related in concept but are used metaphorically (*spirare* = *to breathe* in Latin. **In*spira*ción/in*spira*tion** = *to blow into*, as in give creative life to).
- Folk etymologies: Words can undergo spelling or pronunciation changes when their etymology, or heritage, is misunderstood. For example, the English word **cockroach** is actually a borrowed word from the Spanish ***cucaracha***. However, the word **roach** is also used on its own to refer to these disgusting bugs, treating **cockroach** as if it were a compound word involving the English words **cock** and **roach**. The English word **roach** actually comes from the Middle English word ***roche***, referring to a specific kind of fish.

Language Use

Discourse Analysis

Discourse analysis is the study of linguistic exchanges between individuals, either written or spoken. It seeks to go "beyond the sentence" to look at larger chunks of utterances for patterns and meaning. For example, we can examine how speakers take turns in conversation and how they mark that it is the other speaker's turn or that they are done talking (e.g. **"Well,…" "…what do you think?"** ***"Bueno,…"*** or ***"…¿verdad?"***) Coherence, the use of words and phrases that help the listener/reader to link ideas and understand how they are meant to relate to each other, is another important part of extended discourse (e.g. ***"First…then…later…"*** or ***"Al contrario…de hecho…"*** When you take the speaking and writing sections of your exam, you will be judged on your discourse – how you use language in context, above the sentence level, to clearly communicate your ideas to your listener/reader. Discourse analysis also studies speech acts and pragmatics (see sections below).

Discourse Analysis in Writing

In extended written texts, there are norms for structure that go beyond the structure of each sentence. While these norms are not universally learned and applied like syntactic rules, and can be bent and broken more freely, they exist nonetheless. Your composition teacher may have sought to teach you these norms (e.g. start each paragraph with an introduction sentence and then only include information in that paragraph that is part of the topic you introduced).

Speech Acts

When language is used to perform an action or ask someone else to perform an action, it is called a speech act. Speech acts can be generally classified as commands (**Wash the dishes!/*¡Lave los platos!)***, questions (**Who washed the dishes?/¿Quién lavó los platos?**), and assertions (**The dishes need to be washed./*Hay que lavar los platos.***). A speech act can also be considered either direct or indirect. A direct speech act uses a form for its literal purpose, for example, using a command to give a command as in "**Wash the dishes!/*¡Lave los platos!***" An indirect speech act uses a form to accomplish something other than its literal purpose. For example, in the statement "**The dishes need to be washed./*Hay que lavar los platos.***", while the speech act is formed as an assertion, its purpose could be to command that someone wash the dishes – imagine a mother staring at a child, clearing her throat, and then saying "**The dishes need to be washed./*Hay que lavar los platos.***" In order to analyze and understand speech acts, we engage in many levels of observation and interpretation, using the context, our linguistic and interpersonal knowledge, the force and tone of the utterance, and many other factors.

Pragmatics

Pragmatics is the study of how context contributes to meaning. Demonstrative pronouns are an excellent example of the ubiquity and importance of pragmatics – the word **this** can have an infinite number of meanings and is correctly interpreted only in context. Indirect speech acts, such as the example above of the mother making an assertion that is actually a command, are another example of how context (the mother/child relationship, the mother's tone of voice and facial expression, etc.) can and does affect the meaning of language. Sentences often mean more than they literally say. A mob boss saying **"Nice car you have…it'd be a shame if something happened to it."**, a father saying **"You left the door open!"** and a guest saying **"A drink would be nice."** are all simple statements on face value, but are intended by the speaker to communicate something else (*a threat to harm the car, a command to shut the door*, and *a request for a drink*). Any factor that is a part of the non-linguistic context can influence the meaning of a linguistic utterance. Pragmatics are employed for a variety of reasons – ease of speech, avoiding taboos, diminishing the way a command or request imposes on another individual, or allowing the speaker or listener to save face. Different cultures employ different levels and types of pragmatic strategies.

Sociolinguistics

Sociolinguistics studies the relationships between language and society – how they interact, and how they modify and impact each other. Language changes and is modified by social features such as geographical location, socioeconomic class, education level, age group, gender, ethnicity, and contact with or knowledge of other languages. These elements affect all languages to various degrees depending on the particular social factors, constantly altering different parts of the language such as pronunciation, word choice, and sentence structure. With Spanish spoken in so many different countries, geographical location is one of the most significant sociolinguistic factors that affect it, and it is very important to pay attention to local nuances.

Theories of First- and Second-Language Learning

Theories of language learning can be roughly divided into two camps. One camp is of the opinion that language learning occurs the same way any other information or skill is learned. The other camp holds that language learning is unique from all other types of learning because the human brain is "hardwired" to learn language.

First Camp: Language Learning Is Like All Other Human Learning

Behaviorist/Environmentalist

The behaviorist or environmentalist view of language acquisition holds that children develop language the same way that all organisms learn everything. Their early linguistic responses to environmental stimuli are reinforced selectively by adults; children will repeat rewarded responses, while ignored responses are less likely to persist. In this view, learning occurs as children behave certain ways and receive reinforcement or punishment as a response to their behavior.

Skinner's Behaviorist Theory Explains the Process of Language Development

B. F. Skinner was a major proponent of the behaviorist or environmentalist view. According to Skinner's theory of Operant Conditioning, learning is a function of change that occurs in an organism's observable behaviors. Behaviorists see language development as a process of building behaviors through conditioning that occurs through interactions with the environment. Skinner stated that adults selectively reinforce young children's vocalizations which to them resemble recognizable speech and disregard those vocalizations they find irrelevant. Children will repeat reinforced responses. The child's responses gradually become more similar to adult speech through what Skinner called successive approximations. Skinner believed children acquire verbal behavior matching that of their "given verbal community" via this process. As their vocalizations approach recognized speech forms, these "produce appropriate consequences" for the children. Main principles include that positively reinforced behavior recurs, that responses can be shaped through presenting information in small increments, and that reinforcement promotes response generalization to other similar stimuli. Limitations of this view include that the rules and structure of language cannot be derived through sheer imitation, and that children often cannot repeat adult utterances.

APPLYING THE PRINCIPLES OF BEHAVIORIST THEORY REGARDING LANGUAGE LEARNING

In order to teach a new language, a teacher likely would introduce lessons in the target language and academic content subjects in small, manageable portions following the behaviorist principle of presenting new material in small amounts. This practice facilitates more precise shaping of new learned behaviors and enables language students to learn more easily. The educator would demonstrate the target language in spoken and written form in order to provide a model for students to imitate, another behaviorist principle. The teacher would be sure to reward correct student responses following the behaviorist principle of positive reinforcement, thereby increasing the students' likelihood of repeating these responses. Behaviorism finds that only outwardly observable and measurable behaviors can be changed and thus disregards internal states, which it cannot observe, measure, or change. As a result, the teacher would use tests, quizzes, in-class and homework assignments, etc. and score these assessments quantitatively in order to measure correct and incorrect responses. Increases in the former and decreases in the latter would indicate learning, which behaviorism defines as observable, measurable changes in behavior over time.

COGNITIVIST

In contrast to environmentalism and behaviorism, the cognitivist view of learning posits that learning occurs in mental processes, rather than external behaviors. In other words, what a child does is not as important as what a child is thinking. Cognitivism views internal mental activity rather than environmental stimuli as the source of learning.

PIAGET'S COGNITIVE DEVELOPMENTAL THEORY

Piaget was one of the first and most well-known cognitivists. He viewed language acquisition as part of a child's overall cognitive development; therefore he believed that language acquisition follows the stages of intellectual development he proposed. Piaget stated that to acquire any specific linguistic form, a child first must be able to understand its underlying concept. Piaget defined the stages of cognitive development as Sensorimotor, Preoperational, Concrete Operations, and Formal Operations. Children in Sensorimotor and Preoperational stages cannot perceive others' viewpoints; Piaget dubbed them egocentric. Sensorimotor infants first perform reflexive activities, and then learn to coordinate their sensations and motor movements. As they become aware of objects, infants develop object-orientation and object permanence (realizing objects continue to exist when out of their sight), then intentional actions. Infants develop mental constructs (schemata) representing objects. By age 2, they internalize these schemata, thereby enabling symbolic thinking—representing things/concepts with linguistic symbols, i.e. words. Concrete Operations-stage children can perform and reverse mental operations, but only regarding concrete objects. In Formal Operations they grasp and manipulate abstract concepts, including abstract word meanings (semantics) and operations (higher-order syntax, grammar, etc.).

Review Video: Piaget's Cognitive Development Theory
Visit mometrix.com/academy and enter code: 100376

CURRENT COGNITIVE THEORIES

McLaughlin is one of the most well-known modern cognitivists. He also holds that language learning occurs through general cognitive processes, and his ideas are sometimes called the "Information Processing Model". According to McLaughlin's model, some of the general mental skills that we use to learn language are transfer (finding connections with preexisting knowledge), simplification (attending only to what we understand), generalization (identifying patterns and rules), restructuring (changing where and how information is stored in our brains – like a computer), and automatization (being able to complete tasks without attending to them). Modern cognitive theory makes a distinction between declarative knowledge – knowing facts and information, and procedural knowledge - knowing how to do something. While language learning has historically been treated as gaining declarative knowledge, cognitivists argue that it be more helpful to think of language learning as the gaining of procedural knowledge.

Connectionist/Parallel Distributed Processing

In this view, knowledge is connections, not just the units being connected. Learning occurs by forming and traversing these neural connections. Therefore, gaining knowledge is not acquiring facts and abilities but building connections and using them to transmit information. This viewpoint shifts the focus of language learning from discrete pieces of knowledge (e.g. vocabulary or verb endings) to the ability to connect those pieces and use them in context.

Second Camp: Language Learning Is Uniquely Supported by the Brain

Nativist

Noam Chomsky is the major proponent of the nativist theory of language development. He maintains that humans possess an internal Language Acquisition Device (LAD), allowing them to generate linguistic structures more easily and naturally than they could without it. In contrast to behaviorists, Chomsky asserts that environmental factors influence, but do not determine, this process.

Noam Chomsky's LAD and His Syntactic Theory

Chomsky's Language Acquisition Device (LAD) is his theoretical construct representing an innate mechanism or tool set he says all humans possess for learning language. Chomsky asserts that since the brain is part of the body, the mental world is part of the biological world in which we live. As a result, the mental world follows biological processes. He designates language development as "language growth" in that the "language organ" grows in the brain like any other bodily organ. His Syntactic Theory explains that speakers understand internal sentence structure (syntax) via "phrase structure rules." His "poverty of stimulus" argument is that children hear many fragmented/ungrammatical/unstructured adult utterances, yet still construct correct grammars, which he views as evidence of universal, inborn language abilities. He also points out that children having different experiences still form the same linguistic rules.

Chomsky's Theory of Innate Language Development

Chomsky proposed the "Innateness Hypothesis", that all humans have an inborn ability to develop language. This is due to Universal Grammar (UG) or "Generative Grammar"—a set of linguistic rules with which our brains are pre-programmed. Chomsky says that this inherent blueprint or template for language structures explains why even deaf and/or blind children and/or children with deaf and/or blind parents develop language in the same ways, following the same stages, as do all other children. Chomsky has stated that language development is an inevitable occurrence with children rather than a voluntary action. In other words, given a suitable environment, including "appropriate nutrition and environmental stimulation," they will acquire language naturally, similarly to their predetermined physical maturation processes. Chomsky's UG does not contain specific rules of every language. Rather, it contains general "principles and parameters" from which language rules are derived.

Chomsky's Transformational Grammar

Noam Chomsky has proposed that language consists of "deep structures" and "surface structures." Deep structures are the forms in which linguistic concepts originate. He says our minds then perform "transformations" which change these deep structures to surface structures, which are the final forms of our spoken and written language. For example, a basic statement is a deep structure, and we transform it to make it grammatically complete. As a result, we turn the statement into a question or a negative, or both. A deep structure might convey "He is going out." Chomsky proposes that we automatically make transformations to this structure to turn it into a question: "Is he going out?" or a negative: "He is not going out;" or both: "He is not going out, is he?" So for Chomsky, the essential concept is the same, but the semantic changes, i.e. changes in meaning, and syntactic changes, i.e. changes in sentence structure that produce such variations as questions and negatives, are achieved through transformations from the same deep structure to various surface structures.

Approaches of Teaching That Reflects Chomsky's Theory of Language Acquisition

According to Chomsky, learning language is not something that children actually do, but is a natural process occurring universally in children as they develop. Chomsky has stated that we live in a biological world; the body—including the brain, and the "language organ" he believes our brains inherently possess—physically matures over time according to predetermined patterns. Chomsky proposed that we are born with a Language Acquisition Device (LAD) in our brains, thereby facilitating language development. He allowed that children need proper nutrition and environmental stimulation in order to nurture the natural language development enabled by the LAD. Therefore, language teachers would want to ensure their students receive optimal physical nourishment and stimulus-rich environments, under the teacher's influence at school and at home inasmuch as this is possible. Because Chomsky that found all humans share Universal Grammar (UG) regardless of individual languages, language teachers would emphasize basic commonalities between English and the target langugage in order to help students relate the two languages. Differences could be addressed through correcting target langugage errors over time as students' target language proficiency progresses.

Interactionist

Jerome Bruner was the main proponent of Interactionist theory, which says that interactions between the child and parents/caregivers determine the course of language development. This theory draws heavily from the constructivist concept of learning. Piaget often is credited with founding constructivist learning theory – the idea that learning is a process in which learners actively build, or construct, new concepts and ideas upon their foundations of existing knowledge. Piaget focused on the cognitive aspects of this construction and on the learner's interactions with/actions upon the environment, while Bruner focused more on the social aspects of learning and on the learner's interactions with parents and others, reflecting the work of Lev Vygotsky and his sociocultural theory of learning.

Jerome Bruner's Interactionist Theory of Language Acquisition

Bruner emphasizes adult-child interactions as promoting children's language acquisition. Bruner sees child-directed speech (CDS), i.e. the linguistic behaviors of adults in speaking to children, as having a specialized adaptation of supporting the process of language development. Bruner termed such support "scaffolding." Chomsky proposed a universal Language Acquisition Device (LAD) that we all possess, reflecting innate ability to structure language. Bruner countered this proposal with a Language Acquisition Support System (LASS), an innate ability to read and interpret social situations and interactions and hence to understand language and learn it readily. This reflects Bruner's greater emphasis on the interactions of the learning child with the family and social environment and the support they give.

Scaffolding

Wood, Bruner and Ross (1976) concluded from their research that parents and other adults give children "scaffolding," or the temporary support they need to promote their cognitive growth. They found that in everyday interactions involving play, adults provided support structures (analogous to the scaffolds temporarily erected around buildings under construction) in order to help children understand new concepts and perform new tasks. This analogy is consistent with the constructivist theory to which Bruner subscribed, wherein we construct our realities as well as new ideas based on our knowledge. The purposes of scaffolding include making new ideas or tasks simpler and easier for children to understand, giving learning children motivation and encouragement to learn, emphasizing the most important components of a task, correcting any errors they may have made in attempting it, and supplying adult models for children of the behaviors they are engaged in learning, which the children can observe and then imitate. The concept of scaffolding has also been applied to Lev Vygotsky's sociocultural theory of learning, especially his Zone of Proximal Development (what a learner can do not on his/her own but rather what s/he can do with guidance of a more developed learner or adult), and to Stephen Krashen's hypotheses of language acquisition, especially the concept of *i*+1. (See section "Input Theory" below.)

Review Video: Instructional Scaffolding
Visit mometrix.com/academy and enter code: 989759

Review Video: Zone of Proximal Development (ZPD)
Visit mometrix.com/academy and enter code: 555594

Input Theory

Steven Krashen presented the input model of language learning, which has 5 main hypotheses:

- Acquisition/learning distinction: Acquisition is the normal process of "getting" a language, as small children universally do. Learning is formally studying a language in a classroom. Acquisition is subconscious, while learning involves engaging our conscious understanding.
- Input: Language is acquired by receiving comprehensible input, utterances that are above the speaking level of the individual but understandable by them. Comprehensible input is sometimes denoted as *i*+1.
- Natural order: There is a normal order in which rules of language are acquired.
- Monitor: Learning, the formal and conscious study of a language, is primarily useful in monitoring what has been acquired, allowing the individual to make adjustments and corrections. Learning is not a replacement for acquisition.
- Affective filter: Aversive feelings such as discomfort, stress, self-consciousness, and/or lack of motivation can be associated with language learning, most commonly in adults and older teenagers. This can hinder language acquisition.

Similarities and Differences in Learning First and Second Languages

Note: In the field of language acquisition, one's first, or "native" language is referred to as L1. Languages learned later in life are referred to L2 (or L3 for a third language, and so on).

Similarities

Both Constructed from Prior Knowledge

L1 is constructed from experiences: environmental (*all those things that go "**vroom**" are cars*) or social (*"**Hi**" is what people say when they see each other*) and also from prior knowledge in the same language (*Walk**ed** = walk yesterday. Talk**ed** = ?*). Similarly, L2 can be constructed from experiences and prior knowledge of the same language. In addition, L2 can be constructed using prior knowledge of L1. (*I can talk about yesterday by adding **-ed** in L1. What will I add to the end of a word in L2 to talk about yesterday?*)

Same Sources in Natural Situations

A language learner, whether a young child learning L1 or an older child learning L2, can receive natural language input from many sources: home, peers, school, and the cultural environment. If the L2 learner is not immersed in a culture where the target language is spoken, he will have fewer sources of language input. A Spanish-speaking young person living in an English-speaking culture will hear his L2 – English – from peers, at school, and in his everyday environment. An English-speaking young person living in an English-speaking culture will hear his L2 – Spanish – with less frequency, possibly only from his teacher at school.

Learners Use Similar Strategies

L1 and L2 language learners use similar strategies as they learn and to compensate for what they do not know. One example of a learning strategy used by both L1 and L2 learners is overgeneralization (e.g. using typical past tense/preterite endings even for irregular verbs – saying ***goed*** instead of ***went*** or ***tenió*** instead of ***tuvo***). Both types of learners also use circumlocution – talking around a word that they do not know (*I need* ***the thing for washing my hair****...shampoo*).

Learning Follows Predictable Patterns

Krashen's natural order hypothesis suggests that language acquisition will follow a predictable pattern, whether the language being acquired is L1 or L2. This has been supported by research. For example, single words or formulaic phrases are mastered first ("***pool***"), then a simple sentence structure ("***We go to the pool***"), then an understanding of how parts of a sentence can move around ("***Can we go to the pool? Are we going to the pool? I really like going to the pool! Did you go to the pool last summer?***").

Silent Period

L2 learners do well when allowed to listen without responding for a period of time, just like a young child does in first language acquisition, where first words are not uttered for months! However, this "silent period" is not as necessary or prolonged in L2, probably due to increased cognitive skills of an older learner and their preexisting knowledge of L1.

Motherese/How We Speak to Language Learners

The way adults speak to young children ("baby talk" or motherese), with single or repeated words, simple phrases, slow utterance, and a distinct tone of voice, allows children to receive comprehensible input (***Cup? Anna wants a cup of water?***). Modified vocabulary, structure, speed, and tone to provide comprehensible input is similarly helpful to L2 learners, which is why we often speak more slowly and with simpler words when we speak with non-native speakers.

Differences

Critical Period

L1 has a critical period: if for a horrible reason (abuse, abandonment, etc.), a child is not exposed to and does not acquire a first language by a certain age (somewhere between age 5 and puberty), they will never master a language. Research has not supported this for L2 learners – if you have learned a first language, you can learn a second language at any point in your lifespan.

Cognitive Development

L2 learners are older than L1 learners. Therefore, they are more developed cognitively, so they have more cognitive tools at their disposal. For example, they have greater prior knowledge of world, they can learn more quickly, and they have more control over the input they receive– they can ask for repetition or clarification. They can learn and apply rules, they have a first language from which they can transfer, and they have experience using their first language in real-life settings.

Affective Factors

Affective filters play a larger role in L2 acquisition. Older learners are more likely than toddlers to experience inhibitions, anxiety, and motivation (or lack thereof) as they study a language. Family and peer attitudes and behaviors toward the target language and culture (which may be different from their own) can also increase a learner's affective filter.

Transfer and Interference

An L2 learner has already learned a language (L1). Transfer from L1 is not always helpful, either because it does not contain structures or vocabulary that L2 does or because the two languages are syntactically or semantically different in some regards (e.g., preterite and imperfect in Spanish vs. only one past tense in English, false cognates like *carpeta*/folder and carpet/*alfombra*)

Accent

Some evidence shows that with age, it is more difficult to achieve a native-like accent. This is believed to be partially physiological – our palates harden as we approach puberty, making them inflexible to creating sounds not already learned. There is also a neural component to this reality: babies at 6 months of age can distinguish between native language sounds and non-native sounds and pay more attention to native language sounds.

Krashen's Learning/Acquisition Distinction

(See section "Input Theory" above.) While L1 is always acquired, not all students have the opportunity to acquire L2. Classroom learning, no matter how carefully it mirrors L1 acquisition, does not usually provide L2 input 12 hours a day for several years in a variety of contexts and therefore L2 classrooms are a less-effective way to achieve fluency in a language.

Fundamental Difference Hypothesis

This hypothesis posits that L2 learners are not able to access Universal Grammar (UG)/Language Acquisition Device (LAD) (see section "Nativist" above) to the same extent as L1 learners, making it more difficult to learn a second or subsequent language. This is suggested because very nearly all learners of L1 learn it fluently, which is not the case for L2 learners.

Stages and Patterns in Second-Language Learning

Continuum of Learning Theory

The Continuum of Learning theory outlines predictable steps when learning a new language:

- The Silent/Receptive or Preproduction stage can last from a few hours to six months. Students usually don't say much and communicate by using pictures and pointing.
- In the Early Production stage, students use one- and two-word phrases. They indicate understanding with yes or no and who/what/where questions. This stage can last six months.
- The Speech Emergence stage may last a year. Students use short sentences and begin to ask simple questions. Grammatical errors may make communication challenging.
- In the Intermediate Language Proficiency stage students begin to make complex statements, share thoughts and opinions and speak more often. This may last a year or more.

- The Advanced Learning Proficiency stage lasts five to seven years. Students have acquired a substantial vocabulary and are capable of participating fully in classroom activities and discussions.

Patterns Commonly Observed in Second Language Learners

Interlanguage

An interlanguage is a normal stage of language learning, where students exhibit transitional competence – a cohesive, rule-bound use of the target language that is not native. This interlanguage is often colored by transfer from L1. For example, an English-speaking Spanish student may express likes and dislikes by saying "*Me gusta **corriendo**. No me gusta **bailando***" *¿Te gusta **bailando** o **corriendo**?*" This is cohesive – the student has a rule-bound pattern of using the gerund after *me/te gusta*. This is also how the phrase is constructed in English (I like **running**). However, it is non-native, because a native speaker would be more likely to use the infinitive: "*Me gusta **correr**.*"

Fossilization

Fossilization occurs when learners plateau at their interlanguage rather than progressing on to native-like competence. If a learner continues saying "*Me gusta **corriendo***" as above rather than learning to say "*Me gusta **correr***", then fossilization will take place. An L2 teacher should not be surprised by students using an interlanguage, as it is a natural stage of language learning, but the teacher should also help a student avoid fossilization by modeling native competence. ("*Hmm…te gusta **correr**?*")

Codeswitching

Codeswitching is a common practice among language learners and bilingual individuals in which the speaker goes from using one language to another mid-speech (***¿Quieres ir* to the park with me?**). This switch typically involves one word/phrase or occurs in predictable places in sentence structure –at the end of a clause rather than in the middle of it. Since codeswitching is a universal practice among bilingual individuals, experts are divided as to how much a teacher should discourage the practice in the classroom.

Communication Strategies

Language learners employ a variety of communication strategies to compensate for gaps in their ability. Some of these strategies include paraphrasing (repeating a simpler, shorter version of what was said), substituting words (using "***animal***" instead of "***gato***" when you don't know the word for "**cat**"), coining words ("*Mi mama es **nice-o***"), and mediating meaning with their interlocutor (e.g. asking for repetition, paraphrasing and looking for approval, using hand motions or other contextual props)

Communicating with Students

The Four Modalities

There are four modalities in which language is used: listening, speaking, reading, and writing. The following definitions are from The American Heritage College Dictionary.

- Listening is "To make an effort to hear something." To hear is "to be capable of perceiving sound by the ear."
- Speaking is being "capable of speech involving talking, expressing or telling." To speak is "to convey thoughts, opinions or emotions orally."

- Reading is "the act or activity of rendering text aloud." To read is "the ability to examine and grasp the meaning of written and printed material in a given language."
- Writing is "meaningful letters or characters that constitute readable material." To write is "to form letters, words or symbols on a surface such as paper with an instrument such as a pen." (People also use typewriters and computer keyboards.)

The Three Modes of Communication

Interpersonal

The interpersonal mode is two-way, with two (or more) individuals negotiating meaning with each other, typically spontaneously and in order to exchange information of some sort. Spoken conversations and text message exchanges are two examples of interpersonal communication.

Basic interpersonal communication skills encompass two different and distinct styles of communication:

- In context-embedded communication, various visual and vocal props are available to help the student understand that which is being said, including pictures and other objects to graphically explain and communicate demonstratively. The speaker's gestures and tone of voice help the listener understand the words being used. Conversations with speakers who use hand gestures and stories with pictures and props help the learners understand more quickly and easily.
- Context-reduced communication does not have visual clues and cues and therefore the learner must rely on his competency and fluency in the language. Phone conversations, for example, do not allow the listener to see the speaker and thus hand gestures and facial expressions and other visual aides are missing. Reading a note without pictorial guides may make it difficult for the student to understand the written words.

Interpretive

The interpretive mode is one-way, with the language learner being the "receiver" of input in the target language. In the interpretive mode, the individual, in the absence of interaction with the author/speaker/presenter, constructs meaning from the source material. Examples of source material include a public speech or radio program, an article or book, and a TV program or movie.

Presentational

The presentational mode is one-way, with the language learner being the "producer" of output in the target language. The individual engages in communication without directly interacting with the audience. Examples of presentational communication include writing an essay, giving a presentation, or telling a story.

Methods Used to Teach Languages Other Than English

The three methods most commonly used to teach languages other than English are ***grammar-based***, ***communication-based*** and ***content-based***. Grammar-based methods teach students the rules of the target language including structure, function and vocabulary. Emphasis is on the "why" and "how" of the language. Communication-based methodology teaches students how to use the target langugage in every-day, realistic situations. This approach emphasizes practical conversational usage. Content-based methodology teaches students grammar and vocabulary and uses speaking and writing assignments in order to practice these skills. This approach includes using the target langugue as the main method of classroom communication between the teacher and the student and amongst students. This method emphasizes an integrated approach to learning the target langugage.

Instructional Strategies

Comprehensible Input

Comprehensible input, according to Krashen's language learning hypotheses, is the level of language that is understandable by learners but contains words and grammatical structures that they have not yet learned or mastered. It is often called ***i*+1**, with *i* representing the learner's current language ability. If a student is only exposed to *i*, that student's language ability may stagnate. If a student is only exposed to *i* +3 (several steps beyond their current ability), they will not be able to pick up on the new words and structures as easily. Following are two examples of comprehensible input in a second language classroom. A teacher may use the vocabulary that a student already knows to introduce new words (e.g., *Ella es mi abuela. Ella es la madre de mi padre.*) If students know everything except the word *abuela*, they will be able to comprehend *abuela*. A teacher may also use comprehensible input to introduce new grammatical structures (e.g., *Yo no juego con juguetes ahora. Cuando tenía seis años, yo jugaba con juguetes todos los días*). A student who has not yet learned the imperfect tense but knows the present tense and the vocabulary in this utterance can learn from this input the difference between present tense verbs and imperfect tense verbs.

Total Physical Response (TPR)

Developed by James J. Asher in the 1960s, Total Physical Response (TPR) uses physical activity to reinforce the words and phrases being taught. Depending upon the age and level of language proficiency, students are given a series of simple to complex commands and/or instructions. They are expected to respond appropriately. TPR is a tool that is effective when incorporated with other methods. In a first-year language class, this might look similar to a game of Simon Says, where the teacher says "Put the pencil on top of the book," showing the students what to do. The students then mimic the teacher. Other school supplies and prepositions can be added in gradually (for example, "Put the pencil under the book" or "Put the folder on top of the book") and the teacher will begin to not demonstrate but see if the students can comprehend the commands without visual cues.

Scaffolding

Second language teachers must accurately gauge all the prerequisite skills students will need to successfully complete a task set before them. This is especially true when activities or assessments are cooperative, project-based, or based on realia or cultural artifacts. For example, if a teacher wants students to make a booklet or a presentation introducing members of their families, students will need to know some specific vocabulary (terms for referring to family members - mother, father, etc., adjectives for describing their physical and personality traits - tall, smart, etc., verbs for describing what they like to do or do frequently) and some specific grammatical structures (phrases for introducing someone, using *ser* for characteristics, matching adjectives to nouns they describe in number and gender, using infinitives with *gustar* or conjugating verbs in the present 3rd person to indicate consistent action). These words and structures must be taught and practiced in smaller chunks before asking students to combine them and create with them. Students will quickly become frustrated by high-level tasks when they are not confident they have the skills to complete the tasks successfully.

Cooperative Learning

Opportunities to interact and speak are vital to language learning. The interpersonal mode requires two or more speakers working together to construct meaning. In the classroom, teachers can arrange cooperative learning experiences that allow students the chance to communicate together in meaningful ways. Below are some examples of cooperative learning activities for an L2 classroom.

- Jigsaw: Students work in small groups to complete unique parts of an assignment (e.g., read and summarize a section of a story or article, learn about a holiday in one country that speaks the target language). The students in each small group (You can call them groups, A, B, C...) become "experts" on their section or topic. Then the teacher creates new groups (You can call them groups 1, 2, 3...) that contain one person from each of the previous groups (So, group 1 has one person from group A, one person from group B...). Each student is now responsible to communicate to her peers what she learned about her section or topic and answer questions that her peers have about the new material she has presented.
- Information gap: One student has information that another student needs to find out. Perhaps one student has a map showing where the library is located and must give directions to the other student so he can correctly identify the library on his own blank map.
- Interview: A teacher can provide questions or ask students to write their own questions and then students interview each other.

Use of Realia/Cultural Artifacts

Realia and cultural artifacts are an excellent way to teach language in its cultural context. For example, when completing a unit on clothes, prices, and shopping, a teacher can print a department store ad from a store in the target culture and ask students to interact with it. This allows students to experience the language as they might when immersed in the target culture. It can be challenging to make sure these pieces are age and language-learning-level appropriate - keep the idea of comprehensible input in mind!

Interdisciplinary Learning/Connections to Other Classes and to Home Life

Language learning truly lends itself to interdisciplinary learning! Strategies that students have learned for reading comprehension in L1 can be applied in L2 and reading strategies that help students in the L2 classroom can be applied in L1 as well. Learning about L2 culture(s) and history can create connections with the social studies and literature classrooms. As students' language skills increase, content knowledge from other subject areas can be delivered, discussed, and assessed in the target language.

Speaking an unfamiliar, non-native language is easier for LOTE students when the subject matter is familiar and personal to them. Therefore, asking students to talk about or write about themselves and their home life can encourage L2 production. Students also find it interesting to compare their experiences with those of students in other locations and cultures, providing connections between their personal life and the target culture.

Project-Based Teaching

Project-based teaching can be practiced in the L2 classroom. For example, after learning the preterite and imperfect tenses, students can be asked to give a presentation about their own childhood. When learning about cities and giving directions, students can be given a project in which they use online resources to explore a city where the target language is spoken, perhaps identifying places of interest and giving directions in the target language for how to get from one place to the next. It is important to provide students with projects that they can complete with their language skills, otherwise they will be easily frustrated at their inability to do what is asked of them. For example, a student who has not learned any past tenses should not be asked to tell a story about when she was younger.

Student-Centered Learning

Student-centered learning is an excellent way to foster successful language learning. Teachers should encourage self-evaluation and self-monitoring, helping students learn to identify their own strengths and weaknesses and to correct their own mistakes. Students can select learning strategies that are meaningful and helpful to themselves (e.g., a teacher can teach or model multiple ways to approach a text in the foreign language or multiple ways to learn and recall new vocabulary words, then let students choose which way works best for them).

Extra-Curricular Experiences

Extra-curricular experiences are of great value in the language classroom as well. Any environment that encourages authentic communication and engagement with the cultural context of the target language will be of assistance in language learning. Writing with pen pals or skyping with speakers of the target language, visiting a restaurant or festival that is owned/hosted by the target culture, or even traveling to a country in the target culture will enhance the language-learning experience.

Assessment Strategies

Technical Quality of Assessments

One issue that must be considered when developing academic assessments is the technical quality of the examination. The National Center for Research on Evaluation, Standards and Student Testing (CRESST) developed the following criteria to evaluate technical quality:

- Cognitive Complexity: requires problem-solving, critical thinking and reasoning ability.
- Content Quality: correct responses demonstrate knowledge of critical subject matter.
- Meaningfulness: students understand the value of the assessment and the tasks involved.
- Language Appropriateness: clear to the students and appropriate to the requested task.
- Transfer and Generalization: indicates ability to complete similar tasks and the results permit valid generalization about learning capabilities.
- Fairness: performance measurements and scoring avoid factors irrelevant to school learning.
- Reliability: consistently represents data added to students' background knowledge.
- Consequences: it results in the desired effect on students, instructors and the educational system.

Standards for Assessments

A variety of activities such as written assignments, oral presentations, and class participation should be incorporated into the classroom assessment scheme in order to obtain a broader, more realistic view of the student's understanding of the material. The assessment process should be fully explained so that the student knows what is expected. He is evaluated using one or all of the following standards:

- self-referenced —based on his previous level of progress
- criterion-referenced — a defined, school, district-wide, or program-wide standard
- norm-referenced — based on the progress of groups of students the same age or grade level

Using a combination of standards instead of relying on one method presents a clearer, more accurate picture of the student's growth.

Informal and Formal Assessment

Assessment can be classified as informal or formal. Formal assessment employs an assessment tool that has been tested and standardized in some fashion. The AP Spanish Language test or an ACTFL assessment are examples of formal assessments. Informal assessment encompasses all non-standardized assessment tools and should occur in an ongoing fashion in every classroom. Informal assessment includes a broad range of assessment strategies: teacher observation, assigned homework or classwork, in-class responses or discussions, monitoring of progress toward a performance goal, and locally-written quizzes and tests. Most project-based assessment and rubrics are informal assessment.

It is vital that classroom instruction, informal assessment, and formal assessment are aligned. If students are going to take a formal assessment (e.g., the AP Spanish Language test) at the end of Spanish IV, then the informal assessments constructed and administered in Spanish I-IV should assess whether or not students have mastered the material they need to be successful on the formal assessment. In addition, some (not all) of the informal assessments should help students prepare for the format and structure of the formal assessment. These informal assessments must then be aligned with the instruction in the classroom. For example, if students are going to be asked to write a personal narrative in the target language on the formal assessment, then instruction in the classroom should teach them the vocabulary and grammar necessary for this task. Informal assessments given in the classroom must test if students have learned the vocabulary and grammar they need, and at some point, an informal assessment should require students to write under the constraints they will experience when they take the formal assessment (time limit, not using a dictionary, etc.). In order for this process to be successful, teachers must be familiar with local and state/national standards as they develop both assessment and instruction. Some localities or states may not have clear L2 standards that are tested formally, and in this case a teacher should familiarize himself with the standards for the formal assessment his students may ultimately take (Advanced Placement, International Baccalaureate, etc.).

Formative and Summative Assessment

Another way to conceptualize assessment is to categorize it as formative or summative. Summative assessment is assessment that occurs at the end of a chapter, unit, semester, year, or course of study (or any defined period) and is intended to evaluate student learning against standard(s) that were taught during that period. A summative assessment should allow the teacher to answer the question "Has the student learned what he was expected to learn?" Summative assessments can be informal (a teacher-written chapter test) or formal (the AP Spanish exam).

Formative assessment is designed not to evaluate learning at the end of the learning process but to diagnose how the learning process is going while it is underway. It allows teachers and students to collect information on student strengths and weaknesses and measure progress toward the standard(s) that will be measured on the summative assessment. Formative assessment is integrated into the instructional process and provides feedback in a timely fashion so that adjustments in instruction and learning can be made quickly. Student responses to teacher questions, completed homework, classroom assignments and activities, and student self-reflections are all examples of formative assessments. Formative assessment is typically informal, but formal assessments can be used in a formative fashion rather than summative (e.g., using a standardized test at the beginning of a unit to measure a student's starting point toward the learning goals).

As stated above, the key to effective instruction and assessment is alignment. A teacher should teach with the end goal in mind, and the end goal should be accurately measured by the summative assessment(s). Formative assessment along the way should check student progress toward the end goal, allowing teachers to adjust instruction to maximize student learning and allowing students to reflect on their own learning process and progress.

> **Review Video: Formative and Summative Assessments**
> Visit mometrix.com/academy and enter code: 804991
>
> **Review Video: Assessment Reliability and Validity**
> Visit mometrix.com/academy and enter code: 424680

Assessment in Each Modality/Mode of Communication

Interpersonal

Assessing a student's interpersonal communication will primarily involve speaking tasks, and possibly writing tasks. For example, students can be asked to interview one another, have a conversation with another student or with the teacher, take part in a debate, play a role in a communicative situation (e.g., store clerk and customer), or respond to an email or text,

Interpretive

To assess a student's interpretive communication, the teacher will provide text in the target language, either spoken or written, and then assess the student's ability to interpret that text. A student could listen to a recorded conversation or song, watch a movie, or read an article or story before answering questions about what she understood and learned from the text.

Presentational

Presentational communication can be assessed by asking students to speak or write about a given topic. A "how-to" speech, a persuasive essay, a presentation about extended family members and their likes and dislikes, or a personal narrative are all examples of assessment tasks in the presentational mode.

Types of Assessment Tools

Pen and Paper Tests

Matching and true/false questions are an excellent way to quickly assess how well students remember specific facts, as well as their ability to memorize data. Multiple choice and short-answer questions require a little deeper knowledge of the subject and better reasoning and thinking skills. These four testing options are reasonably quick and easy to grade. Open-response questions can be used to evaluate in depth content knowledge, the use of critical thinking skills, and the ability to communicate thoughts and ideas through the written word. This option requires more time, effort, and concentration to evaluate fairly, and is a more effective tool in some situations and courses than it is in others.

Rubrics and Checklists

Rubrics and checklists are used for measuring performance or proficiency. In a checklist, either the attribute/skill is displayed or it is not (e.g., Did the student use at least 5 vocabulary words in his story?). In a rubric, points are awarded on a sliding scale based on descriptors of increasing demonstration of attribute/skill (e.g., The student used more than 10 vocabulary words in his story = 5 points. The student used 7-9 vocabulary words in his story = 4 points. The student used 4-6 vocabulary words in his story = 3 points...). ACTFL (The American Council on the Teaching of Foreign Language) has published categories and descriptors that can be helpful to language teachers in developing rubrics. These measures can provide a level of objectivity to the assessment process when complex skills are being assessed.

Task Completion

A task completion assessment measures if a task can be successfully undertaken in the target language. This type of assessment is holistic – it focuses on realistic situations and judges a student not on every step of the process but on the completion of the goal. For example, if a student is given directions only in Spanish, can she arrive at the correct classroom? It does not matter if she understands every word used in the directions given (as might be measured with a multiple-choice or fill-in-the-blank test question), but that she can use what she does understand to successfully complete the task. Task completion assessments can measure a student's interpretive skills as in the example above or their interpersonal or presentational skills (e.g., can the student successfully order a desired meal from a menu in Spanish?)

Portfolio

A portfolio is a collection of the student's work assembled over a period of time (e.g., six week grading period, one semester, the entire year). Various items can be included: contracts, copies of completed activities such as papers; presentations and pictures of props; performance assessments made by the student, his peers, and the teacher; copies of class work and homework; classroom tests; and state-mandated exams. A portfolio is a powerful aide in assessing the student's progress and an excellent format to present to parents so they can review their child's progress. The decision on what to include should be a collaboration between the student and the teacher. What will be included: examples of best work, worst work, typical work, or perhaps some of each? Will the student keep a copy as a reference point? Decisions need to be made and rules established as early as possible in the process so that progress is accurately and fairly recorded.

Once decisions have been made about what will be included, it is important to begin with baseline data for comparison as the portfolio grows. Selected material can be placed in a folder or large envelope with the student's name on the front. Each addition needs to be dated with an explanation attached stating why the item was included and what features should be noted. Teachers who use portfolios will often create assignments with the intention of including it in the package. As the contents grow, it may become necessary due to space limitations to review the items and remove some daily work, quizzes, or tests. Once the portfolio is complete, the teacher needs to have a method to evaluate the contents and review the student's progress in areas such as creativity, critical thinking, originality, research skills, perseverance, responsibility, and communication effectiveness. A checklist or rubric can be useful.

Phonology

Phonetic Language

Spanish is a phonetic language, which means that every letter (vowels as well as consonants) and some combinations of letters each have an associated sound. This associated sound is used every single time that this particular letter or combination of letters appears in a word. Therefore, as in all phonetic languages, if you know how to spell a word, you know how to pronounce it. The only exceptions are foreign or borrowed words, which are sometimes pronounced the same way they are pronounced in the original language (for example, *los jeans*).

Spanish Pronunciation of Vowels

Spanish has five vowels, the same as in English, but they are different from English in the sense that they make one and only one sound regardless of their position in the word or which letters come before and after them. For example, the vowel **a** in Spanish is always pronounced like a shorter version of the **a** in c**a**r. There is no difference in the way it sounds whether it is at the beginning of the word (*amanecer*), between two consonants (*caro*), between a consonant and a vowel (*caer, teatro*) or at the end of the word (*mesa*). The same consistency of pronunciation is true of the vowels **e**, **i**, **o**, and **u**: there is only one sound for each of them. **e** is pronounced similarly to the short **e** in b**e**d (*entrar*); **i** is pronounced like a long or double **ee** as in s**ee** (*hijo*); **o** is pronounced like a long **o** in g**o** (*dormir*); and **u** is pronounced similarly to **oo** or **ue** as they appear in the English words g**oo** or s**ue** (*usar*).

Pronunciations of the Letter C in Spanish

The letter **c** has two different pronunciations depending on which letter follows it, much like in English. If followed by an **a** (*camino*), **o** (*correr*), **u** (*cuñado*), or a consonant (*conectar*), the letter **c** sounds like the English hard **c** in **c**oneand **c**amera or like the **k** in brea**k** and **k**ite. If followed by the vowels **e** (*centro*) or **i** (*cigarillo*), the letter **c** sounds like the English soft **c** in fa**c**e and **c**elery or like the **s** in **s**afe or be**s**t. In some regions of Spain, **c** followed by **e** or **i** is not pronounced **s**, but rather **th** as in the English words **th**ink or wi**th** (e.g., *centro* is pronounced **the**ntro).

When a Spanish word contains a double **c** (*occidente, collección, diccionario*), each **c** individually follows the rules above. The first **c**, which is followed by a consonant, has the strong sound of **k**. The second **c**, which is usually followed by the vowel **i**, will be pronounced **s** or **th** depending on the region. Therefore in most of the Spanish-speaking world, **cc** will sound similar to its pronunciation in the English words a**cc**ident and a**cc**ess, or like the **x** sound found in e**x**it. In some parts of Spain, *diccionario* would be pronounced di**cth**ionario.

When the letter **c** is followed by the consonant **h** (*chico*), it forms the new letter/phoneme **ch**.

Pronunciation of the Letters CH in Spanish

The Spanish **ch** is always pronounced one way. It has the exact same sound as found in English words such as **ch**urch, **ch**arcoal, and mar**ch**. Spanish dictionaries have a separate section for the **ch**, which is located after the letter **c**. A few common words in Spanish that use **ch** are ***chancho*** (pig), *mu**ch**o* (much), ***ch**ico* (boy), and ***ch**aqueta* (jacket).

Pronunciation and Spelling of the Phoneme F in English and Spanish

The sound of the phoneme **f** in Spanish is the same its sound in English as found in words such as **f**amily and **f**uture. It is never pronounced with the **v** sound found in the English word o**f**.

The phoneme **f** is obtained in Spanish only by the use of the letter **f**, while in English the same sound appears in words with **f** (**f**ace), **ff** (co**ff**in), and **ph** (**ph**otograph). The letter **f** is never doubled in Spanish and the **ph** combination does not exist in Spanish. In some foreign words the **ph** has been replaced by a single **f** (tele**ph**one-*telé**f**ono*, tro**ph**y-*tro**f**eo*).

Pronunciations of the Letter G in Spanish

When followed by a consonant (*re**g**la, ne**g**ro*) or by the vowels **a**, **o**, or **u** (***g**ato, a**g**osto, **g**usto*), the sound of the letter **g** in Spanish is similar to its hard sound in English words such as **g**ood and **g**ame. If the letter **g** is followed by the vowels **e** or **i** (***g**enerar, re**g**istro*), its sound is like the sound of the Spanish **j** (a strong English **h**; see section "Pronuciation of the letter j in Spanish" below for regional variations). If there is a **u** between the letter **g** and the vowels **e** or **i** (***gu**erra, **gu**iso*), the **u** is not pronounced and the letter **g** recovers its hard sound.

Pronunciation of the Letter H in Spanish and English

In English, the letter **h** has a soft, aspirated sound (**h**appy). In Spanish, by contrast, it is almost always silent. Most of the words that contain a letter **h** in Spanish have Latin or Greek roots, and the

h has only been kept for etymological reasons. The only time **h** is pronounced is in foreign words with no equivalent spelling in Spanish such as ***H**awaii*, ***h**ámster*, and ***h**obby*. In those cases, the letter **h** sounds like the Spanish letter **j** (see section "Pronuciation of the letter j in Spanish" below).

Recall that when the letter **h** follows the letter **c** (*mu**ch**o*, ***ch**an**ch**o*), it forms a unique phoneme, **ch**. (See section "Pronunciation of the letter ch in Spanish" above.)

Pronunciation of the Letter J in Spanish

The letter **j** has a completely different pronunciation from that of the same letter in English, and its sound is not found in English. The sound in English that most approximates the Spanish letter **j** would be an extremely hard and strong **h**, an exaggeration of the sound in words such as **h**ot and **h**ome. In some regions, the **j** is pronounced slightly softer than it is in other regions. Remember that in Spanish, the letter **g**, when followed by the vowels **e** as in ***ge**nero* (genre) and *di**ge**rir* (digest) or **i** as in *re**gi**strar* (register) and *hi**gi**ene* (hygiene), has the same strong sound as the letter **j** (See section "Pronunciations of the letter g in Spanish" above).

Regional Differences in Pronunciation of the Double L

Double l, or **ll**, is considered its own letter in Spanish. The way the double l is pronounced varies by regions, and sometimes even within the same country. In most Spanish speaking areas, the **ll** has a soft sound similar to the English **y** in **y**es or **y**ellow. In many parts of Argentina and Uruguay, however, the double l is much stronger and is pronounced like the **zh** phoneme found in English in words such as mea**s**ure and plea**s**ure. In other regions, it is pronounced somewhat like the English letter **j** as it sounds in **j**elly or **J**apan. Common words that have the **ll** phoneme are ***ll**uvia* (rain), ***ll**ave* (key), ***ll**orar* (cry), and ***ll**egar* (arrive).

Existence of the Letter Ñ in Spanish

The letter **ñ** does not exist in English but is considered its own separate letter in Spanish. The letter **ñ** can be found in words such as *ma**ñ**ana* (morning or tomorrow), *a**ñ**o* (year), *se**ñ**or* (mister), and *ni**ñ**a* (girl). The most similar sounds in English that resemble the **ñ** in Spanish are the **ny** or **ni** phonemes as found in words such as ca**ny**on, o**ni**on, or opi**ni**on. In the Spanish alphabet the **ñ** is located after the letter **n**.

Letter Q in Spanish

In Spanish, the letter **q** has the sound of the English letter **k**. The letter **q** is always followed by a **u** (**qu**) and then either an **e** (***que**rido, **que**brar, **que**mar, **que**dar, **que**jido*) or an **i** (***qui**zá, **qui**tar, **qui**nce, **qui**eto*). There are very few exceptions (***qua**ntum, **quo**rum*), all of which have foreign roots.

Pronunciation of the Letter R in Spanish

The letter **r** has two distinctively different pronunciations in Spanish: a soft one, similar to the English **tt** or **dd** sounds, and a strong, rolling one. The soft sound is used whenever a single letter **r** is in the middle of a word between two vowels (*ca**r**o, pu**r**o, ai**r**e*), between a vowel and most consonants (*t**r**en, ja**r**dín, pa**r**te*), or at the end of a word (*camina**r**, come**r**, recibi**r***). At the beginning of a word (***r**eto, **r**ápido, **r**ojo*) or after the consonants **l**, **n**, and **s** (*al**r**ededor, son**r**isa, Is**r**ael*), the single letter **r** is pronounced with the strong trilling sound used in the double **r** or **rr** phoneme (See section "Pronunciation of the double r in Spanish" below").

Pronunciation of the Double R in Spanish

The double **r** or **rr** is not considered a separate letter, but it is a very frequently used phoneme in Spanish. Some common words that include the double **r** are *co**rr**er, pe**rr**o, a**rr**iba*, and *ca**rr**o*. The **rr** has a trilling sound that can be achieved by flapping the tongue against the front of the mouth. If properly "rolled," the **rr** sound should be similar to the one you get when you try to imitate a motor. Be aware that the **rr** is used only between vowels. A similar trilling sound at the beginning of a word or after certain consonants (**l**, **n**, **s**) is spelled with a single **r** (See section "Pronunciation of the letter r in Spanish" above).

Letter W in Spanish

The letter **w** is not native to the Spanish language, and it appears only in words that come from other languages. Depending on the country, it is called *uve doble*, *v doble*, *doble u*, or *doble v*. Words in Spanish with a **w** have mostly English roots (***w**aterpolo, ha**w**aiano, **w**hisky*) and are usually pronounced with the English **w** sound as found in **w**ater and **w**inter. In some countries, however, the **w** is pronounced with a very lightly pronounced **g** added before the English **w** for a **gw** sound.

Pronunciation of the Letter Y in Spanish

In Spanish, the letter **y** can be treated as a vowel or a consonant. At the end of a word (*re**y**, mu**y**, so**y***), it is always pronounced as the Spanish vowel **i**. If the letter **y** is before a vowel (***y**o, **y**a, **y**arda*), in most countries it is also pronounced as the Spanish vowel **i**. However, in Argentina and Uruguay, the letter **y** before another vowel sounds more like the English phoneme **sh** as found in words such as **sh**ower and **sh**ow or the **zh** phoneme found in English words such as mea**s**ure and plea**s**ure. In other regions, the letter **y** before another vowel will sound similar to the English **j**, making the Spanish word *yo* sound like the English word **J**oe.

Letter Z in Spanish

In Spanish the letter **z**, regardless of which letter comes after it, has the same sound as the letter **c** before an **e** (*c**e**na*) or **i** (*coc**i**na*). Therefore, in most of Latin America countries, it sounds like the **s** in English words such as **s**ilence and in**s**tant, while in most of Spain it sounds like the **th** in English words such as **th**ink and **th**under. In Spanish, the letter **z** is typically not used before an **e** or **i** except in words of foreign origin (***z**epelin, **z**igzaguear*). Due to this rule, the letter **z** is replaced by a **c** when forming the plural of words ending in **z** (*lápi**z**/lápi**c**es, tapi**z**/tapi**c**es*) and in certain verb conjugations (see section "Spelling changes in plurals and derivatives" below).

Dipthongs and Tripthongs

Spanish has several dipthongs – two vowels blended together to make a sound that begins as one vowel sound and ends as another. They are listed below, along with examples of words that contain them.

ai/ay	*b**ai**le, h**ay***
ei/ey	*s**ei**s, r**ey***
oi/oy	***oi**go, est**oy***
ui/uy	*r**ui**do, m**uy***
au	*p**au**sa, **au**tor*
eu	***Eu**ropa, d**eu**da*
ia	*anc**ia**no,med**ia***
ie	*v**ie**jo, s**ie**mpre*
io	*suc**io**, delic**io**so*
iu	*c**iu**dad, v**iu**da*
ua	*ig**ua**l, c**ua**tro*
ue	*b**ue**no, j**ue**go*
uo	*antig**uo**, monstr**uo***

If one of the vowels carries an accent mark, the vowel pair is no longer a dipthong (*me**dia*** vs. *com**ía***).

Tripthongs are primarily found in second person plural forms of verbs in Spanish. They can occur with an accented middle vowel or without an accented middle vowel.

***iai/iái**: r**iai**s, camb**iái**s*

***iei/iéi**: gu**ie**s, camb**iéi**s*

***uay/uái**: Parag**uay**, averig**uái**s*

***uéi/üéi**: habit**uéi**s, averig**üéi**s*

Other tripthongs are infrequent and occur in slang or onomatopoeias. For example, ***uau*** in *g**uau*** (a dog barking)

Syllable Structure in Spanish

Spanish syllables are primarily CVC (consonant, vowel, consonant) or CV (consonant, vowel). As in English, every syllable must contain a vowel. The most common dividing point for Spanish syllables is a consonant followed by a vowel. (*cuchara=**cu-cha-ra***). When two consonants occur next to each other, they are split into two separate syllables unless the second consonant is an **l** or an **r** (*cuando* = ***cuan-do***, *trabajo* = ***tra-ba-jo***). When three consonants occur together, they are typically split with the first in one syllable and the second two in another syllable (*inglés* = ***in-glés***). When two vowels occur next to each other, keep dipthongs together in one syllable and split other vowel pairs or accented vowels into separate syllables (*baile* = ***bai-le***, *feo* = ***fe-o***, *sucio* = ***su-cio***, *tío* = ***tí-o***)

Rules for Determining Stress

For words that end in a vowel, **-n**, or **-s**, the stress falls on the penultimate syllable. (e.g., *nada=**NA-da***, *zapato* = ***za-PA-to***, *limonada* = ***li-mo-NA-da***). Stress for words ending in consonants other than -**n** or **-s** falls on the last syllable (e.g., *ciudad* = ***ci-u-DAD***, *doctor* = ***doc-TOR***). Exceptions are noted with a written accent mark (e.g., *lápiz=**LA-piz***, *comió= **com-i-O***). (See section "Rules for the written stress or accent mark" below.)

Morphology

Verb Inflections

Spanish verbs are inflected by changing endings. These conjugations mark number, person, tense, mood, and aspect. Verb inflections will be described in the Syntax section.

Noun Inflections

Spanish nouns are divided into two grammatical "genders" and are marked for number. Only pronouns are marked for case (subject vs. object vs. object of preposition). Articles and adjectives are inflected to match the nouns they modify in both number and gender.

Gender in Spanish Words

There are two genders in Spanish (masculine and feminine) for nouns, adjectives, and articles. Every noun has a gender; there is no neuter in Spanish (the English pronoun "it" is an example of a neuter). Even inanimate objects and other nouns that have no connotations with biological gender have a grammatical gender, and the two conceptions of gender have little relation. For example, the word for a dress (*vestido*) is masculine!

Rules for Determining the Gender of Nouns

With very few exceptions, nouns that end with the letter **o** are masculine (*carr**o**, libr**o***) , and nouns that end with the letter **a** are feminine (*cas**a**, mes**a***).

There are some special rules regarding the gender of nouns:

- nouns ending in **-dad**, **-tad**, **-tud**, **-umbre**, **-ión**, **-ie**, **-cia**, **-ez**, and **-eza** are usually feminine (***la** ciu**dad**, **la** liber**tad**, **la** certid**umbre**, **la** canc**ión**, **la** ser**ie**, **la** diferen**cia**, **la** sencill**ez**, **la** trist**eza***)
- nouns ending in **-aje**, **-ambre**, **-or**, and **-án** are usually masculine (***el** equip**aje**, **el** cal**ambre**, **el** val**or**, **el** refr**án***)

Other groups of noun that are masculine are:

- the days of the week (***el** martes, **el** jueves*)
- the months of the year (***el** enero, **el** agosto*)
- languages (***el** griego, **el** inglés*)
- numbers (***el** uno, **el** diez*)
- colors (***el** gris, **el** blanco*)
- infinitives (***el** contaminar, **el** caminar*)
- rivers, seas, and oceans (***el** río Nilo, **el** mar Rojo, **el** océano Pacífico*)

Forming the Feminine Version of a Noun

Nouns that refer to people or animals generally have two versions: one ending in **-a** for the female (*niñ**a**, gat**a**, perr**a***), and one ending in **-o** for the male (*niñ**o**, gat**o**, perr**o***).

There are other rules used in Spanish to form the feminine of a noun referring to an animate being:

- nouns that end in **-or**, **-án**, **-ón**, and **-ín** are usually masculine and form the feminine by adding an **-a** (*doct**or**/doct**ora**; alem**án**/alem**ana**; campe**ón**/campe**ona**; bailar**ín**/bailar**ina***).
- nouns ending in **-ista**, and **-nte** stay the same for both the feminine and the masculine but the article and any adjective used changes (***el** art**ista**/**la** art**ista**; **el** canta**nte** alt**o**/**la** canta**nte** alt**a***).

Sometimes, as in English, the female and male of the same animate object use different nouns rather than two versions of the same noun (woman/man, *mujer/hombre*) but the gender assignment is consistent with the gender they represent (***la** mujer, **el** hombre*).

Some nouns have the same form for the feminine and the masculine, but their meaning is different depending on the gender (***el** capital* = money/***la** capital* = city; ***el** frente*=front/***la** frente*=forehead; ***el** orden*=neatness/**la** *orden*=command)

Forming the Plural of a Noun

The process to form the plural of a noun from the singular version is very similar in Spanish and English. In Spanish, all nouns ending in a vowel are made plural by adding an **-s** at the end of the word. (*libr**o**/libr**os**; herman**a**/herman**as***).

When the noun ends in a consonant, instead of adding an **-s**, the noun is pluralized by adding **-es** (*mes/mes**es**; ley/ley**es**; árbol/árbol**es**, pescad**or**/pescad**ores***) just as is done in English with words that end in **-s**, **-ch**, **-sh**, **-x**, or **-o** (fox/fox**es**). Be aware of required spelling changes when adding **-es** (*pez/peces; lapiz/lápices*) (See section "Spelling changes in plurals and derivatives" below)

Some nouns, such as *los anteojos* (glasses) and *las tijeras* (scissors), are always used in plural in Spanish. Others, such as l*as afueras* (outskirts), *las ganas* (willingness), and *los bienes* (assets), are generally used in the plural but might be occasionally used in the singular.

Nouns that have more than one syllable and end with an unstressed vowel plus an **-s** do not have a different form for the plural (***la*** *crisis/**las** crisis*; ***el*** *jueves/**los** jueves*; ***el*** *paraguas/**los** paraguas*).

Family names are not pluralized in Spanish (***La familia García*** *vive en esta casa* = **The García family** lives in this house; *Mi hermana conoce a **los García*** = my sister knows **the Garcías**)

Agreement

Articles and Adjectives

In Spanish, the article and the adjective used with a noun must agree in gender and number with the noun they refer to (***el*** *coche roj**o**, **los** coches roj**os**, **la** blusa amarill**a**, **las** blusas amarill**as***). The rules for inflecting adjectives for number and gender are contained in the chart below:

Masculine		Feminine	
Singular	**Plural**	**Singular**	**Plural**
ends with **-o** (*alto*)	**-os** (*altos*)	**-a** (*alta*)	**-as** (*altas*)
ends with **-e** (*interesante*) ends with **-ista** (*egoísta*)	**-es** (*interesantes*) **-istas** (*egoístas*)	**-e** (*interesante*) **-ista** (*egoísta*)	**-es** (*interesantes*) **-istas** (*egoístas*)
ends with consonant (*gris*) exception: ends with **-z** (*feliz*)	**-es** (*grises*) **z** changes to **c** before adding **-es** (felices)	-consonant (*gris*) **-z** (*feliz*)	**-es** (*grises*) **z** changes to **c** before adding **-es** (*felices*)
ends with **-or, ón, -in** (*trabajador*)	**-es** (*trabajadores*)	**-a** (*trabajadora*)	**-as** (*trabajadoras*)

Nouns and Verbs

The subject of the sentence and the verb associated with that subject must agree in person and number (***el niño*** *llor**ó**; **los niños** llor**aron**; **yo** ten**go** frío; **nosotros** ten**emos** frío; **tú** vien**es** esta noche; **ustedes** vien**en** esta noche*). There are also rules for the agreement of verb tenses and modes. These forms and rules will be discussed in the Syntax section.

Comparisons

Superiority and Inferiority

In English, comparisons are often made by creating new word forms (nice/**nicer**, fast/**fastest,** good/**better/worse**) In most cases, comparisons in Spanish are denoted by the expressions ***más...que*** and ***menos...que*** with the adjective, adverb, or noun placed in between (*Juan es **más grande que** Pedro; yo trabajo **más rápidamente que** Tomás; tenemos **más confianza que** tú; mi jardín está **menos iluminado que** el del vecino; Susana tiene **menos dinero que** Ana*).

There are a few Spanish words that have their own comparative forms. The most notable are ***menor*** (younger), ***mayor*** (older), ***mejor*** (better), and ***peor*** (worse). These words replace the ***mas...*** or ***menos...*** in the previous construction (*yo soy **menor que** mi hermano; mi hermano es **mayor que** yo; Pedro tiene **mejor voz que** Juan; Juan tiene **peor voz que** Pedro*).

Equality

To express a comparison of equality, the Spanish language uses the expression ***tan...como*** with the adjective or adverb in between (*Juan es **tan alto como** Pedro; Juan escribe **tan bien como** Pedro*).

If the comparison includes a noun, the expression ***tanto...como*** is used (*este vaso tiene* ***tanto jugo como*** *ése*). In this expression, ***tanto*** has to agree in gender and number with the noun it refers to (*tengo* ***tanto frío*** *como ustedes; Juan tiene* ***tantos juguetes*** *como Pedro; la montaña recibió* ***tanta lluvia*** *como el valle; tengo* ***tantas hermanas*** *como Juan*).

Relative Superlative

The relative superlative describes a noun in the context of a group. In English, relative superlatives are noted by placing the words **most** or **least** before the adjective, adverb, or noun, or adding the suffix **-est**. (Maria is **the most beautiful** of her sisters, Juan is **the least qualified** in the department, Pedro is **the** fast**est** runner on his team) The superlative degree of adjectives in Spanish is expressed by using the comparative form of the adjective (***más lindo, menos inteligente*** – see section "Superiority and inferiority" above) preceded by the definitive article (***el*** *más lindo,* ***el*** *menos inteligente*). The definite article has to agree in gender and number with the noun it refers to (***María*** *es* ***la más bonita*** *de las hermanas;* ***Pedro y Juan*** *son* ***los menos autoritarios*** *del grupo;* ***estas casas*** *son* ***las más caras*** *de la zona*). This rule also applies to the irregular comparatives such as *mejor, peor, mayor*, and *menor* (***la mejor*** *carne de la región;* ***el peor*** *alumno de la clase,* ***las mayores*** *distancias del país;* ***los menores*** *detalles de la pintura*).

Absolute Superlative

The absolute superlative describes a noun without comparing it to a group and is communicated with the words **very** or **extremely** in English (Pedro is **very** intelligent). One way to denote the absolute superlative in Spanish is by adding ***muy*** or ***extremadamente/sumamente*** before the adjective (*Pedro es* ***muy*** *inteligente; Juan es* ***extremadamente*** *cuidadoso*). Another option is to add the suffix ***-ísimo*** to the adjective (Pedro es ***inteligentísimo***) in accordance in gender and number with the noun it refers to (***ísima, ísimos, ísimas***). Adjectives ending in a vowel lose that vowel when the suffix ***-ísimo*** is added (*much**o**/muchísimo; car**a**/carísima; mal**os**/malísimos; pequeñ**os**/pequeñísimos*). Be aware of spelling changes required to comply with spelling rules (*ri**co**/ri**qu**ísimo; lar**go**/lar**gu**ísimo; feli**z**/feli**c**ísimo*). (See section "Spelling changes in plurals and derivatives" below.)

Word Derivatives and Derivational Suffixes

Derivate Words

A derivate word is one that has been formed using an existing word as its base. Derivatives are not variations of a word, like different conjugation forms of the same verb (**eat/eats/eating**) or the plural of a noun (**house/houses**). Rather, they are new words coming from a "base" word (**clear/clearly/unclear, respect/respectful/disrespect**). These new words are often formed with derivational prefixes and suffixes in English. The concept is the same in Spanish (***persona/personalmente/impersonal, conocer/conocimiento/desconocer***).

However, in English, many words are used interchangeably as nouns and verbs. For example, **I ride a bike**: **ride** is a verb. **My friend gives me a ride**: **ride** is a noun. In Spanish, even these derivate words will be marked differently for different parts of speech. (I **love** my mom = *Yo* ***amo*** *a mi mamá.* **Love** is important = ***El amor*** *es importante.*)

Common Derivational Suffixes

Some examples of suffixes that form nouns from verbs in Spanish are ***-dor*** (*trabajar – trabaja**dor***) and ***-miento*** (*pensar – pensa**miento***). Some examples of Spanish suffixes that form adjectives are ***-ble*** (*amar – ama**ble***) and ***-tivo*** (*competir – compete**tivo***). Sometimes the noun or adjective will contain spelling changes that the verb undergoes (***juego*** = game, similar to spelling changes in the verb *jugar*) or be related to the past participle of the verb (***el puesto, el dicho***). If you don't recognize a word immediately, you can consider different forms of a verb that appears to be related to help you identify the "word family" of a given word.

Adverb Formation

To form an adverb from an adjective in Spanish, the suffix ***-mente*** is added to the feminine singular form of the adjective (*rápido/rápida**mente**; lento/lenta**mente***). This is similar to the addition of **-ly** to an adjective to form an adverb in English (quick/quick**ly**; sad/sad**ly**). Adjectives that are the same in the feminine and in the masculine add ***-mente*** to their singular form (*fácil/fácil**mente**; triste/triste**mente***). As in English, some adjectives do not change form to become adverbs (e.g., *alto, bajo, fuerte*). *Demasiado, más, menos, mucho, poco, mejor, peor,* and *tanto* also do not change from their adjective form (*vayamos **más** rápido; es el sitio **peor** iluminado*). The adverb that corresponds to *bueno* is ***bien***, and to *malo* is ***mal*** (*el hotel está **bien** ubicado*).

Possession

Spanish does not have the **'s** to express possession that is employed in English. It uses the preposition ***de*** instead (**Tom's** book/*el libro **de Tom***; my **parents'** house/*la casa de **mis padres***). In some instances ***de*** is followed by the definite article. In those cases, the article has to agree in gender and number with the noun that follows (*el libro **de la niña**; el gato **de los vecinos***). For phonetic reasons when ***de*** is followed by ***el***, the two words are contracted into ***del*** (*el libro **del** niño*).

To inquire about possession, ***de quién*** is equivalent to **whose** (*¿**de quién** es este libro?*/**whose** book is this?). In those cases where you know there is more than one possessor, ***de quiénes*** is used in the interrogative form (*¿**de quiénes** es este libro?*/**whose** book is this?). In the interrogative form, there is no difference between feminine and masculine.

Diminutives

Diminutives are used to denote smallness or to express affection, and are usually formed in Spanish by adding the suffix ***-ito*** at the end of the noun. If the noun ends in an unaccented vowel, the vowel is dropped (*libro/libr**ito**; perro/perr**ito***). If the noun ends in **e**, **n**, or **r**, a **c** is added to the suffix, making it ***-cito*** (*padre/padre**cito**; joven/joven**cito**; mujer/mujer**cita***). The suffix has to agree with the gender and number of the noun being modified (***el** camión/camioncit**o**; **los** collares/collarcit**os**; **la** blusa/blusit**a**; **las** sillas/sillit**as***). Other spelling changes that need to be taken into account are for nouns that have **g** or **c** in the last syllable; they change to **gu** and **qu** (*lago/laguito*; *Paco/Pa**qu**ito*) See section "Spelling changes in plurals and derivatives" below.

Compound Words

Spanish compound words usually consist of a verb and a noun together. While English words tend to have the noun first and then the verb (**dishwasher, skyscraper**), Spanish compound words typically have the verb first and then the noun (***lavaplatos, abrelatas, rascacielos***).

Contractions

Spanish has two standard contractions: the preposition *a* + the article *el* form the contraction ***al,*** and the preposition *de* + the article *el* form the contraction ***del*** (*vamos **a el** partido = vamos **al** partido, el sombrero **de el** señor = el sombrero **del** señor*).

Pronouns Added to the End of a Word

When object and reflexive pronouns are used with infinitives, present participles, and affirmative commands, they are added to the verb to create one word. See the sections "Pronouns in the imperative mood" and "Position of pronouns when using the present participle and infinitives" below for examples and details.

Cognates

Cognates are words in different languages that have the same etymological origin and similar meaning, spelling, and pronunciation. Some English/Spanish cognates are identical (***doctor, terrible, hospital, cruel***) and some have minor differences (**religion/*religión*, Canada/*Canadá*, novel/*novela*, dentist/*dentista*, president/*presidente*, information/*información***). Some other cognates have bigger differences but still have the same root (**abandon/*abandonar*, decide/*decidir*, university/*universidad***). False cognates are words that have some similarities in spelling and pronunciation but do not share the same origins and do not have the same meaning Some examples of false cognates are **exit**(*salida*) and ***éxito***(success), **hay**(*heno*) and ***hay***(there is), **large**(*grande*) and ***largo***(long), **pie**(*pastel*) and ***pie***(foot), **rope**(*soga*) and ***ropa***(clothes), **embarrassed**(*avergonzada*) and ***embarazada***(pregnant).

Instances Where the Same Word Is Used Both in Spanish and in English

All languages incorporate words and phrases from other languages. Spanish and English are no exceptions. English words related to technology have crossed over to a wide range of languages and words like ***e-mail***, ***clic*** (**click**), and ***DVD***, for example, have been absorbed into Spanish, becoming a part of it. Spanish words have made their way into English, too. For some of them there is another English word that can be used as well (***fiesta*/party, *patio*/courtyard**), but some have no equivalent in English (***adobe, armadillo, tango***). Both languages also share the use of some French words (***amateur, ballet, boulevard***). Examples of loan words from Italian used both in English and Spanish include many musical terms (***aria, cadenza, opera, piano, viola***). Many of words borrowed from German are used in philosophy in Spanish and in English (***angst, ersatz, gestalt, geist***).

Orthography

Capitalization

Capitalization is not employed in Spanish as frequently as it is in English. The first word of a sentence is always capitalized. Proper names of people (*Jorge Luis Borges, María*), companies (*Sony, Chevron*) and places (*España, Madrid, el río Nilo*) are capitalized. Abbreviations of personal titles (*Sr., Dr.*) are capitalized but if the full word is used, it is written in lower case (*el señor Aguilar, el doctor Fuentes*). For titles of books, stories, poems, essays, songs, films, etc., only the first letter is capitalized (La odisea, La guerra de las galaxias). The days of the week (*lunes, viernes*) and the months of the year (*enero, abril*) are not capitalized. Nationalities (*argentino, australiano*) and languages (*latín, inglés*) also are not capitalized.

Writing Dates

In Spanish the days of the week and the months of the year are not capitalized unless they are at the beginning of a sentence. The proper way to write a date is ***18 de diciembre de 1948*** in contrast to the usual format of **December 18, 1948** in English. However, the form ***diciembre 18, 1948*** has started to appear in Spanish as well. When using dashes or slashes, the order is not the same: in English it is **month/day/year** while in Spanish is **day/month/year**. The correct meaning is obvious in some instances. There is no doubt that **25/12/2018** means **December 25, 2018** (as there is no 25th month). But in some cases this difference can be confusing. **3/7/2018** is **July 3, 2018** in Spanish and **March 7, 2018** in English. Be aware of this difference when reading and writing.

Writing Numbers

The English language uses a period to denote the decimal point in a number and commas every 3 digits (**21,097.83**). Different regions of the Spanish speaking world use different systems of marking numbers. Sometimes a comma is used to denote the decimals, sometimes a period, and occasionally an apostrophe. So, the first three digits of π could be written one of the following ways: ***3,14/3.14/3'14.*** Commas, periods, or spaces can be used every 3 digits. Therefore, the number ten thousand can be written one of the following ways: ***10,000/10.000/10 000.***

When writing or reading a definite number, the words **hundred**, **thousand**, and **million** in English are always in singular. In Spanish, the words ***cien*** and ***millón*** use the singular or the plural form in accordance with the number, while the word ***mil*** is always in singular (200 = *dos**cientos***; 1.000.000 = ***un millón***, 5.000.000 = *cinco **millones***; 3000 = *tres **mil***).

Special Interrogation and Exclamation Marks

In Spanish, as in English, questions end with the interrogation mark **?**, and exclamations end with the exclamation mark **!**. But in Spanish, for both types of sentences, an inverted mark is required at the beginning of the sentence. Therefore, all questions in Spanish begin with **¿**, and all exclamations begin with **¡**. (*¿Dónde estás?, ¡Estoy aqui!*) Computer keyboards for the English language do not have a key for these symbols, and there are different options you can use to insert them depending on the program you are using. A test that requires you to write in Spanish will use a particular user interface for inserting these symbols that you can familiarize yourself with ahead of time by accessing the website for that specific test.

Rules for the Written Stress or Accent Mark

The Spanish language uses a written stress or accent mark on vowels to denote exceptions to its stressing rules (See section "Rules for determining stress" above). Words with a stress in the last syllable will have a written stress or accent mark if they end in a vowel (*mamá, café, así*) or the consonants **-n** (*camión, común, jamón*) or **-s** (*jamás, francés, anís*). For those words stressed in the second-to-last syllable, an accent mark is needed when they end in any consonant (*ángel, álbum, cadáver, lápiz*) except **-n** and **-s**. For words stressed in the third-to-last syllable, a written stress is always required, regardless of the last letter (*apéndice, códigos, diplomático*).

There are a few special rules when it comes to the written stress or accent mark in Spanish:

- Written accent marks are only placed on vowels.
- One-syllable words never have a written accent except when there are two possible different meanings: *el* (the) and *él* (he), *si* (if) and *sí* (yes), *tu* (your) and *tú* (you), *mas* (but) and *más* (more).
- An written accent is used when two adjacent vowels that would otherwise form a dipthong are to be pronounced separately (*media* vs *hacía*).
- Adverbs such as *cuándo* (when), *dónde* (where), and *cómo* (how) as well as pronouns such as *quién* (who), *qué* (what), and *cuál* (which) require an accent mark when used as interrogatives. This accent mark is not present when the word is not used as an interrogative. (*¿Dónde está el libro? Yo voy donde mi esposo va.*)
- Adverbs formed by adding *-mente* to an adjective that has a written stress keep the accent mark (*fácil–fácilmente, cortés–cortésmente*).
- When pronouns are added to the end of a verb form, to keep the accent as it was in the infinitive form - see section "Pronouns" below. (*Estoy buscándolo, ¡Cepíllate los dientes!*)

Special Cases for the Spelling of Conjunctions

For phonetic reasons, the conjunction ***y*** (and) changes to ***e*** when the word after the conjunction starts with ***i*** or ***hi*** (*español **e** inglés, padre **e** hijo, Susana **e** Isabel*). Something similar occurs with the conjunction ***o*** (or), which is changed to ***u*** when the word that follows it starts with **o** or **ho** (*setenta **u** ochenta, casas **u** hoteles, Carlos **u** Honorio*).

Spelling Changes in Plurals and Derivatives

When an e, i, or y is placed next to a **c**, **g**, or **z** that was previously the end of the word or followed by an **a**, **o**, or **u**, there is a spelling change, primarily to maintain the pronunciation of **c**, **g**, or **z**.

c changes to **qu**. (*buscar: bus**qu**é, rico: ri**qu**ísimo*)

g adds a **u** (*pagar: pa**gu**é*)

z changes to **c** (*almorzar: almorcé, lápiz: lápices*)

Spelling Changes in Verb Conjugations

Spelling Changes in Verbs Ending in -Car

In Spanish, the letter **c** has a hard sound like the letter **k** in English when is it followed by an **a** (*carro*), **o** (*colegio*), or **u** (*curva*), and a soft sound like the **c** found in English in words such as **ce**ntury and **ci**gar, when it is followed by the vowels **e** (*celoso*) or **i** (*cien*). (See section "Pronunciations of the letter c in Spanish" above.) To keep the hard sound of the letter **c** found in the infinitive of a verb ending in **-car** (sa**car**, to**car**, bus**car**), whenever a verb ending places an **e** or **i** next to the **c**, the letter **c** is replaced by **qu** (*yo sa**qué**, ¡no to**ques**!, espero que bus**quemos***).

Spelling Changes in Verbs Ending in -Gar

When followed by a consonant (*regla, negro*) or by the vowels **a**, **o**, or **u** (***ga**to, a**go**sto, **gu**sto*), the sound of the letter **g** in Spanish is similar to its hard sound in English words such as **g**ood and **g**ame. If the letter **g** is followed by the vowels **e** or **i** (***ge**nerar, re**gi**stro*), its sound is like the sound of the Spanish **j** (a strong English **h**, see section "Pronuciation of the letter j in Spanish" above for regional variations). To keep the hard sound of the letter **g** found in the infinitive of a verb ending in **-gar** (*jugar, pagar, llegar*), whenever a verb ending places an **e** or **i** next to the **g**, a **u** is added after the **g** (*yo ju**gué**, ¡no pa**gues**!, espero que lle**guen***).

Spelling Changes in Verbs Ending in -Zar

In Spanish, the letter **z** is never used before **e** or **i** and is typically replaced with a **c** when a plural ending or a verb ending places an **e** or **i** next to the **z**. To be consistent with this rule, for those verbs ending in **-zar** (*empe**zar**, alcan**zar**, utili**zar***), the **z** is replaced by a **c** whenever a verb ending places an **e** or **i** next to the **z** (*yo empe**cé**, espero que alcan**ces**, ¡no utili**cen**!*). Also, because of this rule, there are no verbs ending in **-zer** (second conjugation) or **-zir** (third conjugation).

Spelling Changes in Verbs Ending in -Cer and -Cir

Verbs in Spanish that end in **-cer** (*cono**cer**, pare**cer**, mere**cer**, ofre**cer**, cre**cer***) or **-cir** (*condu**cir**, lu**cir**, tradu**cir**, produ**cir***) preceded by a vowel are irregular in the present tense of the indicative for the first person singular (*yo*) form. Since the **o** hardens the sound of the **c**, (see section "Pronunciations of the letter c in Spanish" above), these verbs add a **z** before the **c** in the present indicative *yo* form (*yo cono**zc**o, yo ofre**zc**o, yo cre**zc**o, yo condu**zc**o, yo tradu**zc**o, yo produ**zc**o*). The same addition is made in the present of the subjunctive tense for all persons as well as in most of the imperative forms, since in all these cases an **a** is being placed next to the **c,** which changes its sound. (*que él mere**zc**a, que ellos apare**zc**an, ¡produ**zc**an!, ¡no condu**zc**as!*). The same rules apply to all other verbs derived from those mentioned above (*desconocer, desaparecer, aparecer, desmerecer, deslucir*).

Spelling Changes in Verbs Ending in -Ger and -Gir

The letter **g** in Spanish has a hard sound like the same letter in English in words such as **g**arnet and **g**ray before **a** (***g**aviota*), **o** (***g**overno*), and **u** (*a**g**udo*), but a Spanish **j** sound before **e** (***g**erente*) and **i** (*a**g**itar*). In those verbs ending in **-ger** (*esco**ger**, reco**ger***) and **-gir** (*ele**gir**, diri**gir***), to be consistent and keep the soft sound, whenever a verb ending places an **a** or **o** next to the **g** (the *yo* form of the present indicative, all forms of the present subjunctive, most forms of the imperative), the the letter **g** is replaced by the letter **j**, (*yo esco**jo**, quiero que reco**jan**, ¡eli**ja**!*).

Changes in Spelling for Verbs Ending in a Vowel and -Er or -Ir

When a verb ends in a vowel followed by **-er** or **-ir**, certain spelling changes occur to avoid forming a dipthong or tripthong where there was not one before. When a verb ending would place three vowels in a row, (third person forms of the preterite, present participles), the middle **i** is changed to a **y**. (*ellos le**y**eron, el jugador se ca**y**ó, cre**y**endo*). When a verb ending would place only an **i** next to the vowel at the end of the verb stem (first and second person forms of the preterite, past participles), the **i** receives an accent (cre**í**mos, le**í**ste, cre**í**do). An exception/special case is noted below in the section "Changes in spelling for verbs ending in -uir".

Changes in Spelling for Verbs Ending in -Uir

Verbs of the third conjugation ending in **-uir** (*incl**uir**, h**uir**, constr**uir**, contrib**uir**, destr**uir***) have a **y** added in the present tense (*yo inclu**y**o, tú hu**y**es, él constru**y**e, ellos contribu**y**en*) before all endings except those beginning with an **i** (*nosotros destru**í**mos*). Notice that the **i** carries an accent mark in this situation. The same rules apply for the preterite and present subjunctive tenses (*él constru**y**ó, tú contribu**í**ste, que nosotros destru**y**amos*).

Syntax

Word Order in Sentences

Both English and Spanish are basically SVO languages; languages in which the more common sentence structure is Subject + Verb + Object (**The boy eats bread/*El niño come pan***). English is more structured and allows variations in word order primarily for questions or as a literary or poetic device. Spanish is more flexible, and it is very common to find sentences where the verb or the object is at the beginning of the sentence (***Pedro leyó este libro/Leyó Pedro este libro/Este libro lo leyó Pedro***). The meaning of the sentence remains basically the same but with some subtle variations on emphasis. Also, when object pronouns are used to replace an object in Spanish, they are customarily placed before the verb rather than after the verb (*Pedro leyó* ***el libro***/*Pedro* ***lo*** *leyó*). It is important to note that the subject is frequently omitted in Spanish since the verb ending indicates the subject. (*Lleg**amos** tarde*/**We** arrived late).

Interrogative Form

The structure of sentences denoting interrogation is very similar in English and in Spanish. If the questions include interrogative adjectives, pronouns and adverbs such as *quién, cuál, cómo*, etc., the questions begins with those words (*¿**Quién** vino?, ¿**Cuál** es tu casa?, ¿**Cómo** estás?*). In all other cases the question will begin with the verb followed by the subject. (*¿**Llegaron los niños** de la escuela?*). Be aware that many times the subject is omitted (*¿**Llegaron** de la escuela?*). In their interrogative form, the interrogative adjectives, pronouns, and adverbs mentioned above always have a written stress or accent mark. Questions in Spanish require an interrogation mark at the beginning (¿) as well as at the end (?).

Exclamatory Form

Exclamations in Spanish can be expressed with ***qué*** in a very similar manner as English does with **what** (*¡**Qué** día tan bonito!*/**What** a beautiful day!) and **how** (*¡**Qué** bonito!*/**How** beautiful!). The exclamatory form is also use to denote a warning (*¡Cuidado!*/Careful!), an order (*¡No hable!*/Don't talk!) and emotions (*¡Por fin llegaste!*/You finally arrived!) in the same way as the English language does. As with interrogatives, adjectives, pronouns and adverbs such as *qué, cómo, cuánto*, etc., have a written stress or accent mark. In Spanish, all exclamations require an exclamation mark (¡) at the beginning as well as at the end (!).

Adjectives

Adjectives That Go After the Noun

In Spanish, descriptive adjectives are usually placed after the noun they modify (*la casa **blanca**, el hombre **alto***).

Adjectives That Go Before the Noun

Some adjectives are placed before the noun they modify. Their categories are:

- Adjectives that denote quantity such as *alguno, ambos, bastante, mucho, poco, suficiente, varios* (*presentó **algunas** ideas; **ambos** estudiantes son alemanes; tengo **bastante** dinero*).
- Adjectives that refer to number or order such as *primero, segundo, cinco*, etc. (*la **segunda** casa a la derecha, **cinco** libros*).
- Some adjectives that indicate quality such as *bueno, malo, mejor* and *peor* can be placed before or after the noun (***buena** comida/comida **buena**; el **peor** caso/el caso **peor***).
- Possessive and demonstrative adjectives (See sections "Possessive adjectives" and "Demonstrative adjectives" below.

Bueno, malo, alguno, ninguno, primero, tercero, and *grande* drop their final **-o** or **-e** when placed before a masculine singular noun they are modifying (***buen** trabajo/trabajo **bueno**, **gran** estadio/estadio **grande***).

Adjectives Before or After the Noun

Some adjectives have different meanings depending on whether they are placed before or after the noun they modify. Examples are:

- *la **antigua** capital*/the **former** capital—*la capital **antigua***/the **old** capital
- *una **cierta** condición*/a **certain** condition—*una condición **cierta***/a **sure** condition
- ***diferentes** ideas*/**various** ideas—*ideas **diferentes***/**different** ideas
- ***gran** universidad*/**great** university—*universidad **grande***/**big** university
- *el **mismo** jefe*/the **same** boss—*el jefe **mismo***/the boss **himself**
- ***pobre** hombre*/**unfortunate** man—*hombre **pobre***/**destitute** man
- *un **simple** carpintero*/**just** a carpenter—*un carpintero **simple***/a **simple** carpenter
- *la **única** oportunidad*/the **only** opportunity—*la oportunidad **única***/the **unique** opportunity
- *mi **viejo** amigo*/my **longtime** friend—*mi amigo **viejo***/my **elderly** friend

Possessive Adjectives

	Masculine Singular	Feminine Singular	Masculine Plural	Feminine Plural
my	*mi*		*mis*	
your (singular informal)	*tu*		*tus*	
his/her/its/your (singular formal)	*su*		*sus*	
our	*nuestro*	*nuestra*	*nuestros*	*nuestras*
your (plural informal)	*vuestro*	*vuestra*	*vuestros*	*vuestras*
their/your (plural formal)	*su*		*sus*	

In Spanish, possessive adjectives refer to the possessor but, like all adjectives, must agree in gender and number with the noun they modify (***mi** hijo, **mis** hijos; **nuestra** casa, **nuestras** casas*). Note that Spanish uses ***su/sus*** for the third person regardless of the gender and number of the possessor (**Her** son—***su** hijo*; **their** house—***su** casa*; **her** books—***sus** libros*; **its** food—***su** comida*). ***Su/sus*** is also used for the formal second person singular (you brought **your** book/*usted trajo **su** libro*) and for the formal second person plural (you all drink **your** coffee/*ustedes toman **su** café*).

Demonstrative Adjectives

In Spanish there are three possible demonstrative adjectives: ***este***, ***ese***, and ***aquel***, compared to the two that exist in English (**this, that**). ***Este*** refers to anything close. ***Ese*** denotes a certain distance. ***Aquel*** indicates farther away or over there. Demonstrative adjectives, like all adjectives in Spanish, have to agree in gender and number with the nouns they modify (*este libr**o***/this book; *aquell**a** cas**a***/the house over there; *es**os** gat**os***/those cats; *est**as** sill**as***/these chairs). The different forms of the demonstrative adjectives can be found in the chart below

Masculine singular	Feminine singular	Masculine plural	Feminine plural
este	*esta*	*estos*	*estas*
ese	*esa*	*esos*	*Esas*
aquel	*aquella*	*aquellos*	*aquellas*

Verbs

Verbs can be marked for number, person, tense, mood, and aspect in Spanish.

Infinitive Form

In English, the infinitive form of a verb is denoted by the particle **to** that precedes it (**to** walk, **to** cry, **to** run). In Spanish, the infinitive forms of verbs are denoted by the endings **-ar** (*camin**ar**, llor**ar**, est**ar***), **-er** (*corr**er**, vend**er**, s**er***), or **-ir** (*escrib**ir**, dec**ir***). These can be called “first, second, and third conjugations”, or “-ar, -er, and -ir verbs”, and all Spanish verbs belong to one of these three groups. Each group has its own forms for each tense which apply to all regular verbs that belong to that particular conjugation “group”. Conjugated forms for irregular verbs vary from group to group and even within the same conjugation.

Indicative Mood

The indicative mood communicates objective statements. The present, preterite, imperfect, future, progressive, and perfect tenses are considered indicative.

PRESENT INDICATIVE, FORMATION

Drop the infinitive ending of the verb and use the endings in the table below to form the present of the indicative for all regular verbs of the three conjugations.

	-AR	-ER	-IR
yo	*-o*	*-o*	*-o*
tú	*-as*	*-es*	*-es*
él	*-a*	*-e*	*-e*
nosotros	*-amos*	*-emos*	*-imos*
vosotros	*-áis*	*-éis*	*-ís*
ellos	*-an*	*-en*	*-en*

Examples:

-ar verbs (e.g., *hablar, cantar, estudiar*)

yo hablo I talk	*nosotros hablamos* we talk
tú hablas you talk	*vosotros habláis* you all talk
él habla he talks	*ellos hablan* they talk

-er verbs (e.g., *comer, correr, leer*)

yo como I eat	*nosotros comemos* we eat
tú comes you eat	*vosotros coméis* you all eat
él come he eats	*ellos comen* they eat

-ir verbs (e.g., *abrir, asistir, permitir*)

yo abro I open	*nosotros abrimos* we open
tú abres you open	*vosotros abrís* you all open
él abre he opens	*ellos abren* they open

Present Indicative, Verbs with Irregular First-Person Singular Forms

The following verbs are irregular in the first person singular of the present indicative but follow the regular patterns for the other forms of the present indicative.

Verb	First person singular form
caer	***caigo***
dar	***doy***
hacer	***hago***
poner	***pongo***
saber	***sé***
salir	***salgo***
traer	***traigo***
valer	***valgo***
ver	***veo***

Present Indicative, Verbs with a Stem Change

There are three groups of verbs that have a stem change in all singular forms and the third-person plural form of the verb in the present indicative. The endings remain regular.

e changes to **ie** (e.g., *querer, pensar, perder, empezar, preferir, despertarse*)

*yo qu**ie**ro*	*nosotros queremos*
*tú qu**ie**res*	*vosotros queréis*
*él qu**ie**re*	*ellos qu**ie**ren*

e changes to **i** (e.g., *pedir, vestirse, servir, repetir*)

*yo p**i**do*	*nosotros pedimos*
*tú p**i**des*	*vosotros pedís*
*él p**i**de*	*ellos p**i**den*

o changes to **ue** (e.g., *dormir, encontrar, poder, contar*) *Jugar* changes **u** to **ue**.

*yo d**ue**rmo*	*nosotros dormimos*
*tú d**ue**rmes*	*vosotros dormís*
*él d**ue**rme*	*ellos d**ue**rmen*

Some verbs have both an irregular first-person singular form and stem changes or spelling changes in other forms of the verb.

tener (e-ie)

*yo **tengo***	*nosotros tenemos*
*tú t**ie**nes*	*vosotros tenéis*
*él t**ie**ne*	*ellos t**ie**nen*

venir (e-ie)

yo ***vengo***	*nosotros venimos*
tú ***vie****nes*	*vosotros venís*
él ***vie****ne*	*ellos* ***vie****nen*

decir (e-i)

yo ***digo***	*nosotros decimos*
tú ***di****ces*	*vosotros decís*
él ***di****ce*	*ellos* ***di****cen*

oír (added y)

yo ***oigo***	*nosotros oímos*
*tú o****y****es*	*vosotros oís*
*él o****y****e*	*ellos o****y****en*

PRETERITE INDICATIVE, FORMATION

Drop the infinitive ending of the verb and use the endings in table below to form the preterite of the indicative for all regular verbs of the three conjugations.

	-AR	-ER	-IR
yo	*-é*	*-í*	*-í*
tú	*-aste*	*-iste*	*-iste*
él	*-ó*	*-ió*	*-ió*
nosotros	*-amos*	*-imos*	*-imos*
vosotros	*-asteis*	*-isteis*	*-isteis*
ellos	*-aron*	*-ieron*	*-ieron*

Examples:

-ar verbs (e.g., *caminar, regresar, llamar*)

yo caminé I walked	*nosotros caminamos* we walked
tú caminaste you walked	*vosotros caminasteis* you all walked
él caminó he walked	*ellos caminaron* they walked

-er verbs (e.g., *aprender, beber, depender*)

yo bebí I drank	*nosotros bebimos* we drank
tú bebiste you drank	*vosotros bebisteis* you drank
él bebió he drank	*ellos bebieron* they drank

-ir verbs (e.g., *vivir, escribir, recibir*)

yo viví I lived	*nosotros vivimos* we lived
tú viviste you lived	*vosotros vivisteis* you all lived
él vivió he lived	*ellos vivieron* they lived

Preterite, Verbs That End in -Car, -Gar, -Zar

See section "Spelling changes in verb conjugations"

Preterite, Verbs That Have a Vowel Followed By -Er or -Ir

See section "Changes in spelling for verbs ending in a vowel and -er or -ir"

Preterite, Verbs That Have a Stem Change in the Present Tense

Stem-changing verbs that end in **-ar** and **-er** have no stem change in the preterite tense

yo desperté	*nosotros despertamos*
tú despertaste	*vosotros despertasteis*
él despertó	*ellos despertaron*

yo perdí	*nosotros perdimos*
tú perdiste	*vosotros perdisteis*
él perdió	*ellos perdieron*

Stem-changing verbs that end in **-ir** have a stem change in the third person forms of the preterite.

o changes to **u**

yo dormí	*nosotros dormimos*
tú dormiste	*vosotros dormisteis*
*él d**u**rmió*	*ellos d**u**rmieron*

e changes to **i**

yo preferí	*nosotros preferimos*
tú preferiste	*vosotros preferisteis*
*él pref**i**rió*	*ellos pref**i**rieron*

Preterite, Irregular Verbs

The following verbs have irregular stems in the preterite. To create their forms in the preterite, use the irregular stem and add the following irregular endings:

andar	***anduv-***
estar	***estuv-***
tener	***tuv-***
caber	***cup-***
haber	***hub-***
poder	***pud-***
poner	***pus-***
saber	***sup-***
querer	***quis-***
venir	***vin-***

yo	***-e***
tú	***-iste***
él	***-o***
nosotros	***-imos***
vosotros	***-isteis***
ellos	***-ieron***

The following verbs have irregular stems in the preterite that end in **-j**. To create their preterite forms, use the same endings as above, but without the **i** in the third-person plural form.

conducir	***conduj-***
decir	***dij-***
producir	***produj-***
traer	***traj-***

yo	***-e***
tú	***-iste***
él	***-o***
nosotros	***-imos***
vosotros	***-isteis***
ellos	***-eron***

The following verbs are irregular in the preterite

Ser and ***ir*** (share the same forms in the preterite)

yo fui	*nosotros fuimos*
tú fuiste	*vosotros fuisteis*
él fue	*ellos fueron*

hacer

yo hice	*nosotros hicimos*
tú hiciste	*vosotros hicisteis*
él hizo	*ellos hicieron*

dar

yo di	*nosotros dimos*
tú diste	*vosotros disteis*
él dio	*ellos dieron*

ver

yo vi	*nosotros vimos*
tú viste	*vosotros visteis*
él vio	*ellos vieron*

Preterite, Uses

The preterite is used to express:

- One-time actions in the past (ayer yo **me lastimé** el codo, el año pasado **fuimos** a Chile)
- A sequence or chain of events in the past (primero **se despertó** y entonces **se duchó** y **se vistió**)
- An action, emotion, or condition that is considered completed (**me puse** muy triste cuando **perdimos**)
- Actions that interrupt another action in progress, or actions that are completed while another action continues in the background (cuando montaban en bicicleta, Juan **se cayó**, mientras mi mama lavaba los platos, yo **me acosté**)

Imperfect Indicative, Formation

Drop the infinitive ending of the verb and use the endings in the table below to form the imperfect of the indicative for all regular verbs of the three conjugations.

	AR	ER	IR
yo	*-aba*	*-ía*	*-ía*
tú	*-abas*	*-ías*	*-ías*
él	*-aba*	*-ía*	*-ía*
nosotros	*-ábamos*	*-íamos*	*-íamos*
vosotros	*-abais*	*-íais*	*-íais*
ellos	*-aban*	*-ían*	*-ían*

The imperfect can be translated with the English simple past (**I traveled**) but also with verb phrases such as "**I used to travel**", **"I would travel"**, or "**I was traveling**".

Examples:

-ar verbs (e.g., *viajar, regresar, cepillar*)

yo viajaba I traveled/used to travel/would travel/ was traveling	*nosotros viajábamos* we traveled/used to travel/would travel/ were traveling
tú viajabas you traveled/used to travel/would travel/ were traveling	*vosotros viajabais* you all traveled/used to travel/would travel/ were traveling
él viajaba he traveled/used to travel/would travel/ was traveling	*ellos viajaban* they traveled/used to travel/would travel/ were traveling

-er verbs (e.g., *vender, responder, comprender*)

yo vendía I sold/used to sell/would sell/was selling	*nosotros vendíamos* we sold/used to sell/would sell/were selling
tú vendías you sold/used to sell/would sell/were selling	*vosotros vendíais* you all sold/used to sell/would sell/were selling
él vendía he sold/used to sell/would sell/was selling	*ellos vendían* they sold/used to sell/would sell/were selling

-ir verbs (e.g., *describir, discutir*)

yo discutía I discussed/used to discuss/would discuss/ was discussing	*nosotros discutíamos* we discussed/used to discuss/would discuss/ were discussing
tú discutías you discussed/used to discuss/would discuss/ were discussing	*vosotros discutíais* you all discussed/used to discuss/would discuss/ were discussing
él discutía he discussed/used to discuss/would discuss/ was discussing	*ellos discutían* they discussed/used to discuss/would discuss/ were discussing

There are no spelling changes in the imperfect indicative.

IMPERFECT, IRREGULAR VERBS

There are three verbs with irregular forms in the imperfect:

ser

yo era	*nosotros éramos*
tú eras	*vosotros erais*
él era	*ellos eran*

ir

yo iba	*nosotros íbamos*
tú ibas	*vosotros ibais*
él iba	*ellos iban*

ver

yo veía	*nosotros veíamos*
tú veías	*vosotros veíais*
él veía	*ellos veían*

Imperfect, Uses

The imperfect is used to express:

- habitual actions in the past (*cuando **era** niño, siempre **jugaba** en el parquet; **íbamos** de vacaciones a Canadá cada verano*)
- age in the past (***tenía** 9 años cuando conocí a Pedro; ¿cuántos años **tenías** cuando entraste a la escuela*)
- time in the past (*¿qué hora **era** cuando empezó el partido?; **eran** las nueve de la noche cuando llegué a casa*)
- physical and emotional characteristics that are considered permanent in the past (*Ana **era** muy alta de niña; mi tío **era** un hombre muy simpático*)
- continuous actions interrupted by another action in the past (*yo **leía** una novela cuando sonó el teléfono; Juan **dormía** cuando empezó el incendio*)

Gerund/Present Participle, Formation and Usage

The gerund, or present participle (in English,the **-ing** form of a verb), is formed in Spanish by dropping the infinitive ending of the verb and adding ***-ando*** for **-ar** verbs (*caminar/**caminando**; trabajar/**trabajando***) and **-iendo** for **-er** and **-ir** verbs (*comer/**comiendo**, correr/**corriendo**; salir/**saliendo**; recibir/**recibiendo***).

Verbs that end with a vowel followed by **-er** or **-ir** have a spelling change in the gerund (see section "Spelling changes in verbs that end with a vowel and -er/-ir"): *creer/cre**y**endo*

-er and **-ir** verbs that stem-change in the present tense also have a spelling change in the gerund: **e** changes to **i** and **o** changes to **u**. (*dormir/d**u**rmiendo; pedir/p**i**diendo*).

The gerund is used similarly in Spanish and English.

Progressive Tenses, Formation

Progressive tenses use the verb *estar* as an auxiliary verb with the gerund of the main verb.

- yo **estoy comiendo**: I am eating
- tú **estabas durmiendo**: you were sleeping
- él **está estudiando**: he is studying
- nosotros **estábamos viniendo**: we were coming
- vosotros **estáis trabajando**: you are working
- ellos **estaban pintando**: they were painting

Progressive Tenses, Uses

The progressive tenses are used to denote an action that is or was in progress (***yo estaba durmiendo*/I was sleeping; *nosotros estamos mirando*/we are watching**). Progressive tenses are never used in reference to the future as the English "going to...". For those cases, Spanish uses the future tense or the simple future: ***ir a*** and the infinitive of the main verb (**I am going to do** my homework/***voy a hacer*** *mi tarea*; **they are going to finish** the book/*ellos **van a terminar** el libro*).

Past Participles, Formation and Usage

To form the past participle of **-ar** verbs, drop the ***-ar*** and add ***-ado*** (*hablar/**hablado***); for **-er** and **-ir** verbs, drop the ***-er*** or ***-ir*** and add ***-ido*** (*comer/**comido**, dormir/**dormido***).

-er and **-ir** verbs that have an **a**, **e**, or **o** before the ending of the infinitive require a written accent in their past participles (***caer**/caído; sonr**eir**/sonreído; **oir**/oído*).

Several verbs have irregular past participles:

abrir	***abierto***
cubrir	***cubierto***
decir	***dicho***
escribir	***escrito***
hacer	***hecho***
imprimir	***impreso***
morir	***muerto***
poner	***puesto***
romper	***roto***
volver	***vuelto***
ver	***visto***

Past participles can be used as adjectives. When used as such, the past participle has to agree in gender and number with the noun it modifies (*liberí**a** cerrad**a**, consultori**o** cerrad**o**, tiend**as** cerrad**as**, edifici**os** cerrad**os***). Past participles are also used in the perfect tenses.

Perfect Tenses, Formation

The perfect tenses are formed with a form of the auxiliary verb *haber* and the past participle of a verb.

The verb haber:

	yo	tú	él	nosotros	ustedes	ellos
indicative present	*he*	*has*	*ha*	*hemos*	*habéis*	*han*
indicative imperfect	*había*	*habías*	*había*	*habíamos*	*habíais*	*habían*
indicative preterit	*hube*	*hubiste*	*hubo*	*hubimos*	*hubisteis*	*hubieron*
future	*habré*	*habrás*	*habrá*	*habremos*	*habréis*	*habrán*
conditional	*habría*	*habrías*	*habría*	*habríamos*	*habríais*	*habrían*
subjunctive present	*haya*	*hayas*	*haya*	*hayamos*	*hayáis*	*hayan*
subjunctive imperfect	*hubiera/ hubiese*	*hubiera/ hubieses*	*hubiera/ hubiese*	*hubiéramos/ hubiésemos*	*hubierais / hubieseis*	*hubieran/ hubiesen*

The two forms of the subjunctive imperfect are interchangable, but the ***-ese*** form is typically found in written language rather than in spoken.

Perfect Tenses, Uses

The **present perfect** is used to denote an action that has been completed in the recent past (*yo **he leído** este libro*/I **have read** this book) or to describe a past action that continues into the present time (***hemos vivido** aquí muchos años*/we **have lived** here many years).

The **past perfect** of the indicative is used to denote an action in the past that was completed before a second action in the past (*cuando me desperté, Marta ya **había llegado***/when I woke up, Marta **had already arrived**).

The **future perfect** is used to denote an action that will be completed in the future before a certain time or another action in the future occurs (***me habré graduado** antes de ir de vacaciones*/**I will have graduated** before going on vacation).

The **conditional perfect** is used to denote an action that would have been completed in the past under certain conditions (*ella le **habría dicho** la verdad*/she **would have told** him the truth)

Future Indicative, Formation

To form the future of the indicative of all regular verbs, add the endings shown in the table below to the infinitive, regardless of the conjugation, **-ar**, **-er**, or **-ir**.

	Future
yo	***-é***
tú	***-ás***
él	***-á***
nosotros	***-emos***
vosotros	***-éis***
ellos	***-án***

Examples:

-ar verbs (e.g., *hablar, caminar, regresar*)

yo hablaré I will talk	nosotros hablaremos we will talk
tú hablarás you will talk	vosotros hablaréis you all will talk
él hablará he will talk	ellos hablarán they will talk

-er verbs (e.g., *comer, aprender, correr*)

yo comeré I will eat	*nosotros comeremos* we will eat
tú comerás you will eat	*vosotros comeréis* you all will eat
él comerá he will eat	*ellos comerán* they will eat

-ir verbs (e.g., *escribir, vivir, describir*)

yo escribiré I will write	*nosotros escribiremos* we will write
tú escribirás you will write	*vosotros escribiréis* you all will write
él escribirá he will write	*ellos escribirán* they will write

Future, Irregular Verbs

The following verbs use irregular stems in the future, with the same regular future endings as above:

decir	***dir-***
haber	***habr-***
hacer	***har-***
poder	***podr-***
poner	***pondr-***
querer	***querr-***
saber	***sabr-***
salir	***saldr-***
tener	***tendr-***
venir	***vendr-***

Example:

yo tendré I will have	*nosotros tendremos* we will have
tú tendrás you will have	*vosotros tendréis* you all will have
él tendrá he will have	*ellos tendrán* they will have

CONDITIONAL, USES

The conditional in Spanish is used in the same way the conditional is used in English:

- with the subjunctive in true "conditional if" clauses (*si yo fuera Juan, no* ***iría*** *a la fiesta*/if I were Juan, I **wouldn't go** to the party; *si lloviera, el jardín no se* ***vería*** *tan feo*/if it rained, the garden **wouldn't look** that ugly)
- in indirect speech, when the main verb is in the past and the second verb denotes a future action in the past (*Juan dijo que* ***hablaría*** *con ella*/Juan said **he would talk** with her; *Pedro me informó que* ***iría*** *al cine*/Pedro informed me **he would go** to the movies)

CONDITIONAL, FORMATION

To form the conditional of all regular verbs, add the endings shown in the table below to the infinitive, regardless of the conjugation, **-ar**, **-er**, or **-ir**.

	Conditional
yo	***-ía***
tú	***-ías***
él	***-ía***
nosotros	***-íamos***
vosotros	***-íais***
ellos	***-ían***

Examples:

-ar verbs (e.g., *hablar, caminar, regresar*)

yo hablaría I would talk	*nosotros hablaríamos* we would talk
tú hablarías you would talk	*vosotros hablaríais* you all would talk
él hablaría he would talk	*ellos hablarían* they would talk

-er verbs (e.g., *comer, aprender, correr*)

yo comería I would eat	*nosotros comeríamos* we would eat
tú comerías you would eat	*vosotros comeríais* you all would eat
él comería he would eat	*ellos comerían* they would eat

-ir verbs (e.g., *escribir, vivir, describir*)

yo escribiría I would write	*nosotros escribiríamos* we would write
tú escribirías you would write	*vosotros escribiríais* you all would write
él escribiría he would write	*ellos escribirían* they would write

Conditional, Irregular Verbs

The following verbs use irregular stems in the conditional, with the same regular conditional endings as above. Notice these are the same irregular stems that are used in the future indicative.

decir	***dir-***
haber	***habr-***
hacer	***har-***
poder	***podr-***
poner	***pondr-***
querer	***querr-***
saber	***sabr-***
salir	***saldr-***
tener	***tendr-***
venir	***vendr-***

Example:

yo tendría I would have	*nosotros tendríamos* we would have
tú tendrías you would have	*vosotros tendríais* you all would have
él tendría he would have	*ellos tendrían* they would have

Subjunctive Mood

The subjunctive is used in subordinate clauses introduced by *que* to express:

- a wish (*quiero que Juan* ***venga*** *a la fiesta*),
- uncertainty or doubt (*es probable que María* ***se case*** *con Juan*),
- a command (*dígale al chofer que* ***esté*** *aquí a las seis*),
- an emotion (*es una lástima que ustedes no* ***puedan*** *venir a visitarnos*),
- preference or need (*es mejor que* ***te pongas*** *un abrigo*),
- approval/disapproval (*está bien que* ***te vistas*** *de negro para el funeral*)

The subjunctive is also used with adverbial clauses introduced by conjuctions

Conjunctions That Sometimes Require the Subjunctive

Some conjunctions such as *aunque, como, donde, de manera que, de modo que, según*, and *mientras*, when used to express the opinion of the speaker, uncertainty or a conjecture, require the use of the subjunctive mood. In all other cases, they are followed by the indicative.

Examples:

- *Aunque* ***tengamos*** *el dinero, no vamos a comprar un auto nuevo*/even **if we have** the money—**we are not sure we do**—we are not going to buy a new car
- *Comemos donde* ***tú quieras***/we'll eat ***where you want*—but we do not know where you want to eat**).

Conjunctions That Always Require the Subjunctive

The conjunctions *antes (de) que, para que, sin que, a fin de que, a menos que, con tal (de) que,* and *en caso de que* are always followed by a verb in the subjunctive mode.

Examples:

- *termina el trabajo antes de que el jefe te lo* ***pida***
- *voy a visitarte para que* ***podamos*** *hablar*
- *hicimos el trabajo sin que ella se* ***diera*** *cuenta*
- *apagué la televisión a fin de que* ***pudieras*** *estudiar*
- *a menos que* ***tengas*** *otra idea, vayamos al cine*
- *con tal de que* ***vengas****, no me importa la hora*
- *en caso de que el plomero* ***llegue****, aquí dejo el dinero para pagarle).*

Compound Relative Pronouns and the Subjunctive

The compound relative pronouns *quienquiera* (whoever), *cualquiera* (whatever/whichever), and *dondequiera* (wherever) are always followed by *que* and then the verb in the subjunctive mode.

Examples:

- *este libro es útil para* ***quienquiera que lo lea***/this book is useful to whoever reads it
- ***cualquiera que sea*** *la causa, el resultado será el mismo*/whatever the cause is, the result will be the same
- ***dondequiera que él vaya****, lo encontraremos*/wherever he goes we will find him

Present of the Subjunctive

To form the present subjunctive of regular verbs, take the first person singular of the present indicative (*yo hablo*), drop the *-o*, and add the endings shown in the table below.

	AR	ER/IR
yo	*-e*	*-a*
tú	*-es*	*-as*
él	*-e*	*-a*
nosotros	*-emos*	*-amos*
vosotros	*-éis*	*-áis*
ellos	*-en*	*-an*

Examples:

-ar verbs (e.g., *hablar, caminar, regresar*)

yo camine	*nosotros caminemos*
tú camines	*vosotros caminéis*
él camine	*ellos caminen*

-er and **-ir** verbs (e.g., *comer, correr, escribir*)

yo corra	*nosotros corramos*
tú corras	*vosotros corráis*
él corra	*ellos corran*

Present Subjunctive, Spelling Changes

Verbs that have an irregular *yo* form in the present indicative will have the same irregularities in all the subjunctive forms (e.g., ***el tenga***).

Verbs that end with **-car**, **-gar**, and **-zar**: see section "Spelling changes in verb conjugations"

Verbs with a stem change in the present indicative also have a stem change in the present subjunctive. **-ar** and **-er** verbs follow the same pattern as the present indicative

Examples:

-ar verbs (e.g., *cerrar, almorzar, contar*)

*yo **cie**rre*	*nosotros cerremos*
*tú **cie**rres*	*vosotros cerréis*
*él **cie**rre*	*ellos **cie**rren*

-er verbs (e.g., *poder, volver, llover*)

*yo **pue**da*	*nosotros podamos*
*tú **pue**das*	*vosotros podáis*
*él **pue**da*	*ellos **pue**dan*

-ir verbs with a stem change in the present indicative have the same changes in the present subjunctive, but also have a change in the *nosotros* and *vosotros* forms: **o** changes to **u** and **e** changes to **i**.

Examples:

*yo pre**fie**ra*	*nosotros pre**fi**ramos*
*tú pre**fie**ras*	*vosotros pre**fi**ráis*
*él pre**fie**ra*	*ellos pre**fie**ran*

*yo **due**rma*	*nosotros **du**rmamos*
*tú **due**rmas*	*vosotros **du**rmáis*
*él **due**rma*	*ellos **due**rman*

Present Subjunctive, Irregular Verbs

The following verbs are irregular in the subjunctive:

dar

yo dé	*nosotros demos*
tú des	*vosotros deis*
él dé	*ellos den*

estar

yo esté	*nosotros estemos*
tú estés	*vosotros estéis*
él esté	*ellos estén*

ir

yo vaya	*nosotros vayamos*
tú vayas	*vosotros vayáis*
él vaya	*ellos vayan*

saber

yo sepa	*nosotros sepamos*
tú sepas	*vosotros sepáis*
él sepa	*ellos sepan*

ser

yo sea	*nosotros seamos*
tú seas	*vosotros seáis*
él sea	*ellos sean*

Imperfect of the Subjunctive

To form the imperfect of the subjunctive of regular verbs, take the third person plural of the preterite of the indicative (*ellos hablaron, ellos comieron*), drop ***-ron***, and add the endings shown in the table below. This pattern holds true for all verbs that have irregular forms in the preterite. The *nosotros* form will carry an accent on the vowel before the ***-ramos*** ending.

	AR/ER/IR
yo	***-ra***
tú	***-ras***
él	***-ra***
nosotros	***-ramos***
vosotros	***-rais***
ellos	***-ran***

-ar verbs (e.g., *hablar, caminar, regresar*)

yo caminara	*nosotros camináramos*
tú caminaras	*vosotros caminarais*
él caminara	*ellos caminaran*

-er and **-ir** verbs (e.g., *comer, correr, escribir*)

yo comiera	*nosotros comiéramos*
tú comieras	*vosotros comierais*
él comiera	*ellos comieran*

Verbs with irregular preterite forms (e.g., *ir, dar, poder*)

yo fuera	*nosotros fuéramos*
tú fueras	*vosotros fuerais*
él fuera	*ellos fueran*

Imperative Mood

The imperative mood is used to express commands, requests, or instructions. In Spanish, commands are marked for formality (informal or *tú* commands and formal or *usted* commands) and number. Informal commands have different forms depending on whether the command being given is affirmative (do it!) or negative (don't do it!)

Informal Commands

Affirmative commands for the informal second person singular (***salta** más alto*/jump higher) are formed with the present of the indicative conjugation of the third person singular (*él salta*). Affirmative informal second person plural commands are formed by removing ***-r*** from the infinitive and adding ***-d***. (***Saltad** más alto*). This form is rarely used in Latin America.

Negative informal commands are formed using the second-person singular of the present of the subjunctive (***no hables** tan fuerte*/don't talk so loudly, ***no comáis** tanto*/don't eat so much). *No* is always placed before the command.

	Singular		**Plural**	
	Affirmative	Negative	Affirmative	Negative
hablar	***habla***	***no hables***	***hablad***	***no habléis***
comer	***come***	***no comas***	***comed***	***no comáis***
escribir	***escribe***	***no escribas***	***escribed***	***no escribáis***
dormir	***duerme***	***no duermas***	***dormid***	***no durmáis***
poner	***pon***	***no pongas***	***poned***	***no pongáis***

Several verbs have irregular informal singular affirmative commands:

decir	***di***
hacer	***haz***
ir	***ve***
poner	***pon***
salir	***sal***
ser	***sé***
tener	***ten***
venir	***ven***

Formal Commands

Formal commands do not have different affirmative/negative forms other than adding "*no*" before the command.

Commands for the formal second person singular (***salte*** *más alto*/jump higher) are formed with the present of the subjunctive of the third person singular (*él salte*). Commands for the formal second person plural (***salten*** *mas alto*/jump higher) are formed with the present of the subjunctive of the third person plural (*ellos salten*)

	Singular		Plural	
	Affirmative	Negative	Affirmative	Negative
hablar	***hable***	***no hable***	***hablen***	***no hablen***
comer	***coma***	***no coma***	***coman***	***no comam***
escribir	***escriba***	***no escriba***	***escriban***	***no escriban***
dormir	***duerma***	***no duerma***	***duerman***	***no duerman***
poner	***ponga***	***no ponga***	***pongan***	***no pongan***

Pronouns in the Imperative Mood

When needed, object and reflexive pronouns are added at the end of affirmative commands (***llámame*** *más tarde*/call me later, ***pónganse*** *los zapatos*/put on your shoes). Be aware that the addition of the pronoun changes the syllabic structure of the word and requires a written accent or stress mark (See section "Rules for the written stress or accent mark")

Negative commands place object and reflexive pronouns as a separate word between no and the verb (***no me llames*** *esta noche*/don't call me tonight, ***no se preocupen***/don't worry).

The Verb Ir

The verb ***ir*** is used as an auxiliary verb in Spanish similarly to the "**going to**" expression in English in forming the continuous tenses (***voy a comer*** *a las dos; ellos* ***iban a completar*** *la tarea a la noche*). The verb ***ir*** is extremely irregular. See the table below for its conjugation for the simple tenses of the indicative.

	Present	Imperfect	Preterite
yo	*voy*	*iba*	*fui*
tú	*vas*	*ibas*	*fuiste*
él	*va*	*iba*	*fue*
nosotros	*vamos*	*íbamos*	*fuimos*
vosotros	*vais*	*ibais*	*fuisteis*
ellos	*van*	*iban*	*fueron*

Articles

Definite Articles

There is only one definite article in English: **the**. By contrast, Spanish has different forms that denote number and gender.

	Singular	Plural
Masculine	*el*	*los*
Feminine	*la*	*las*

The definite article must always be in agreement in number and gender with the noun it precedes (***el*** *libro,* ***la*** *revista,* ***los*** *cigarros,* ***las*** *zanahorias*). The definite article ***el*** does not have a written accent. When written with a stress mark, the word has a different meaning (*él*/he).

Indefinite Article

The equivalent of the English indefinite article **a (an)** and its plural **some/a few** in Spanish is ***un***. It changes to agree in gender and number with the noun it precedes (***un*** *libro,* ***una*** *revista,* ***unos*** *libros,* ***unas*** *revistas*).

	Singular	Plural
Masculine	*un*	*unos*
Feminine	*una*	*unas*

The use of the indefinite article is very similar in both languages, although there are some differences. In general, when talking about religion and profession, there is no need of an indefinite article in Spanish (*Pedro es católico*/Pedro is **a** Catholic; *Juan es médico*/Juan is **a** doctor) unless an adjective also modifies the noun (*Pedro es* ***un*** *católico devoto*/Pedro is **a** devout Catholic; *Juan es* ***un*** *médico excelente*/Juan is **an** excellent doctor).

Pronouns

Subject Pronouns

	Singular	Plural
1st person	***yo***: I	***nosotros(as)***: we
2nd person informal	***tú***: you	***vosotros(as)***: you all
2nd person formal	***usted***: you	***ustedes***: you all
3rd person	***él***: he ***ella***: she	***ellos(as)***: they

Subject pronouns identify the person(s) doing the action in a sentence. Subject pronouns in Spanish are frequently left out, as the verb ending often identifies who is doing the action. The *vosotros* form is primarily used in Spain. The feminine plural pronouns are only used when the group is comprised of all females (***ellas*** *van de compras*/the group of females goes shopping); a mixed group uses the masculine form (***ellos*** *estudian*/the group of males and females studies).

Direct Object Pronouns

	Singular	Plural
1st person	***me***: me	***nos***: us
2nd person informal	***te***: you	***os***: you all
2nd person formal	***lo***: you (masculine) ***la***: you (feminine)	***los***: you all (masculine) ***las***: you all (feminine)
3rd person	***lo***: him/it (masculine) ***la***: her/it (feminine)	***los***: them (masculine) ***las***: them (feminine)

Direct object pronouns replace the recipient of the action. They are placed directly before the conjugated verb or attached to the end of present participles and infinitives (see section "Position of pronouns when using the present participle and infinitives"). When used to replace an impersonal noun, they must agree with the number and grammatical gender of the noun replaced.

Examples:

- ¿Necesitas **el libro**? Si, **lo** necesito. Do you need the book? Yes, I need it.
- ¿Vas a traer **las flores**? Si, voy a traer**las**/Si, **las** voy a traer. Are you going to bring the flowers? Yes, I'll bring them.

Indirect Object Pronouns

	Singular	Plural
1st person	***me***: to/for me	***nos***: to/for us
2nd person informal	***te***: to/for you	***os***: to/for you all
2nd person formal	***le***: to/for you	***les***: to/for you all
3rd person	***le***: to/for him/her/it	***les***: to/for them

Indirect object pronouns answer the question "to whom?" or "for whom" and usually indicate the recipient(s) of the direct object. They are placed directly before the conjugated verb or attached to the end of present participles and infinitives (see section "Position of pronouns when using the present participle and infinitives").

Examples:

- ***Te** digo la verdad:* I am telling you the truth,
- *Estoy preguntándo**le**/**Le** estoy preguntando*: I am asking her.

When used together with a direct object pronoun, the indirect object pronoun is placed first. If ***le*** or ***les*** is used next to ***lo, la, los***, or ***las***, it changes to ***se***.

Examples:

- ***Me lo** dieron:* They gave it to me
- ***Se lo** dieron*: They gave it to him

Some verbs that typically take an indirect object pronoun are: *contestar, dar, decir, explicar, preguntar, regalar,* and *responder.*

Another class of verbs are used primarily in the third person singular or plural with an indirect object pronoun. The most common of these is *gustar* (***Me gusta** el chocolate, **les gusta** bailar, **te gustan** los gatos*), and others include *doler, encantar, enojar, faltar, fascinar, importar, interesar,* and *molestar.* See section "Gustar" below.

Prepositional Pronouns

Prepositional pronouns are used as objects of a preposition. They are the same as the subject pronouns with the exception of ***mí*** and ***tí***

	Singular	Plural
1st person	***mí***: me	***nosotros(as)***: us
2nd person informal	***tí***: you	***vosotros(as)***: you all
2nd person formal	***usted***: you	***ustedes***: you all
3rd person	***él***: him ***ella***: her	***ellos(as)***: them

mí and ***tí*** combine with the preposition *con* to create the forms ***conmigo*** and ***contigo***.

REFLEXIVE AND RECIPROCAL PRONOUNS

	Singular	Plural
1st person	***me***: myself	***nos***: ourselves/each other
2nd person informal	***te***: yourself	***os***: yourselves/each other
2nd person formal	***se***: yourself	***se***: yourselves/each other
3rd person	***se:*** himself/herself/itself	***se***: themselves/each other

Reflexive pronouns indicate that the subject of the sentence does something to himself or herself. Some verbs are almost always reflexive and can be identified by the ***se*** at the end of the infinitive (*levantar**se***). Other verbs can be used reflexively or with a distinct subject and object. (***Me lavo** la cara/**lavo** el coche*). When a reflexive pronoun is used, a possessive pronoun does not need to be used as it is in English (*Pedro **se lavó el** pelo*/Pedro washed **his** hair).

When used as reciprocal pronouns, ***nos***, ***os***, and ***se*** communicate the idea of **each other** (*Alma y Juana **se ayudan***/Alma and Juana **help each other**)

Reflexive and reciprocal pronouns are placed directly before the conjugated verb or attached to the end of present participles and infinitives (see section "Position of pronouns when using the present participle and infinitives").

Examples:

- ***Me** afeito todos los días*: I shave every day
- *Mi hermana está preparando**se**/Mi hermana **se** está preparando*: My sister is getting ready
- ***Nos** vamos después de cepillar**nos** los dientes*: We leave after brushing our teeth.

POSSESSIVE PRONOUNS

Possessive pronouns in Spanish have the same functions as their English equivalent: they replace a possessive adjective and a noun. Possessive pronouns must be in accordance in gender and number with the noun they are replacing (*¿Son **tus libros**? Si, son **los míos***).

	Item(s) owned			
	Singular		Plural	
Owner	Masculine	Feminine	Masculine	Feminine
yo	***el mío***: mine	***la mía***: mine	***los míos***: mine	***las mías***: mine
tú	***el tuyo***: yours	***la tuya***: yours	***los tuyos***: yours	***las tuyas***: yours
usted él ella	***el suyo***: yours/his/hers/its	***la suya***: yours/his/hers/its	***los suyos***: yours/his/hers/its	***las suyas***: yours/his/hers/its
nosotros(as)	***el nuestro***: ours	***la nuestra***: ours	***los nuestros***: ours	***las nuestras***: ours
vosotros(as)	***el vuestro***: yours	***la vuestra***: yours	***los vuestros***: yours	***las vuestras***: yours
ustedes ellos(as)	***el suyo***: yours/theirs	***la suya***: yours/theirs	***los suyos***: yours/theirs	***las suyas***: yours/theirs

POSITION OF PRONOUNS WHEN USING THE PRESENT PARTICIPLE AND INFINITIVES

Object, reflexive, and reciprocal pronouns, when used as the object of a present participle or infinitive, can be attached to the end of the present participle or infinitive to form a single word (*escribiendo**me**, escuchándo**te**, mirar**la**, seguir**nos***). Alternately, they can be placed in front of the conjugated verb when the participle or infinitive is part of a verb phrase. Both forms are correct and are commonly used.

Examples:

- *Pedro **me** estaba diciendo un cuento/ Pedro estaba diciéndo**me** un cuento*: Pedro was telling me a story
- *José **te** va a leer el libro/ José va a leer**te** el libro*: José is going to read you a book
- *Susana **nos** tiene que esperar/ Susana tiene que esperar**nos***: Susana has to wait for us

Demonstrative Pronouns

In Spanish there are three possible demonstrative pronouns (***éste, ése, aquél***) compared to the two that exist in English (**this one, that one**), and they do not have the word **one** following them as in English (**this one/*éste***). They have the same form as the demonstrative adjectives (*este*) but with a written accent (***éste***). Demonstrative pronouns must agree in gender and number with the noun they replace. (*blus**a**—ést**a**; libr**o**—ést**e**; cas**as**—ést**as**; perr**os**—ést**os***). There is also a neuter form (***esto, eso, aquello***). These do not have a written accent, and usually refer to ideas or general phrases (*¿por qué dices **eso**?*/why do you say **that**?; *no hay nada peor que **esto***/there is nothing worse than **this**).

Masculine singular	Feminine singular	Neuter	Masculine plural	Feminine plural
éste	***ésta***	***esto***	***éstos***	***éstas***
ése	***ésa***	***eso***	***ésos***	***ésas***
aquél	***aquélla***	***aquello***	***aquéllos***	***aquéllas***

Distributive Adjectives and Pronouns

Each and **every** are translated as ***cada*** (**each** season has its advantages/***cada** estación tiene sus ventajas*; **every** passenger carried his suitcase/***cada** pasajero cargaba su maleta*).

The equivalent of **everyone** and **everybody** is ***todos*** (**everyone** loves him/***todos** lo aman*; **everybody** was ready/***todos** estaban listos*)

Everything is ***todo*** (**everything** he said was true/***todo** lo que dijo era verdad*).

Relative Pronouns

Relative pronouns connect two clauses. ***Que***, which can be translated **that, who**, or **whom**, is the most common relative pronoun in Spanish. ***Que*** introduces the relative or dependent clause.

- *Leo un libro. El libro es interesante—El libro **que** leo es interesante.*/The book **that** I'm reading is interesting.
- *Las maestras trabajan en esta escuela. Las maestras son buenas.—Las maestras **que** trabajan en esta escuela son buenas.*/The teachers **who** work in this school are good.

In English, you can sometimes omit the relative pronoun (the house I like/the house **that** I like). This omission is not accepted in Spanish (*la casa **que** me gusta*).

Quien(**who/whom**), ***donde***(**where**), ***el cual***(**which**), and ***cuyo***(**whose**) are also used as relative pronouns. ***Quien*** must agree in number with its antecedent, and ***el cual*** and ***cuyo*** must agree in number and gender.

- *Elena es la amiga con **quien** fui al cine ayer*/Elena is the friend with **whom** I went to the movies yesterday.
- *Ellos tienen cuatro perros, dos de **los cuales** se quedan en la casa*/They have four dogs, two **of which** stay in the house.
- *Espana es un lugar **donde** quiero viajar*/Spain is a place **where** I want to travel
- *La artista **cuyas** obras vimos en el museo viene a la clase manana*/The artist **whose** works we saw in the museum is coming to class tomorrow

Prepositions

Idiomatic Nature of Prepositions

Prepositions are highly idiomatic; they are not easily translated from one language to another. For example, the Spanish preposition ***en*** can be translated **in** (*Estoy **en** el carro*/I am **in** the car), **at** (*Estoy **en** casa*/I am **at** home), and **on** (*Estoy* **en** mi bicicleta/I am **on** my bicycle).

Uses of the Preposition A

The Spanish preposition ***a*** can be used to express many different concepts

- Movement: *Vamos **a** la biblioteca* (we go to the library)
- Distance: *La tienda se ubica **a** tres kilomtros* (the store is three kilometers away)
- Time/age: *La fiesta comienza **a** las ocho* (the party begins at eight), *Mi hija aprendio a leer **a** los seis años* (my daughter learned to read at six years of age)
- Manner: *Me gusta el pollo **a** la parrilla* (I like grilled chicken)
- Personal ***a*** - Placed before a name or a personal pronoun when it is the direct object: *Es importante escuchar **a** la maestra* (It is importante to listen to the teacher)

The Preposition Para

The English prepositions **for** and **to** can be translated as ***para***. ***Para*** is used in the following instances

- Direction or destination (*tenemos que salir **para** la oficina*/we have to leave **for** the office)
- Recipient of something (*compré esta blusa **para** mi hermana*/I bought this blouse **for** my sister)
- Purpose (*el plomero vino **para** arreglar la ducha*/the plumber came **to** fix the shower)
- Time/deadline (*siempre vamos a la casa de mis padres **para** Navidad*/we always go to my parents' house **for** Christmas)
- Comparison (*la mesa es demasiado grande **para** la cocina*/the table is too big **for** the kitchen)
- Intended use (*el día es **para** trabajar*/the day is **for** working)

The Preposition Por

In some instance the preposition **for** is translated as ***por***. ***Por*** is also used to replace **through**, **by**, and **per**. ***Por*** is used in the following instances:

- Means of transportation or communication (*lo llamo* ***por*** *teléfono*/I call him **by** phone; *voy a Madrid* ***por*** *avión*/I go to Madrid **by** plane)
- Exchange/substitution (*cambié la blusa grande* ***por*** *una mediana*/I exchanged the large blouse **for** a medium)
- Duration (*los niños jugaron* ***por*** *cuatro horas*/the children played **for** four hours)
- Quantity (*ella gana $400* ***por*** *semana*/she earns $400 **per** week)
- Object of an errand (*voy al mercado* ***por*** *leche*/I go to the market **for** milk)
- Agent (*el libro fue escrito* ***por*** *Pedro*/the book was written **by** Peter)

Interrogatives

Interrogative words are used to ask questions. In Spanish, they are always preceded and followed by a question mark and must carry a written accent. A list of Spanish interrogative words appears below:

¿Qué...?	***What...?***
¿Cuál(es)...?	***Which (one/ones) ...?***
¿Cómo...?	***How...?***
¿Cuándo...?	***When...?***
¿Dónde...?	***Where...?***
¿Por qué...?	***Why...?***
¿Cuánto(s)...?	***How much/many...?***
¿Quién(es)...?	***Who?***

Cuál is sometimes used in place of ***qué*** to ask "what" when it has the sense of "which one", or when the answer will be a selection from a discrete group.

- *¿En* ***qué*** *piensas?* (**What** are you thinking about?)
- *¿****Cuál*** *es tu color favorito?* (**What** is your favorite color?)

Dónde, when used to ask **to where/where to** (describing movement toward a location) is preceded by the preposition ***a***. This a can be added to the beginning of ***dónde*** or left as its own word.

- *¿****Dónde*** *estás?* **Where** are you?
- *¿****A dónde*** *vas?/ ¿****Adónde*** *vas?* **(To) Where** are you going?

In some instances, ***cómo*** is used instead of ***qué*** to translate an expression that uses **what** in English. For example, in some regions, if you don't understand or are incredulous about what is being said, you would say ***"¿Cómo?"***, similar to saying **"What?"** in English. Other expressions include ***¿cómo te llamas?*** (how are you called/what is your name?) and ***¿cómo eres?*** (how are you/what are you like?).

Conjunctions and Adverbs

Different Kinds of Adverbs

Both in English and in Spanish, adverbs modify verbs, adjectives, other adverbs, and clauses (the bird flew **high**/*el pájaro voló* ***alto***; the mountain is **very** high/*la montaña es* ***muy*** *alta*; the student knew the topic **quite** well/*el estudiante sabía el tema* ***bastante*** *bien*). Unlike adjectives, Spanish adverbs are not marked for number or gender. There are several kinds of adverbs:

- of manner: ***rápidamente*** (quickly), ***bien*** (well), ***apropiadamente*** (appropriately)
- of place: ***aquí*** (here), ***allá*** (there), ***alrededor*** (around)
- of time: ***ahora*** (now), ***pronto*** (soon), ***hoy*** (today)
- of frequency: ***nunca*** (never), ***ocasionalmente*** (occasionally), ***a menudo*** (often)
- of degree: ***muy*** (very), ***bastante*** (quite), ***demasiado*** (too)
- interrogative: ***cuándo*** (when?), ***dónde*** (where?), ***por qué*** (why?)
- relative: ***cuando*** (when), ***donde*** (where), ***por que*** (why)

In Spanish, a prepositional phrase will often be used instead of an adverb (*Mi padre no conduce* ***con cuidado****/Mi padre no conduce* ***cuidadosamente***: My father doesn't drive **carefully**).

Cohesive Words and Phrases

The use of conjunctions and cohesive phrases is a mark of advanced thought and language ability (and therefore may result in a higher score on a writing or speaking test). Below is a list of common conjunctions and cohesive phrases in Spanish. You may find it helpful to memorize a few to use in the speaking or writing portion of your test:

a causa de	on account of, because of
a fin de cuentas	in the end, after all
a la (misma) vez	at the same time
a partir de	beginning with
a pesar de (que)	in spite of the fact that
además	besides, furthermore
ahora mismo	right now
a la vez	at the same time
al fin y al cabo	after all
al mismo tiempo	at the same time
al principio	at the beginning
al + infinitivo	upon (action)
así (que)	so
aun	even
aunque	although
como	as, inasmuch as, because
como consecuencia	as a consequence
como punto de partida	as a point of departure
como resultado	as a result
con relación a	in relation to
con respecto a	with respect to, regarding
conviene indicar/señalar	it is suitable to indicate/point out
de antemano	beforehand, in advance
de aquí (ahora, hoy) en adelante	from now on
de ese modo	in that way
de hecho	in fact
de modo que	in such a way that
de todos modos	at any rate, anyhow
debido a	owing to, because of
dentro de poco	shortly, in a short while

después de + infinitivo	after (an action)
durante	during
en cambio	on the other hand
en conclusión	in conclusion
en cuanto	as soon
en cuanto a	regarding
en definitiva	in conclusion, definitely
en fin	finally, in short
en primer lugar	in the first place
en realidad	in reality
en resumen	in summary
es decir	that is to say
entonces	then
finalmente	finally
hace poco	a short while ago
hasta el momento/la fecha	until now
hay que tomar en cuenta que	one must realize that
hoy (en) día	nowadays
lo importante es que	what is important is that
luego	later, then
mientras	while
mientras tanto	meanwhile
ni, ni	neither/nor
ni siquiera	not even
no…sino que	not…but rather
o, o	either/or
o sea	that is to say
para concluir	to conclude
para continuar	to continue
para empezar	to start
para ilustrar	to illustrate
para resumir	to summarize
para terminar	to end
pero	but
por	because of
por consiguiente	therefore
por ejemplo	for example
por eso	therefore
por lo general	generally
por lo tanto	therefore
por medio de	by way of
por otro lado	on the other hand
porque	because
primero	first
puesto que	since, as
si	if
sin embargo	however, nevertheless
si no	otherwise
sino que	but rather
también	also

tampoco	neither, either
tan pronto como	as soon as
una vez que	once (that)
ya que	because of, seeing that, since

Semantics and Pragmatics

Formal and Informal Forms of Address

In English, there is only one second-person singular pronoun, **you**, for both formal and informal ways of addressing people. In Spanish, there are two forms: the formal ***usted*** and the informal ***tú***. The informal ***tú*** has its own particular conjugation for all tenses (***tú vienes, tú fuiste, tú comerás, tú has dormido***). The informal ***tú*** also has its own set of object, possessive and reflexive pronouns (***tu*** *libro,* ***tus*** *hermanos, esta casa es* ***tuya****, Ana* ***te*** *invite al concierto*). The formal ***usted***, on the other hand, uses the same verb conjugations as the third-person singular pronoun *él* (***usted viene, usted comerá, usted ha dormido***). In a similar way, ***usted*** uses the third-person singular object, possessive and reflexive pronouns (***su*** *libro,* ***sus*** *hermanas, esta casa es* ***suya****, Ana* ***lo*** *invitó al concierto*). In different regions, the situations vary in which one form or the other would be used.

The informal second-person plural, ***vosotros***, is primarily used in Spain. In the rest of the Spanish speaking world, the formal second-person plural, ***ustedes***, is used. The informal ***vosotros*** has its own particular conjugation for all tenses (***vosotros venís, vosotros fuisteis, vosotros comeréis, vosotros habéis dormido***). The informal ***vosotros*** also has its own set of object, possessive and reflexive pronouns (***vuestro*** *libro,* ***vuestros*** *hermanos, esta casa es* ***vuestra****, Ana* ***os*** *invite al concierto*). The formal ***ustedes***, on the other hand, uses the same verb conjugations as the third-person plural pronoun *ellos* (***ustedes vienen, ustedes comerán, ustedes han dormido***). In a similar way, ***ustedes*** uses the third-person plural possessive and reflexive pronouns (***su*** *libro,* ***sus*** *hermanas, esta casa es* ***suya****, Ana* ***los*** *invitó al concierto*).

Vos as an Informal Form of Address

In Argentina and Uruguay, the informal second-person singular pronoun ***tú*** is seldom used. Instead, these countries use ***vos***. ***Vos*** has its own conjugation forms. For most tenses, they are the same as the usual second-person singular (*tú comiste/****vos comiste****, tú has ido/****vos has ido****, tú comprarás/****vos comprarás***). It is almost always different in the present of the indicative, though. In the case of regular verbs, the verb form is usually the normal second-person singular but with the stress on the last syllable (*tú comes/****vos comés****, tú llegas/****vos llegás***). Exceptions abound with irregular verbs (*tú vienes/****vos venís****, tú eres/****vos sos****, tú cierras/****vos cerrás***).

High-Frequency Idiomatic Expressions

Hace...Que

To describe an action that starts in the past and continues in the present, the Spanish language, like English, uses the present perfect tense (*yo* ***he estudiado*** *español un año, Juan* ***ha esperado*** *dos horas, nosotros* ***hemos vivido*** *en esta ciudad muchos meses*). Very often, these same types of ideas are expressed with ***hace ...que***, which can be compared to the expression **it's been** in English (***hace*** *un año* ***que*** *yo estudio español,* ***hace*** *dos horas* ***que*** *Juan espera,* ***hace*** *muchos meses* ***que*** *nosotros vivimos en esta ciudad*). When using ***hace...que***, the sentence begins with ***hace***, the **time modifier**, and then ***que***, followed by the **subject and verb**, which is now in the present indicative.

OJALÁ

The Spanish word ***ojalá*** does not have an exact translation in English and is derived from Arabic. It is used to express a wish (***ojalá*** *supiera nadar*/I wish I knew how to swim) or hope (***ojalá*** *que mañana sea un lindo día así podemos ir a la parque*/I hope that tomorrow is a nice day so we can go to the park). ***Ojalá*** is always followed by the subjunctive (***ojalá hubiera*** *sabido esto ayer;* ***ojalá lleguemos*** *a tiempo;* ***ojalá aprobemos*** *el examen;* ***ojalá hubiéramos*** *salido más temprano*).

GUSTAR

Gustar (to like) in Spanish requires a different sentence structure than in English. In English the word order is the **person (subject)**, the **verb**, and then the **object** (**I like this book**). In Spanish an **indirect object pronoun** goes first (representing the person), then the **verb**, and then the **object**, which is actually the subject of the sentence (***Me gusta este libro***). A literal translation of ths sentence in English would be: **This book is pleasing to me**. The thing liked is always a noun or an infinitive verb. If the thing liked is a plural noun, the third-person plural form of the verb is used (*Te gusta***n** ***los gatos***). Other verbs that require the same sentence structure as ***gustar*** are: ***molestar*** (*me molestan los zapatos*/the shoes bother me); ***aburrir*** (*nos aburre la música clasica*/classical music bores us); ***encantar*** (*le encanca cantar*/he loves to sing), ***fascinar; faltar;*** and ***interesar***.

SER AND ESTAR

Ser and ***estar*** are both translated **to be** in English but are not used interchangeably.

Ser is used to describe something that is intrinsic to a person, object, or idea, such as nationality (*Marta* ***es*** *argentina*), origin (*la carne* ***es*** *de vaca*), identification (*Pedro* ***es*** *mi hijo*), physical characteristics (***soy*** *rubia*), generalities (***somos*** *estudiantes*), dates (*hoy* ***es*** *12 de octubre*), time of the day (***son*** *las diez de la noche*), place of events (*la fiesta* ***es*** *en mi casa*), possession (*la casa* ***es*** *mía*), and personality traits (*Ana* ***es*** *simpática*). The verb ***ser*** is very irregular; see the table below for its conjugation for the simple tenses of the indicative.

	Present	Imperfect	Preterite
yo	*soy*	*era*	*fui*
tú	*eres*	*eras*	*fuiste*
él	*es*	*era*	*fue*
nosotros	*somos*	*éramos*	*fuimos*
vosotros	*sois*	*erais*	*fuisteis*
ellos	*son*	*eran*	*fueron*

Estar is used to describe something that can change, or is considered less permanent, about a person, object, or idea. It is used to describe location or position (*el libro* ***está*** *sobre la mesa; Juan* ***está*** *en Nueva York*), physical characteristics (*Susana* ***está*** *bonita con ese vestido*), emotional characteristics (*Pedro* ***está*** *contento*) and actions in progress (*María* ***está*** *cocinando; nosotros*

estamos** tomando cerveza*). The verb ***estar is very irregular; see the table below for its conjugation for the simple tenses of the indicative.

	Present	Imperfect	Preterite
yo	*estoy*	*estaba*	*estuve*
tú	*estás*	*estabas*	*estuviste*
él	*está*	*estaba*	*estuvo*
nosotros	*estamos*	*estábamos*	*estuvimos*
vosotros	*estais*	*estabais*	*estuvisteis*
ellos	*están*	*estaban*	*estuvieron*

Conocer and Saber

There are two different verbs in Spanish, ***conocer*** and ***saber***, with a clear distinction in meaning, that correspond to the verb **to know** in English. ***Saber*** is used when **to know** implies a mental effort, study, or training (she knows how to cook pasta/*ella **sabe** como cocinar pasta*, he knows the lesson/*él **sabe** la lección*, they know to get to the church/*ellos **saben** como llegar a la iglesia*). ***Conocer*** is used when **to know** denotes knowing through familiarity or acquaintance (he knows Mr. Jones/*él **conoce** al Sr. Jones*, she knows this part of the city/*ella **conoce** esta parte de la ciudad*).

Common Verbs with a Different Meaning in the Reflexive

There are several verbs in Spanish that have a different meaning, depending on whether they are used as reflexive verb or not. ***Parecer*** means **to seem** or **to appear** (***parece** que va a llover*/**it seems** it is going to rain) while ***parecerse*** means **to resemble** (*Juan **se parece** a su padre*/Juan **resembles** his father). ***Dormir*** means **to sleep** (*Ana **duerme** ocho horas por día*/Ana **sleeps** eight hours per day) while ***dormirse*** means **to fall asleep** (*Jorge **se durmió** en el tren*/Jorge **fell asleep** in the train). Other examples are ***llamar*** (**to call**) and ***llamarse*** (**to be named**) and ***llevar*** (**to carry**) and ***llevarse*** (**to get along**).

Common Verbs with a Different Meaning in the Preterite

Several verbs have a different meaning when used in the preterite tense:

Infinitive	Translation	Preterite meaning
conocer	to know	**met:** *Yo **conocí** a mi novio en Dallas.*
saber	to know	**found out:** *Su mamá **supe** que Juan recibió un F.*
poder	to be able	**succeeded/failed:** *Finalmente **pudo** montar en bicicleta/**No pudo** completar la tarea.*
querer	to want	**tried/refused:** ***Quise** esquiar/**No quise** comer el bróculi.*
tener	to have	**got:** ***Tuvimos** un trofeo cuando ganamos.*

Quisiera

Quisiera and other forms of the imperfect subjunctive of *querer* are used very often in Spanish followed by an infinitive to express a polite request or desire and to soften a statement (*yo **quisiera hablar** con usted, nosotros **quisiéramos visitar** Francia*). It can be compared to **would like** in English (I **would like to talk** with you, we **would like to visit** France). If a different subject is introduced after ***quisiera*** (*yo **quisiera que usted**...*), then an infinitive clause cannot be used, and it must be replaced by a subordinate clause that uses the imperfect of the subjunctive (*yo **quisiera** que usted me **acompañara**, Juan **quisiera** que el trabajo **fuera** más fácil*).

Passive Se

Instead of using the passive voice (*ser* + past participle) in those cases where the subject of the sentence is an inanimate object or when the performer of the action is not important or is not specified, Spanish employs the passive ***se*** with a third-person verb. This particular structure is most often used in the present tense.

Examples:

- ***se venden flores*** *en esa tienda* instead of ***flores son vendidas*** *en esa tienda;*
- ***se espera una gran lluvia*** instead of ***una gran lluvia es esperada;***
- *¿cómo* ***se dice "grocery store"*** *en español?* instead of *¿cómo* ***es dicho "grocery store"*** *en español?*

Pero and Sino

Both ***pero*** and ***sino (que)*** translate the English word **but**. ***Pero*** is used to link affirmative or negative sentences:

- *Ella tiene mucho dinero* ***pero*** *no lo gasta.*
- *Ella no tiene mucho dinero* ***pero*** *va de compras todos los días.*

Sino (que) contrasts two statements, the first one in the negative and the second one in the affirmative, and can also be translated **on the contrary, rather,** or **instead**.

- *No fuimos a Disney World* ***sino*** *a la playa.*
- *No me gusta tocar el piano* ***sino*** *escucharlo.*
- *Se dio prisa, entonces no caminó* ***sino que*** *corrió.*

Equivalents in Spanish of Some and Any

In English, there are two different words to express the concept of a certain amount: **some**, which is used in affirmative sentences (we have **some** time), and **any**, which is used in negative and interrogative sentences (we don't have **any** ideas; do you have **any** brothers?). The Spanish language uses ***algún*** (***alguna, algunos, algunas***) o ***un poco de*** (*tenemos* ***algún/un poco de*** *tiempo; ¿tienes* ***algún*** *hermano?*) for affirmative and interrogative sentences, and ***ningún*** (***ninguna, ningunos, ningunas***) or ***nada de*** for negative sentences (*no tenemos* ***ninguna*** *idea; no tenemos* ***nada*** *de cambio*). The same rule applies to compound words formed with **some** and **any**. Spanish will use ***alguien*** (somebody/anybody), ***algo*** (something/anything), ***algún lugar*** (somewhere/anywhere, etc.) for the affirmative and interrogative forms, and ***nadie, nada, ningún lugar***, etc., for the negative form.

Equivalents in Spanish of Many/Much and Few/Little

In English, **many** is used before countable nouns (**many** books, **many** things), and **much** before uncountable nouns (**much** money, **much** meat). The Spanish language does not differentiate between countable and uncountable nouns and uses only the word ***mucho***. However, the ending of ***mucho*** will change according to the gender and number of the noun that follows (*much**os** libr**os**, much**as** cos**as**, much**o** diner**o**, much**a** carn**e***). The same thing happens with **few** (**few** mistakes, **few** houses) and **little** (**little** time, **little** milk). In both cases they will be translated as ***poco***, whose ending will agree in gender and number with the noun that follows (*poc**os** error**es**, poc**as** cas**as**, poc**o** tiemp**o**, poc**a** lech**e***).

Laws Regarding Bilingual Education

14TH Amendment and Brown vs. Board of Education (1954)

The 14th Amendment to the United States Constitution was adopted in 1868 as one of the Reconstruction Amendments after the Civil War. The passage of this amendment gave a constitutional foundation to the educational rights of linguistic minority students. It guarantees that no US State can pass or enforce any law that limits the immunities or privileges of its citizens; that no State can deny any person life, liberty, or property without following due process of law; and that no State can refuse equal protection of the laws to any citizen. The 1954 case of Brown vs. Board of Education overruled the 1896 decision in Plessy vs. Ferguson that allowed "separate but equal" education for black students. In Brown vs. Board of Education, the Court ruled segregated public schools unconstitutional and ordered their desegregation. The opportunity for a public school education was declared a right "which must be made available to all on equal terms."

US Legislation Passed in the Decade Between 1964 and 1974

In the Civil Rights Act of 1964, Title VI banned discrimination in federally funded programs. Essentially, Title VI of the Civil Rights Act said all students have the right to effective and meaningful instruction and thereafter was cited frequently in other court cases. Title VII of the Elementary and Secondary Education Act (ESEA) of 1968, and of its 1974 reauthorization, also called the Bilingual Education Acts, allocated supplementary funds for school districts to create programs for meeting the recognized "special educational needs" of many students in the United States identified with limited English proficiency (LEP). On May 20, 1970, the Department of Health, Education, and Welfare (HEW) issued a Memorandum interpreting the regulations of this Title VII to outlaw schools' refusing access to any educational programs based on LEP status. The 1974 Equal Educational Opportunity Act defined the denial of equal educational opportunity, including an agency's failure to "take appropriate action to overcome language barriers that impede equal participation by students in an instructional program."

The Supreme Court's Ruling in Lau vs. Nichols (1974)

In San Francisco, CA, a child of Chinese immigrants was failing in school because he could not understand the lessons, which were taught only in English. An attorney sued on the family's behalf. While lower courts decided against the plaintiffs, appeals to higher courts led to a class-action suit before the Supreme Court on behalf of nearly 1,800 Chinese parents with children struggling in English-only classes due to limited English-language proficiency (LEP). The Court decided that simply having the same schools, teachers, classes, and textbooks did not constitute equal treatment for LEP students because they were prevented from receiving a meaningful education by not understanding English. Moreover, the justices ruled that making basic English skills a prerequisite for participation in educational programs was "to make a mockery of public education" because "Basic English skills are at the very core of what public schools teach...." In 1975, the Department of Health, Education, and Welfare (HEW) issued guidelines for schools regarding LEP students. These so-called "Lau Remedies" were ended by President Reagan's administration in the 1980s.

Civil Rights Language Minority Regulations of 1980, and Castañeda vs. Pickard

The Civil Rights Language Minority Regulations of 1980 stipulated bilingual instruction be delivered by qualified teachers and that bilingual education consist of four essential ingredients: identification, assessment, services, and exit. These regulations established the sequence of procedures still followed today by schools relative to providing education for linguistic minority students. The US Supreme Court's decision in Castañeda vs. Pickard (1981) established the standard used by the Courts for the examination of educational programs provided by schools for students with limited English proficiency (LEP). The ruling stipulated that school districts must have:

- A "pedagogically sound" educational plan for LEP students
- Enough staff qualified to implement this plan, which included both training their currently employed teachers and hiring new, qualified teachers
- A system in place for assessing the program's effectiveness

The wording of this decision did not require specifically "bilingual education" programs, but programs that took "appropriate action to overcome language barriers" to LEP students' educational participation.

1980s US Supreme Court on Educational Programs for LEP Students

The US's State Departments of Education first were officially assigned the legal responsibility for monitoring public school districts' implementation of educational programs for LEP (Limited English Proficient) students through the decision in the case of Idaho vs. Migrant Council (1981). The case of Illinois vs. Gómez (1987) further specified this state responsibility to include setting and enforcing the minimum requirements for implementing language remediation programs. This decision also established requirements for re-classifying LEP students as FEP, or Fluent English Proficient, when their English language proficiency has progressed to fluency. Two Supreme Court cases that used the earlier decision in Castañeda vs. Pickard (1981) to evaluate school districts' educational programs for LEP students were Denver vs. School District No. 1 (1983) and Teresa P. vs. Berkeley Unified (1987).

20th-Century Legal History of Bilingual Education in California

California has the largest proportion of linguistic minority students in the United States, making the legal history of its bilingual education significant to the entire nation. In 1967, Governor Ronald Reagan signed SB 53, overturning an 1872 law mandating English-only instruction and permitting California's public schools to use other instructional languages. In 1974, transitional programs of bilingual education were established through the Chacón-Moscone Bilingual-Bicultural Education Act. These programs adhered to the Federal guidelines for identifying and placing LEP (Limited English Proficient) students and for re-designating LEP students as FEP (Fluent English Proficient) when they attained fluency. In 1981, the Bilingual Education Act was strengthened by the explicit, detailed specification of public school districts' responsibilities to LEP students. However, in 1986 Governor Deukmejian vetoed a bill to legalize bilingual education. In 1987 he vetoed a reauthorization bill, thereby permitting the Bilingual Education Act to expire. Even without the legal mandate, California public school districts continued enforcing the Chacón-Moscone Bilingual-Bicultural Education Act for nearly another decade.

California Legislative Events Regarding Bilingual Education

California's Board of Education had been sued in 1997 by plaintiffs claiming that Limited English Proficient (LEP) students' rights were violated by the Board's granting waivers to school districts allowing English immersion to replace bilingual education. The judge's 1998 ruling was

- that the State Board of Education did not have the authority to grant such waivers
- that California state law did not apply to bilingual education and only Federal laws applied

The first part of this ruling restricted state departure from bilingual education programs; however, the second part conversely restricted enforcement of state laws to provide bilingual education. Also in 1998, California's governor vetoed State Senate Bill 6. On one hand, SB6 incorporated many provisions of the 1974 Chacón-Moscone Bilingual-Bicultural Education Act, which had initiated transitional bilingual education programs meeting Federal guidelines for identifying, placing, and re-classifying LEP students. On the other hand, SB6 also allowed local school districts flexibility in choosing bilingual or English-immersion programs. As a result, its veto both impeded and protected bilingual education.

Proposition 227

Proposition 227 was the culmination of a movement against bilingual education in California. In 1967, using languages of instruction other than English was legalized there, transitional bilingual education programs were authorized in 1974, and the Bilingual Education Act was reinforced in 1981 by more detailed definitions of school district responsibilities to linguistic minority students. However, this trend was reversed later in the 1980s by a governor who vetoed bilingual education laws and allowed the Bilingual Education Act to expire. This reversal was exacerbated in the 1990s by various state laws allowing schools to substitute English immersion for bilingual instruction despite a citizens'-rights lawsuit on behalf of LEP students and another governor's vetoing pro-bilingual law. Proposition 227 virtually outlawed all public-school bilingual education excepting certain special conditions, mandated English immersion for LEP students, and moreover limited English-immersion programs to one year, followed by mainstreaming.

Proposition 227 was passed in California in June 1998. This legislation basically prohibited bilingual education in that state's public schools, except under defined special circumstances. It required public schools in the state to place all limited English proficient (LEP) students in "sheltered English immersion" programs, requiring further that these programs last only one school year, after which students must be mainstreamed into English-speaking classes. In July 1998, in San Francisco US District Court case Valeria G. vs. Wilson, an injunction against implementing Proposition 227 was requested but denied by the judge. The precedents cited for denial were set in the Supreme Court case Castañeda vs. Pickard (1981). These precedents permitted sequential programs that taught English first, subsequently teaching content subjects in English, resembling provisions of Proposition 227 for designing "structured English immersion" programs. A more favorable part of the judge's ruling involved obligating schools to compensate for any academic deficits incurred by LEP students while learning English within a reasonable time until they met grade/peer levels.

In 1999, the California State Board of Education adopted English Language Development (ELD) standards, which are aligned with the Content Standards for Language Arts and Reading. These standards furnish a structure for public school educators in designing instructional programs and in developing and procuring supportive teaching materials. These standards apply equally to all students, reinforcing Proposition 227's (1998) elimination of bilingual education programs and use of English immersion programs requiring linguistic minority students to develop English proficiency as quickly as possible. However, on the heels of Prop 227, a judge who refused an injunction against implementing it also ruled that schools were obligated to remedy any academic deficiencies in ESL students caused by English instruction to the temporary exclusion of content instruction. Therefore, schools also can use the state standards to fulfill their obligation to ESL students through program designs and materials that help assure English proficiency. Founded on the 1996 Escutia Bill, the state also sponsored development in 1999 of an ELD test conforming to its ELD standards.

Legislation for Education in the State of California in 1996-1998

California's bilingual education laws affect the entire USA, both because certain state laws must comply with Federal laws and because, with the nation's highest percentage of linguistic minorities in California, its laws influence the rest of the country. In 1996, the California State Board of Education granted waivers to four school districts which exempted them from complying with the Bilingual Education Act, permitted them to undo their bilingual education programs, and allowed them to create "sheltered English immersion" programs to replace students' native languages with English as quickly as possible. In Quiroz et al vs. State Board of Education (1997), the plaintiffs asserted that school district waivers allowing English-only instruction violated the rights of LEP (Limited English Proficient) students when they sued the Orange Unified School District in the California State Court's Sacramento location. In 1998, the judge ruled that the State Board of Education was not authorized to grant the waivers to school districts; and only federal laws, but not California state laws, applied to linguistic minority education.

Legislation Enacted After Proposition 227 Was Passed

The passage of Proposition 227 virtually had eliminated bilingual education programs in California. While a US District Court judge had refused to issue an injunction against implementing Proposition 227, he also had ruled that public schools must make up for any academic losses to linguistic minority students while they were being taught English without content subject instruction. Previously, the re-designation of students from limited English proficiency (LEP) to fluent English proficiency (FEP) had been established and regulated first by Federal law in the Supreme Court case of Illinois vs. Gómez (1987) and then by California state law in the 1974 Chacón-Moscone Bilingual-Bicultural Education Act. However, in 1999, the California State Board of Education removed these reclassification provisions. Instead, it assigned each of the state's >1100 school districts the responsibility to set its own criteria for re-designating LEP students as FEP, making this process locally determined rather than regulated by Federal or State laws.

Models of Bilingual Education

Dual-Language Instruction

In this model, students receive language and subject content instruction in two languages (usually English and Spanish in the USA). The split between the two languages can be equal (50% of class is conducted in each language) or weighted (e.g. 80% in one language and 20% in the other). The weights used depend on the purpose of the dual-language program. Programs utilizing dual-language instruction can be set up in a variety of ways; for example, one bilingual teacher may be the only teacher, or teachers may teach in a pair, with one teacher teaching in one language and another teacher in the other language.

Transitional Bilingual Education

The goal of transitional bilingual education is to use a student's home language as they achieve literacy and transition to the target language of instruction quickly. In a transitional bilingual program, the weight of each language used will be shifted as the students mature in order to increase proficiency in the target language and decrease use of the home language (e.g. begin with 80% Spanish and 20% English in kindergarten and move toward 80% English and 20% Spanish by 3rd grade and 100% English by 5th grade).

Maintenance Bilingual Education

The goal of maintenance bilingual education is to maintain and improve students' home language skills while simultaneously teaching the target language. In maintenance bilingual education, students will continue to receive instruction in their home language and the target language throughout their education. As described above, this can be accomplished by one bilingual teacher or a team of two teachers, each one delivering content in a different language. A program may have students use both languages in every subject every year (e.g. Mondays and Wednesdays, all subjects are taught in Spanish and Tuesdays and Thursdays all subjects are taught in English) or the program may switch languages at the ends of units, semesters, or years (e.g. math is taught in English in the fall and Spanish in the spring, while science is taught in Spanish in the fall and English in the spring).

Two-Way Immersion

In two-way immersion, a dual-language program is employed to provide a bilingual education to students with different home languages. For example, a two-way immersion class could contain 12 students whose home language is English and 12 students whose home language is Spanish. The goal of two-way immersion is to produce students who are literate in both languages. A two-way immersion program may be set up similarly to a maintenance bilingual education program, with students receiving instruction in both languages throughout their school career.

One-Way Immersion

In this model, the target language is employed almost exclusively from the beginning. In the USA, one-way immersion programs usually consist of students whose home language is not English, receiving (almost) all instruction in English, whether in a separate classroom for non-native English speakers or mainstreamed into a regular English-speaking classroom with or without support from an aide or pull-out teacher. Some one-way immersion programs are created for students whose home language is English, providing (almost) all instruction in Spanish (or another language), but these programs usually add English back in eventually, becoming more of a dual-language program in the upper grades.

Heritage Language Education

Heritage language learners have a broad range of abilities in their heritage language. A child growing up in an English-speaking culture with Spanish-speaking relatives may only understand a little Spanish and not be able to speak it at all, may speak Spanish with incomplete dominance, or may be able to speak Spanish fluently. Heritage speakers may not have any literacy skills in their heritage language. Heritage language education seeks to increase students' abilities in their heritage language. This can be accomplished with programs similar to maintenance bilingual education programs in the younger grades, or with targeted classes for heritage speakers in upper grades (e.g. instead of taking Spanish I with students who have never heard Spanish, heritage speakers may take a separate Spanish I class focused on improving their fluency and literacy).

Perspectives on Bilingual Education

Bilingual education can be approached from a subtractive/deficit perspective or from an additive/enrichment perspective. A subtractive/deficit perspective focuses on a student's lack of ability in the target language (usually English in the USA) and seeks to remedy the "deficit" as quickly as possible. In this perspective, the student's home language is more of a liability than an asset and instruction in that home language is taking away precious instruction time in the target language. A school district that operates with a subtractive or deficit perspective will choose one-way immersion or transitional bilingual education, moving away from the students' home language and toward English immediately or as quickly as possible.

An additive/enrichment perspective celebrates a student's preexisting language abilities, even if they are not in the target language. In this perspective, the student's home language is an asset that can be leveraged for literacy and learning rather than a liability. A school district that operates with an additive or enrichment perspective will be more likely to offer maintenance bilingual or two-way immersion programs, continuing to build on a student's home language as well as teaching the target language.

Developmental Processes in Bilingualism and Biliteracy

Stages of Bilingual Development

Silent Period

Whether a student is acquiring a first or second language, there are stages of language learning that she will pass through. For example, a young child does not utter her first words in her first language until she is nearly a year old! A student receiving instruction and input in her second language may have a similar "silent period" where she hears and understands the second language but does not respond with utterances of her own. This is a completely normal stage of language development.

Delayed Production or Literacy

There is some evidence that bilingual children may have a short period where they lag behind their monolingual peers in language production or literacy. For example, a child who hears two languages at home may not say his first words until a little later than his friend who hears one language at home. This delay is not permanent.

Language Mixing

A bilingual child will mix languages, using words or phrases from two languages even when the listener only speaks one of those languages (e.g. responds in a mix of English and Spanish to an art teacher who only speaks English or to her grandmother who only speaks Spanish). As the child increases in linguistic ability in each language, this language mixing will decrease, and she will speak one language at a time with monolingual speakers.

Codeswitching

Codeswitching occurs when a speaker goes from using one language to another mid-speech (***¿Quieres ir* to the park with me?**) while talking to someone who speaks both languages. This switch typically involves one word/phrase or occurs in predictable places in sentence structure – at the end of a clause rather than in the middle of it. Unlike language mixing, which indicates incomplete dominance of one or both languages, codeswitching is a universal practice between bilingual individuals who are fluent in the same two languages and is not a developmental stage.

Interlanguage

Interlanguage is another common developmental stage in bilingual students. In interlanguage, students exhibit transitional competence – a cohesive, rule-bound use of the target language that is not native. This interlanguage is often colored by transfer from the home language. For example, a Spanish-speaking student learning English may say "**My uncle is doctor. My dad is lawyer**". This is cohesive – the student has a rule-bound pattern of stating a profession without an indefinite article. This is also how the phrase is constructed in Spanish (*Mi tío es médico*). However, it is non-native, because a native English speaker would be more likely to use an indefinite article: "**My uncle is *a* doctor.**"

Simultaneous vs. Sequential Bilingualism

Simultaneous bilingualism is when a child has been exposed to two languages from birth. In sequential bilingualism, a child encounters the second language for the first time later in life (perhaps in the classroom). These two groups of bilingual students may demonstrate some differences. There is research to suggest that in sequential bilingualism, the two languages are stored and accessed differently in the brain (with the advantage going to the first language), whereas with simultaneous bilingualism the two languages are stored and accessed similarly. There is also the affective factor – a student's emotional relationship to each language and its speaker(s) and culture(s) will influence his learning and usage of the language. Which language becomes dominant is an outcome of these factors and more – which language is the dominant cultural language? Which language is the language of education? How often and in what contexts does the student use each language? So, while there are some differences between simultaneous and sequential bilingualism, a student's bilingual experience is profoundly shaped by a variety of factors.

Transferring Linguistic Knowledge Between Languages

The skills that a student has gained in her first or home language will transfer, to some extent, as she learns a target language. For example, a student who is literate in her home language will find it easier to begin to read in the target language than a student who has no literacy skills (which is one of the arguments for a dual-language model of bilingual education). The amount of transferrable knowledge and skills depends heavily on the similarities and differences of the first and target languages. If the two languages share an alphabet, as English and Spanish do, literacy skills are easily transferred. If the student's home language uses a different writing system than the target language, the transfer advantage is not as large.

Contrastive Analysis

Contrastive analysis is the awareness of similarities and differences between a student's home language and the target language. This awareness is useful in shaping instruction. In places where the two languages are similar, teachers can draw on students' prior linguistic knowledge, as in the literacy example above. This is called positive transfer. Where the two languages differ, teachers can anticipate student errors and interlanguage caused by negative transfer as in the example "**My uncle is doctor**" above. Teachers can also encourage student metacognition (thinking about their own thinking) by drawing their attention to the similarities and differences between the two languages. This metacognition can help students tap into their first language knowledge as well as use the target language in a native-like way.

Role of Culture

Cultural Similarities and Differences

Language Use

Cultures have many different norms for language use (both oral and written) and nonverbal communication. A few examples include: What is the appropriate amount of eye contact and physical distance between speakers? What volume of speech is appropriate? How long/complicated is an ideal utterance or sentence? A bilingual teacher must be aware of these differing norms and be careful not to value one set of cultural practices over the other. The best way to do this is for the teacher to use each language authentically. When speaking each language, use that language's norms. This can demonstrate to students that, just as both languages are valued, so are both sets of cultural norms. Teachers can also directly teach these norms (e.g. *"When we talk to each other in English, it is considered polite to look at the eyes of the speaker or listener."*)

Cultural Context of Language and Learning

Beyond language use, different cultures have different perspectives on other factors that will affect the bilingual classroom. For example, how should teacher/student interactions be conducted?

What about teacher/parent interactions? Markers for respect, attention, and care may differ from culture to culture. Is cooperation or competition more highly valued in each culture? Does the culture emphasize that the individual or the group is more important? The answers to these questions will shape what happens each day in the classroom and may explain "difficulties" that a student is having. Instruction and interactions with students and parents must be both linguistically and culturally inclusive.

Affective Filter

Affective filter is a part of Stephen Krashen's theory of language acquisition and learning. It refers to aversive feelings such as discomfort, stress, self-consciousness, and/or lack of motivation. These feelings can hinder language acquisition in many ways. For example, if a student's home language and culture are not valued in the classroom or school, he may have a high affective filter (experiencing the feelings listed above) and therefore be less likely to succeed in school and/or less likely to continue to speak his home language. Family and peer attitudes and behaviors toward the target language and culture (which may be different from their own) can also increase a learner's affective filter. If parents or friends do not value the target language or culture, the student may either agree with them and struggle to acquire the target language or may begin to have a negative attitude toward his home language and culture. To avoid interference from a student's affective filter, teachers and parents should welcome and value both languages and cultures and seek to make the student at ease in his environments.

Role of the Home Environment

As stated above, the home environment impacts a student's learning. Parents are the primary language teachers for the first 5 years of a child's life! This does not change just because a student begins to attend school. If true bilingualism is the goal, then the school should encourage use of the home language and communicate that the home language and culture are valued, even (and especially!) when they are not dominant. For example, when a student lives in a Spanish-speaking home in an English-dominant culture, the opportunity to speak and learn Spanish will occur primarily at home and should not be missed. Similarly, parents can encourage and support students as they seek linguistic and cultural fluency in both languages and cultures. Schools and homes alike should have an additive mindset toward bilingualism rather than a subtractive one. This can also be aided by clear communication between home and school as regards expectations, student progress, affective issues that parents or teachers see, and more. If the student knows that school and home are both on his team, his learning will be positively affected.

Target Language Instruction in the Bilingual Classroom

One of the bilingual teacher's responsibilities is teaching students the target language. Following are some research-based strategies for target language instruction.

Provide Comprehensible Input

Comprehensible input, according to Krashen's language learning hypotheses, is the level of language that is understandable by learners but contains words and grammatical structures that they have not yet learned or mastered. It is often called ***i*+1**, with *i* representing the learner's current language ability. If a student is only exposed to *i*, that student's language ability may stagnate. If a student is only exposed to *i*+3 (several steps beyond their current ability), they will not be able to pick up on the new words and structures as easily. Following are two examples of comprehensible input in a bilingual classroom. A teacher may use the vocabulary that a student already knows to introduce new words (e.g. *She is my grandma. She is my dad's mom.*) If students know everything except the word *grandma*, they will be able to comprehend *grandma*. A teacher may also use comprehensible input to introduce new grammatical structures (e.g. *I walked to school yesterday. I walk to school every day*). A student who has not yet learned the past tense but knows the present tense and the vocabulary in this utterance can learn from this input the difference between present tense verbs and past tense verbs.

Access Students' Prior Knowledge

One of the benefits of teaching older language learners is that they have a richer set of prior knowledge than a young toddler does. This knowledge may be linguistic, academic, or experiential. A teacher can call on students' knowledge of their home language to help them understand a word or structure in the target language (e.g. *"How do you change "**camino**" to say that you did it yesterday?"*). If a student already knows how to add and subtract but does not know the words **"add"** and **"subtract"** in the target language, the teacher can have the student complete the math problem with manipulatives and then teach the target language words for the academic knowledge the student already has. Providing target language texts and books that allow students to access their own prior life experiences is a way to leverage that knowledge to teach the target language.

Create a Language-Rich Environment

A teacher can support student acquisition of the target language by making the classroom a language-rich environment. This could include labelling classroom objects in the target language, posting word walls or other displays with key words and phrases on them, completing classroom routines in the target language, reading aloud to students, making books in the target language readily accessible to them, speaking to students individually and in groups in the target language, providing students with other native interlocutors, and any other strategy that increases the students' exposure to the target language.

Give Explicit Instruction in Context

As students interact with content in the target language, a teacher can use that content to explicitly teach the target language. He may draw students' attention to language structures (e.g. *"Do you see the word **unhappy** in our story? **Un-** is called a prefix. It's stuck on the beginning of the word "happy" to make it mean something new. Can you think of another word with **un-** at the beginning? Can you find another word with a prefix on page 3?"*), forms (e.g. registers – *"Look at how these two characters talk to each other. Can you tell they are friends just by the way they talk?"*), and functions (e.g. informing vs. persuading – *"Why did the writer write this science article? What does she want to happen when we read it?"*) present in the text that students are reading.

Teach to and Integrate the Four Domains of Language

A bilingual teacher should be sensitive to students' needs to learn and practice all four domains (listening, speaking, reading, and writing). This can be done by purposefully varying classroom activities to make sure that students are employing all the domains on a consistent basis. The domains should also be integrated with each other. Allowing students to use two domains at once (e.g. listening to a read-aloud and following along in their own copy of the book) can help the language acquisition process. Another research-based practice is to give students time to prepare a response in one domain before giving it in another (e.g. discussing in a small group before writing a response or writing answers before responding to teacher questions). The domains can also be integrated by giving input in one domain and asking students to produce output in another (e.g. read a story and then retell it to a friend).

Plan Meaningful and Purposeful Literacy Activities

Teaching literacy in the bilingual classroom should not be a theoretical exercise. Providing older language learners with activities that are language-appropriate but not developmentally appropriate (e.g. having 3rd grade students read texts intended for preschoolers) can raise their affective filter. It is best practice to provide students with texts that are meaningful and purposeful. These texts could be meaningful because the students connect with the theme or subject matter, or purposeful because, along with literacy skills, they will also allow the students to gain content knowledge.

Scaffold Literacy Activities

The challenge of choosing meaningful and purposeful literacy activities is that the texts available may be above the language level of students. A teacher can scaffold for students by breaking literacy tasks into smaller tasks (e.g. *"Read just the paragraph headings in the social studies textbook. Now read the words that are in bold in the first paragraph. Now read the first paragraph…"*), providing students with needed skills before encountering a text (e.g. introducing the bold words in a class activity before beginning to read the text) or giving students a limited purpose in interacting with the text (e.g. instead of reading the entire page of the science book, just read the captions under the pictures). Scaffolding can also include helping students access their prior knowledge and experiences that will be of use in relating to and interpreting the text.

Differentiate

Every child comes to a classroom with different prior knowledge and learns and develops at a unique pace. This is true in every classroom, but the range of abilities may be especially broad in a bilingual classroom. Therefore, it is vital that a bilingual teacher provide differentiation for students – modifying and adjusting the content and pace of the curriculum to meet the individual needs of students. Some simple differentiation strategies include asking different levels of questions (e.g. yes/no questions to the novice language learner and open-ended questions to the more advanced language learner), providing different levels of texts that cover the same material, using grouping strategies, giving a novice learner extra time to prepare a response, or giving an advanced learner a self-directed project.

Content Instruction in the Bilingual Classroom

A bilingual teacher will not only need to teach the target language, but also to successfully deliver content instruction in the target language. Following are some research-based strategies for content instruction in the target language

Focus on Content-Specific Language Functions

In each content area, students will need to accomplish certain tasks with the target language. These tasks can be identified in state or local standards. For example, consider the standard **"Students will compare and contrast the seven classes of animals."** The task students will need to complete is **"compare and contrast"**. What vocabulary and structures will students need to complete this task? Compare and contrast words like **"but, same, similar, different, because"** will be important, as will specific scientific vocabulary such as **"skeleton, warm-blooded, hair, feathers, legs"**. These words can be taught explicitly. Students can practice compare and contrast sentences with words they already know – *"Mark and Ana have blue jeans but Sarah and Juan have shorts."* – before moving to using the content-specific vocabulary in the same structures.

Include State Standards

Even when state standards seem out of reach for the beginning bilingual student, they can be integrated into the classroom. A good first way to do this is by teaching academic and subject-specific vocabulary and register. In order to do math and talk about math, students will need to learn the words for **"add"**, **"subtract"**, **"how many"**, etc. The bilingual classroom may need to teach these words in both the home and target languages, as academic vocabulary and register may not be used at the student's home (families may not chat about math with their preschoolers).

Linguistic scaffolding is also an important tool in helping students work toward state standards. This occurs when teacher language and the language in materials and activities are modified to provide students with comprehensible input. Rather than change the topic being studied, teachers change the level of language used to study that topic. In the science example above, the teacher and students may use simpler words and structures to communicate the same concepts (e.g. *"Mammals have hair but birds have feathers"* rather than *"One defining feature of mammals is that they have hair. Birds, on the other hand, always have feathers."*)

Employ Different Participation Structures

Structuring classroom activities in a variety of ways can help elicit student output and give them opportunities to negotiate meaning. Make sure that students have the opportunity to receive input from the teacher, from written material, and from other students. Vary the way that students are asked to respond to that input. Very simple response structures like *"Thumbs up if this is correct"* can allow for the silent period that language learners pass through. Teacher questions to students can be varied in language and cognitive level as each student needs. Cooperative learning activities have a more complex response structure, where students must respond to each other, but this allows them to negotiate meaning with each other and practice in an environment with less pressure. Students may have less affective filter if they are given time to interact with the language and subject material on their own or in a small group before they are asked to respond to the teacher or speak while the whole class is listening.

Foster Higher-Order Thinking

One challenge of language learning is that it takes more complex language skills to express higher-order thinking in speech or writing. A bilingual teacher must remember, however, that even if a student lacks the language skills to express higher-order thinking, they do not lack the cognitive skills to undertake that thinking in the first place. Using the student's home language in a dual-language model can allow students to express their advanced cognitive skills while their target language skills increase. Linguistic scaffolding and focusing on subject-specific language functions (as mentioned above) are key tools to keeping higher-order thinking present in a bilingual classroom. In the science standard example above, **"compare and contrast"** is a higher-order thinking skill, but it is easily attainable for language learners when the teacher provides comprehensible input, gives students a chance to exhibit the cognitive skill using words they already know (e.g. comparing and contrasting clothes students are wearing), and teaches the subject-specific words they need to complete the task.

Review Video: ESL/ESOL/Second Language Learning
Visit mometrix.com/academy and enter code: 795047

Spanish Geography

Spain

Spain is in the Iberian Peninsula and has 50 provinces. It can also be divided into 17 autonomous regions. Its five main rivers are the Ebro, the Duero, the Tajo, the Guadiana, and the Guadalquivir. Spanish (Castilian) is the official language of the country, although in some parts of the country other languages are spoken, for example Catalan in Catalonia, Galician in Galicia, and Basque in the Basque Country. The Spanish language originated in Spain.

Spanish Possessions

Two major groups of islands belong to Spain: the Balearic Islands and the Canary Islands. The Balearic Islands are in the Mediterranean Sea. Their main islands are Mallorca, Menorca, Ibiza, and Formentera. The Canary Islands are in the Atlantic Ocean. The largest of the Canary Islands is Tenerife. Spain also has sovereignty over two small enclaves bordering Morocco, Melilla and Ceuta.

Spanish History: 700-1492

The Muslims in Spain

In 711 Muslims from the north of Africa (sometimes referred to as Moors) invaded the Iberian Peninsula and conquered most of it. What is known today as Spain was under Arab control until 1492. Because Arab culture has had such a long history in Spain, its influence can still be easily seen today. Many of the Spanish words that begin with *al-* have Arabic roots, for example, *álgebra, aldea, alguacil, alférez, azulejo, alcoba, algodón,* and *alcahofa*. The expression *ojalá*, comes from the Arabic phase "Should Allah will it". The Moors' reign on the peninsula also resulted in a lasting architectural legacy. Many buildings from this era still survive. Some of the most famous of those buildings are the mosque of Córdoba and the Alhambra.

Alhambra

The Alhambra was built between the 9th and 13th century in Granada when the Moors occupied Spain. After the Spaniards recovered their land, the Catholic kings built their own palaces in the Alhambra, therefore it has Islamic and Christian architectural elements. The Alhambra is a large complex, containing several buildings. There are also courts, fountains, and gardens within its walls. It is famous for its decorations, which are made from marble, stucco, and tile. Today it continues to be a very important tourist attraction, and in 1984 it was declared a UNESCO World Heritage Site.

Reconquista

The Reconquista refers to the attempt on the part of the Spaniards to recover their land from the control of the Muslims, who had invaded Spain in 711, and to restore a united faith (Christianity, specifically Catholicism). Almost immediately after the invasion, the Spaniards began the process of reconquering the country. The process took from 712 to 1492. In the 720s, the Christians recovered Asturias, their first major victory. The city of Granada was the last to be reconquered by the Spaniards in 1492.

Alfonso X

Alfonso X or Alfonso el Sabio (the Wise) was king of Castilla-León from 1252 to 1284. Alfonso X is known for his decision to use Castilian (*castellano*) as the official language of his kingdom. Castilian became more important than other languages or dialects spoken in the territory, beginning the linguistic unification of Spain. The language we call Spanish is still known as *castellano* in much of the Spanish-speaking world. Alfonso X also sponsored the writing of a number of literary and historical works in Castilian. The *Primera crónica general de España,* assembled in part from his court documents, is very useful in understanding medieval Spanish history.

Spanish Literature and Art During the Middle Ages

El Cantar del Mio Cid

El Cantar del Mio Cid was anonymously written in the 12th century. It is in the style of a singing poem, a very popular form in medieval Spain. *El Cantar del Mio Cid* takes place during the Reconquista, when the Spanish Christians were trying to regain control of their land from the Arabs who had ruled the country since 711. The main character is Rodrigo Díaz de Vivar, who is trying to recover his honor after being exiled by the king Alfonso VI. He takes part in the battle of Valencia and after he recovers his honor, his two daughters marry the heirs of the house of Carrión, relatives of the king. These men mistreat the girls and almost kill them. The Cid fights against the bad husbands and after he defeats them, his daughters marry the heirs of the house of Navarra and Aragón.

Spanish History: 1492-1807

Isabel y Fernando

Isabel and Fernando, also called "The Catholic Monarchs", married in 1469. Their marriage effectively unified Spain, as Fernando originally reigned over Aragon and Isabel over Castile, the two largest states in what is modern Spain. Under their reign, many other seminal events took place: the Reconquista ended, the Inquisition was established, and Spain began to send explorers to unknown parts of the world.

End of the Reconquista

With the unification of Castile and Aragon, the Reconquista moved forward. In 1492, the Catholic forces of Isabel and Fernando took the city of Granada, an event which marked the end of the Reconquista. They sought to establish a unification of religion as well, and eventually all Jews and Muslims who did not convert to Catholicism were expelled from Spain. Those Jews and Muslims who did convert were watched carefully by the Inquisition.

Inquisition

The Inquisition was a court established during the reign of Fernando II of Aragon and Isabel I of Castile in 1478. The purpose of the Inquisition was to discover and punish false converts and

Christian heretics. Because Jews and Muslims had been expelled from Spain, there existed the possibility of Jewish and Muslim believers who claimed conversion but had not truly converted. The court also investigated crimes against the faith, including witchcraft, bigamy, blasphemy, and possession of forbidden books. Inquisition courts used torture during their interrogations. The Inquisition operated in Spain and in Nueva España. The Inquisition was abolished in 1834.

Spanish Armada

The Spanish Armada was a strong fleet composed of more than 130 ships and 20,000 sailors. At its strongest, it was considered invincible. But, in 1588, when King Felipe II sent it to England to try to destroy Queen Elizabeth I of England, the fleet was defeated. The defeat of the fleet is considered the historical point when the Spanish empire started to decline. Spain would never have the same political and economic importance in Europe as before the defeat.

Bourbons

The house of the Bourbons has had great influence in Europe. Their reign in Spain began when Carlos II of Spain (a Hapsburg) designated Felipe V (Duke of Anjou), a Bourbon, as his successor. The death of Carlos II and the subsequent crowning of Felipe V started the War of the Spanish Succession in 1701. Other important Bourbons in Spain were Luis I, Fernando VI, Carlos III, and Carlos IV. The Bourbons implemented reforms to consolidate power and strengthen the efficiency of the bureaucracy in Spain and their colonies in the New World. These reforms were not popular in the colonies. The dissatisfaction they created was one of the factors that led to the revolutionary movements in Latin America.

Royal Spanish Academy

The Real Academia Española (Royal Spanish Academy) was created in 1713 and is responsible for regulating the Spanish language. Its motto is *"Limpia, fija y da esplendor"* ("It cleans, sets and gives splendor"). The academy concentrates in linguistic planning to provide linguistic agreement and a common standard among all the Spanish-speaking regions. It has a formal procedure to incorporate new words, and it periodically publishes dictionaries and grammars. The academy has sometimes been criticized as too conservative and slow to react to change. It is located in Madrid and is affiliated with other national language academies in 21 Spanish-speaking countries. Its website is www.rae.es.

Spanish Literature and Art: 1492-1807

La Celestina (1499)

La Celestina, also known as *La Tragicomedia de Calisto y Melibea*, was written by Fernando de Rojas in 1499. Many consider *La Celestin*a the first Spanish novel although it is not strictly a novel as it is written as a dialogue between the characters. Like a work of theater, the piece is divided into acts. It is representational of the Spanish Renaissance. Rather than focus on divine themes, it bears similarity to Italian humanist comedies. The work also demonstrates revived attention to ancient Roman comedies.

El Siglo de Oro

El Siglo de Oro, or "The Golden Century" refers to a flourishing of Spanish art, literature, and music that took place under the reign of the Hapsburgs (who were great supporters of the arts) in the 1500s and 1600s. During this time period, the Spanish arts were influenced by the art being produced in the rest of Europe but also began to establish their own styles. The artists and works of art listed below are considered a part of *el Siglo de Oro*.

Garcilaso de la Vega (1501-1536)

Garcilaso de la Vega is the poet most credited with bringing Italian poetry forms such as sonnets and elegies to Spain and adapting them to the Spanish language, as well as establishing traditional Spanish forms of poetry such as *estancias* and *liras*. As such, he had a great impact on Spanish poetry and subsequent Spanish poets. His work deals with themes of love and the meaning of life, although religion as a theme is notably absent.

El Greco (1541-1614)

Born Domenikos Theotokopoulos in Greece, El Greco studied art with the Renaissance masters in Italy, but returned to Spain and developed a very unique, expressionistic style of painting. His works are marked by bold brushstrokes and bright colors, more emotional than many works of his time. Not always understood or appreciated in his lifetime, he was recognized in the 20th century as one of the main precursors of impressionism and cubism. He painted many altarpieces and other works with religious themes, as well as portraits. He also did some sculpture. Some of his most well-known works are *The Assumption of the Virgin*, *The Opening of the Fifth Seal*, and his landscapes titled *Toledo.*

Miguel de Cervantes Saavedra (1547-1616)

Miguel de Cervantes Saavedra is most well-known for his novel, *El ingenioso hidalgo Don Quijote de la Mancha*, which was published in two parts, the first one in 1605 and the second one in 1615. In *Don Quijote de la Mancha*, Cervantes recounts the adventures of Alonso Quijano, an old man who goes crazy after reading too many chivalric novels. In his altered state, he believes he is Don Quijote de la Mancha, a traveling knight. Cervantes narrates Don Quijote's adventures and his search for love. The most famous scene is when Alonso fights against windmills, believing they are giants. The book is considered a parody of the chivalric books of the times. In addition to *Don Quijote de la Mancha*, Cervantes wrote *La galatea*, *Novelas ejemplares*, and *Los trabajos de Persiles y Segismunda*, but those works were never as popular as *Don Quijote.*

Félix Lope de Vega y Carpio (1562-1635)

Félix Lope de Vega was a prolific Spanish writer who did much to shape Spanish literary tradition. He produced works in every genre of his time – novels, poetry (epic, religious, and lyric), and works for theatre. He proscribed the form of the Spanish 3-act comedy and wrote his characters with a new level of depth. His plays (of which there were more than 1500) dealt with themes as wide-ranging as religious doctrine, history and legends, and social conditions of the day. Some of his most famous comedies (such as *Fuenteovejuna* and *El mejor alcalde el rey*) describe the unjust uses of power among the nobility in Spain. In addition to revolutionizing theater, Lope de Vega codified many traditional Spanish poem forms.

Francisco de Quevedo y Villegas (1580-1645)

Quevedo was one of the most prolific poets of the *Siglo de Oro*. He was highly involved in politics – he was alternately a court writer or in exile for much of his life and died in jail. His poetry is known for its *conceptismo*, or brief but deep style, in contrast to the more flowery poetry of many of his peers. His sonnets are perhaps most representative of his style and skill as a poet. His work was at times unsympathetic to the excesses of the nobility for whom he wrote, and he also mocked many subgroups of Spanish society in his writings. In addition to poetry, he is known for his satirical works such as *Sueños y discursos.*

Diego Velázquez (1599-1660)

Diego Velázquez was a Spanish painter of the 17th century. Born in Seville, he moved to Madrid where he became the court painter for King Philip IV. He spent time in Italy (which greatly influenced his style) but returned to Madrid, where he lived until his death. He was mainly a portraitist, producing historical and cultural depictions of royalty, notables, and commoners. His most famous painting is *Las Meninas*, a baroque portrayal of the Infanta Margarita, one of the daughters of the king, surrounded by maids of honor and other members of the court. It is now at the Museo del Prado in Madrid. Impressionists and realists of the 19th century as well as modern painters such as Picasso and Dalí have been influenced by Velázquez and use his art as a model for their work.

Bartolomé Esteban Murillo (1618-1682)

Murillo was a Spanish painter who studied under Spanish masters Castillo and Zurbarán, eventually developing a soft, muted style that appealed to the ruling classes and the Catholic church. He completed several works for the monastery and cathedral in Seville and was one of the founders of the Academia de Bellas Artes. While he completed many religiously themed works (the most famous of which may be his *Assumption of the Virgin*), he is also known for his paintings of children in everyday life and his portraiture.

Zarzuela

The zarzuela is a particular work of performing art that mixes theater and music. In the zarzuelas singing and speaking take turns. The zarzuela originated in Spain in the 17th century, and the pieces were very popular with the kings and other members of the privileged class. In Spain, its popularity started to decline with the arrival of opera. Nevertheless, zarzuelas kept on being popular in other countries such as Cuba. In the 19th and 20th century, they became popular again in Spain. The most famous composers of zarzuelas are Amadeo Vives, Federico Chueca, José Serrano, and Jacinto Guerrero.

Spanish History: 1808-1935

Peninsular War and War for Independence

From 1807-1814, the Peninsular War and the Spanish War for Independence took place. The Peninsular War, Napoleon's attempt to take over the Iberian Peninsula, began when Spain and France attacked Portugal together in 1807. It morphed into the Spanish War for Independence when France abandoned Spain as an ally and sought to occupy it instead. The people of Madrid pushed back in the famous *Dos de mayo* uprising on May 2, 1808, and the war between the two empires lasted for 6 more years before the French fully withdrew from Spain.

Latin America

Spain's colonies took advantage of the political and social turmoil on the continent during the Peninsular War. Fueled by the rising democratic sentiment in the western world, the independence movements across Latin America took place during the early 19th century (1810-1833). Spain's colonies in Central and South America revolted against Spanish rule, fought for, and won their independence. The effective end of this global empire had a profound destabilizing effect on Spain in conjunction with the wars and unrest on the peninsula. Spain had been a leader in trade and the world economy, but the loss of many of its colonies resulted in a slower and more isolated economy for Spain.

Cuba, Puerto Rico, and Philippines

In the second half of the 19th century, Spain's colonies in the Indies also declared their independence from Spain. These independence movements were eventually supported by the United States in the Spanish-American War in 1898. The USA involved themselves after rumors of

Spanish-enacted atrocities in the colonies and the sinking of the USS *Maine* in the Havana harbor. The loss of its last colonies effected Spain, not as much economically but rather in its self-conception, since at this point Spain effectively lost its status as an empire and a world power. The writings of the Generation of '98 (see below) were influenced by this historical event.

Spanish Literature and Art: 1808-1935

Francisco Goya (1746-1828)

Francisco Goya was a prominent Spanish painter and printmaker. His career and style spanned many styles: baroque, rococo, and then neoclassicism and expressionism. He worked in the Real Fábrica de Tapices de Madrid designing tapestries and was later appointed court painter. He was a great influence for modern artists as he was one of the first artist to paint what he wanted and not what the king or the church told him to paint. His portraits are known for their realism rather than their flattery. Many of his most famous works are historical or political in nature. His piece *El tres de mayo 1808* shows the execution of Spanish soldiers by the French army. His sets of etchings *Los desastres de la guerra* and *Los caprichos* provide social commentary on the war between France and Spain and many of the social ills in Spain at the time.

El Romanticismo

In the first half of the 1800s, Romanticism held sway in the literature of Spain. It consisted of a rejection of neoclassicism and of conservative social order and a turn toward expressing emotion. Romantic authors dealt with grand, sweeping themes in a mystical and flourishing manner. Romanticism was quickly replaced with Realism in Spain.

Gustavo Adolfo Becquer (1836-1870)

Becquer's writing bridges the gap between Romanticism and modern poetry in Spain. His *Rimas,* written in free verse, deal with themes of love and life. His most famous *rima* is known for the line "***Poesia...eres tu***". His collection of prose pieces, *Leyendas*, are exemplary of Romantic prose, dealing with myth, love, life and death in a mystical, lyrical style.

El Realismo

Realism was the prevailing literary style in Spain during the second half of the 19th century. Realist authors wrote about common themes and people rather than the grandiose ideas dealt with in Romanticism. In realism, styles of language employed by different classes and regions were included, even if they were not "correct". Realist authors often had strong feelings about the social issues of their day and used their writings to explore, praise, and condemn the way these problems were handled in Spain. Two famous Realist authors are described below.

Benito Pérez Galdós (1843-1920)

Benito Pérez Galdós was a Spanish author who wrote realist novels, dramas, and chronicles. He was heavily influenced by the work of Dickens in England and Balzac in France. His characters came from all classes and regions of Spain. His greatest project was *Episodios nacionales* – a set of 46 novels that could best be described as historical fiction. In them, Galdós explores the 19th -century history of Spain through the eyes of several different characters. Some of the stand-out novels from this body of work include *Dona Perfecta, Fortunata y Jacinta*, and *Misericordia.*

Emilia Pardo Bazán (1852-1921)

Emilia Pardo Bazán, also known as the Countess, was very important novelist from the last decades of the 19th century. She tried to introduce naturalism in Spain but rejected the determinism that was at the time connected to naturalism. She also took part in the women's liberation movement of her day. Pardo Bazán wrote stories, novels, and poetry, as well as social studies and commentaries, many of which were published in periodicals. Most of her works deal with the life and customs of Galicia, and the author uses her characters and situations to study the human condition. She wrote more than 500 pieces; the best known are *Los pasos de Ulloa*, *La madre naturaleza*, *Cuentos de la tierra*, and *La tribuna*.

LA GENERACIÓN DEL 98

The generation of 98 was a group of Spanish writers, essayists, and poets who were affected by the moral, political, and social crises in Spain in the last decades of the 19th century. Spain struggled to regain stability after the Napoleanic wars, and the 19th century was marked by rapid, sometimes violent changes from one regime to another. As mentioned above, Spain lost its colonial holdings during this time as well. These authors reacted to what they saw as overbearing, unacademic conservatism in the arts and academia in Spain. Miguel de Unamuno, Antonio Machado, and Pío Baroja are well-known writers from this group.

MIGUEL DE UNAMUNO (1864-1936)

Miguel de Unamuno was an author from the generation of 98. He was a philosopher and professor who was deeply engaged in the intellectual debates of the day. In his best known essay, *Del sentimiento trágico de la vida*, Unamuno explores what it meant and what it should mean to be a Spaniard. His best known novels are *Paz en la guerra, Niebla, Abel Sánchez, La tía Tula,* and *San Manuel Bueno, mártir.*

ANTONIO GAUDÍ (1852-1926)

Antonio Gaudí is arguably Spain's most well-known architect. His work takes from many architectural traditions (Gothic, Romantic, Modern, Oriental) as well as from patterns he observed in nature, creating a very unique style. His celebrated *Basilica de la Sagrada Familia* is still under construction today in Barcelona. Other works, primarily located in Barcelona, include the *Parc Güell*, the *Casa Milà* and the *Casa Batlló*, all of which have been designated UNESCO World Heritage sites.

LA GENERACIÓN DEL 27

The generation of 27 was a group of Spanish poets who rose to prominence before the Spanish Civil War. While their poetry represents diverse styles, they tended to employ free verse and sought to bridge the gap between Spanish folk tradition, classical poetry, and the up and coming styles of poetry in the rest of Europe. Many of them opposed Franco and were killed, jailed, or exiled during or after the Spanish Civil War. Their work influenced writers in Latin America (notably Pablo Neruda and Jorge Luis Borges) and artists (Salvador Dalí identified with the group) as well.

FEDERICO GARCÍA LORCA (1898-1936)

Federico García Lorca, perhaps the most famous of the *Generación de '27*, wrote poetry and works for theatre and was also a musician. In his works, García Lorca offers a separate world with creations that oscillate between stylized reality and surreal fantasy. Among his dramas are *Bodas de sangre*, *Yerma*, and *La casa de Bernarda Alba*. His well-known collections of poetry include *Libro de poemas, Canciones, Romancero gitano, Poema del cante jondo,* and *Poeta en Nueva York.* He lived for a while in New York and studied English at the University of Columbia. He returned to Spain in 1930. In 1936, García Lorca was assassinated a few days after the Spanish Civil War started.

Juan Gris (1887-1927)

Born in Madrid, Gris spent most of his adult life and career as an artist in Paris. His paintings and collages were influenced by the cubism of Picasso and Braque and by the bright colors of Matisse. His version of cubism is more "pure" or mathematical than that of Picasso. Some of his most famous works include *Portrait of Picasso* and his many still lifes (e.g., *Violin and Guitar, Bottle of Rum and a Newspaper*).

Spanish History: 1936-Present

General Francisco Franco (1892-1975)

In 1934, General Francisco Franco led a campaign against the Republican government which had abolished the monarchy, thereby dividing Spain into two factions: the Franquistas or Nationalists and the Republicans or Loyalists. Franco and his faction defeated the Republicans and established an absolute dictatorship. Under Franco, the Catholic Church, the army, and the state were aligned. The dictatorship was defined by its oppression, lack of freedom, fidelity to the Catholic Church, and support from the Spanish financial oligarchy. Political prisoners include scientists, artists, writers, teachers, and professors. Franco continued as dictator until his death in 1975.

Civil War (1936-1939)

The Spanish Civil War was between the Nationalists, under the leadership of General Franco, and the Republicans, composed of anarchists, communists, and socialists, and anyone who opposed Franco. The Nationalists had the support of the fascist governments in Europe – Italy and Germany. The Republicans were supported by Mexico and the Soviet Union. The war divided communities, families, and friends. Many atrocities against civilians were committed. One of the most well-known of these is the bombing of the city of Guernica by the German Luftwaffe. The war ended on April 1, 1939, shortly after the Nationalists took over Madrid. April 1, 1939. Franco then established his dictatorship.

Spain Under Franco

Spain was under the dictatorship of Franco until his death in 1975. His rule was marked by religious and cultural conservatism and autocratic decision-making. He sought to homogenize Spain linguistically and culturally and to keep Spain free from foreign influence, both economic and cultural. Some of the specific policies that demonstrated these goals included the *permiso marital*, which severely limited the legal and economic rights of women, the ban of the public use of regional languages like Catalan and Euskera (the Basque language), and heavy reliance on internal production rather than free trade.

ETA

ETA, or *Euskadi Ta Askatasuna* (Basque Country and Freedom), was an armed leftist group that was founded in 1959, seeking to gain autonomy from Spain for the Basque Country. The Basque country is located in the south of France and the north of Spain and has traditionally resisted assimilation into the larger culture, partially due to the geographic isolation provided by the Pyrenees mountain range and partially due to strong cultural identity. The Basque language is not related to any known European language. While Spain has traditionally allowed for some regional and linguistic self-determination, under Franco this was not the case. ETA was formed to push back against Franco's attempt to homogenize the language and culture of the region. The group employed terrorist attacks to accomplish their goal and only recently (2018) announced their dissolvement.

Post-Franco Spain

After Franco's death in 1975, several leaders ruled for a short amount of time. After a few years of political turmoil, a constitutional democracy was set up and has been successfully maintained since 1982. A cultural movement, often referred to as *La Movida,* occurred after Franco's death as well – the religious and social conservatism that Franco had kept in place was thrown off, and Spaniards reveled in their new freedom of expression on many fronts (art/music, speech, breaking moral taboos, etc.).

Spanish Literature and Art: 1936-Present

Pablo Picasso (1881-1973)

Pablo Ruiz Picasso was a Spanish painter. Born in Málaga, he spent most of his life in Madrid, Barcelona, and Paris. He was inspired by the earlier ground-breaking Spanish painters El Greco and Francisco Goya. Picasso is arguably the most influential artist of the 20th century. Together with Juan Gris, he developed and defined Cubism. Many of his work have political inspiration - Picasso hated the fascist government of Franco. He was a prolific artist and many of his works are in museums all over the world today. His best-known works include *Guernica* (commemmorating the bombing during the Civil War) and *Les Demoiselles d'Avignon.*

Joan Miró (1893-1983)

Joan Miró was a Spanish painter influenced by surrealism and Dada but whose work resists classification. His early works were influenced by Cézanne and then Kandinsky. Miró's works contain more experimental techniques and modern representation (as opposed to classical representation) than his peer Dalí's. He was a sculptor as well as a painter. Some of his best-known works are the sculpture *Pájaro lunar* and the paintings *Carnaval de Arlequín and Granja.*

Salvador Dalí (1904-1989)

Salvador Dalí was a Spanish surrealist painter. He began his career as a cubist but soon, under the influence of other artists in Paris, began to explore surrealism. His work is marked by classical technique as well as his wildly imaginative images. Among his best-known pieces are *La cesta del pan, El hombre invisible,* and *La persistencia de la memoria.*

Spanish Cinema

The successful history of Spanish cinema started in the 1930s with Luis Buñuel, who was the first Spanish director to be recognized internationally through such films as *Belle de Jour, El discreto encanto de la burguesía,* and *Ese oscuro objeto del deseo.* He was associated with the surrealist movement and worked in Spain, France, Mexico, and the United States. Carlos Saura (*La Madriguera, Cría Cuervos, Sweet Hours*) was another Spanish director known globally. Because of the censorship of the Franco era, however, it was difficult for Spanish filmmakers to attract international attention for many decades. Today, Pedro Almodóvar's works (*Mujeres al borde de un ataque de nervios, Todo acerca de mi madre, Volver*) are well known internationally and have made household names of some of the actors (Antonio Banderas) and actresses (Penélope Cruz) who have worked in his films.

Spanish Architecture

Spanish architecture is varied and reflects its history. It had a significant Roman influence from when it was part of the Roman Empire. It then incorporated, especially in Andalucia, Arab features while under the Moors' domination. After the Reconquista, Romanesque and gothic elements were integrated with the Arab styles, sometimes in the same buildings. The 20th century brought

Modernism to architecture, with Antoni Gaudí and Barcelona as its center. Contemporary Spanish architects are internationally recognized, among them Rafael Moneo (*Cathedral of Our Lady of the Angels* in Los Angeles, *Wellesley College* in Massachusetts, *Audrey Jones Beck building* in Houston), and Santiago Calatrava (*Milwaukee Art Museum* in Wisconsin, *Ciutat de les Arts i les Ciències* in Valencia, Spain, *Turning Torso building* in Malmo, Sweden).

Spanish Cultural Practices and Perspectives

Political and Economic Facts About Spain Today

Today, Spain is a democracy under a parliamentary constitutional monarchy with a hereditary monarchy and a bicameral parliament. It is a member of the European Union and its currency is the euro. Spain's population was estimated at 47 million in 2018, and its capital is Madrid. Other important cities include Barcelona, Bilbao, Valencia, Seville, and Zaragoza. Due to Spain's climate, rich historic and cultural quality, and geographic position, tourism has become one of the main sources of income for the country. Spain is also one of the most important developers and producers of renewable energy, in particular solar power.

Metric and Imperial Measurement Systems

Spanish speaking countries primarily use the metric system for measurements. Although some units such as those of time (seconds/*segundos*, hours/*horas*, days/*días*, etc.) and angles (degrees/*grados*) are the same, other units are different. For longitude and distances, the metric system uses centimeters (*centímetros*), meters (*metros*), and kilometers (*kilómetros*), while the imperial system uses inches (*pulgadas*), feet (*pies*), yards (*yardas*), and miles (*millas*). Gram (*gramo*), kilogram (*kilogramo*), and ton (*tonelada*) will be the units used in in the metric system for weight; the imperial units are ounce (*onza*), pound (*libra*), and ton (*tonelada*). When it comes to volume, the metric system uses milliliter (*mililitro*), centiliter (*centilitro*), and liter (*litro*), while the imperial system uses ounce (*onza*), cup (*taza*), quarter (*cuarto*), and gallon (*galón*). Units in both systems are not directly equivalent and have to be converted from one system to another according to their particular relationship. For example, 1 pound is 454 grams, 1 inch equals 2.54 centimeters, and 1 gallon is 3.785 liters.

Religion

The Catholic church has played a large role in the history of Spain. It served as one of the forces that unified several medieval states into modern Spain. The Inquisition is an example of the social and political power that the Catholic church possessed in Spain's early history. More recently, the Church aligned itself with Franco and as a result held great sway over the cultural and moral order during Franco's reign. While the Catholic church is still the majority religion in Spain, many who identify as Catholic could be described as cultural adherents rather than religious. Secularization is strong in Spain, with a large percentage identifying as atheistic, agnostic, or as non-practicing Catholics.

Family and Lifestyle

Spain is a diverse country with many different practices in regard to family and lifestyle. Bearing this in mind, following are some generalizations about Spanish culture. Family is highly valued – even the noon meal is often eaten at home with family. Due in part to the valuing of family and partially to the economic woes in the early 2000s, many young people live with their immediate family into their 20s and 30s if they have not married. In the southern and rural parts of the country, a *siesta*, or afternoon nap is still traditional, and stores and restaurants may even close for a period in the afternoon. Dressing well is important – the standards for casual and formal are a bit elevated in Spain when compared to the USA.

FESTIVALS AND TRADITIONS

Spain has many famous traditional festivals. *La corrida*, or the running of the bulls in Pamplona for the celebration of San Fermin, is perhaps the best-known of these. Throughout Spain, Holy Week, or *Semana santa* is celebrated with parades and a variety of religious festivals. *Carnaval* is similar to the French-American celebration of Mardi Gras and also takes place nation-wide. Local traditions include the *Fallas* in Valencia (parade of large paper floats that are set on fire at the end), the *Tomatina* (everyone throws tomatoes at each other), also in Valencia, and the *Feria* in Seville. Spain is also the location of a famous pilgrimage, the *Santiago de Compostela*.

LANGUAGE

Throughout Spain's history, there has been a debate about the importance of linguistic unity versus preserving the linguistic heritage of the autonomous communities. What we call "Spanish" is technically *castellano* – descended from the language of Castile. In several regions, a local language is still spoken instead of or in addition to *castellano*. *Catalán, euskera*, and Gallego are the languages with the largest groups of speakers. The debate about how to preserve and use these languages is ongoing. Policies such as what language of instruction should be used in school and which languages to use in public spaces (on signs, for example) and in local government are still being formed. The fight for linguistic self-determinism is often linked to a fight for political self-determinism (notably in the case of the Basques), which makes language choice a delicate issue for many Spaniards.

Latin American Geography

NORTH AMERICA

MEXICO

The official name of Mexico is Estados Unidos Mexicanos. The country is in North America, and borders with the United States in the north, and Guatemala and Belize in the south. Its territory is three times the size of Texas. The capital is Ciudad de México, and the currency is the Mexican peso.In Pre-Colombian times, it was inhabited by the Aztecs in the region's center, the Mayans in Yucatan in the south, and the Chimichecas in central area and north. After the arrival of the Spaniards, the Viceroyalty of New Spain was established, In 1519, Hernán Cortés began the conquest of the Aztec Empire. The Viceroyalty of New Spain was later established. In 1821, Mexico declared its independence. Agriculture, industry, mining, and tourism are strong areas of Mexican economy.

ANTILLES

The Antilles (also known as the West Indies) is the archipelago in the Caribbean Sea between North and South America. The Greater Antilles consist of Cuba, Hispaniola (Dominican Republic and Haiti), Jamaica, Puerto Rico, and the Cayman Islands. The Lesser Antilles are the islands on the east of the Caribbean Sea and include Guadeloupe, Dominica, Martinique, Saint Lucia, Barbados, Granada, Trinidad, and others. In Pre-Colombian times, they were inhabited by the Arawak and the Caribs and they were the first land Colón put his foot on in 1492. Sugar production flourished in the Antilles after European colonization, and, with it, slavery. The islands are very diverse ethnically, and, due to the imports of slaves, the influence of African culture is clearly seen.

Dominican Republic

Dominican Republic is on the island of Hispaniola, which it shares with Haiti. The capital is Santo Domingo, and the currency is the Dominican peso. The island was named by Colón when he landed there in 1492. In Pre-Colombian times, it was inhabited by the Taino (an Arawak people group). Santo Domingo was founded by the Spanish in 1496 and was the first permanent European settlement in the New World. The country passed between Spanish and French rule until declaring independence in 1821. The Dominican Republic has had a tumultuous political history, with many dictators and military leaders, Trujillo being perhaps the most infamous. The economy of the Dominican Republic is based on agriculture, mainly sugar cane.

Cuba

Cuba is the largest island in the Greater Antilles. It is to the south of Florida in the United States and to the west of the Bahamas. The capital is Havana, and the currency is the peso. The most important indigenous groups that inhabited the island was home to the Taíno and the Guanahatabey. In 1511, Diego Velásquez de Cuéllar (not the painter) began the conquest of the island. Cuba was under Spanish rule until 1898 (one of the last Spanish holdings in the Americas). In 1952, Fulgencio Batista established a dictatorship, and in 1959, Fidel Castro overthrew him and took control of the country. Under Castro, Cuba had a close relationship with the Soviet Union.

Puerto Rico

Puerto Rico is one of the islands of the Greater Antilles. It is southeast of the United States, and it is an unincorporated territory of the United States. The capital is San Juan, and the currency is the dollar. In Pre-Colombian times, it was inhabited by the Arawak people. In 1493, in his second trip to the new world, Cristobal Colón explored the island. He named it San Juan Bautista. Juan Ponce de León lead the conquest of the island, and it was under Spanish control until 1897, when it sought autonomy from Spain. In 1898, it was occupied by the army of the United States. In 1899 it became part of the United States after the Treaty of Paris ended the Spanish-American War. In 1952, it was designated a commonwealth of the United States.

Central America

Central America is the region between North and South America. It generally begins at the southern border of Mexico and extends to Panama. The Spanish-speaking countries in Central America are: Guatemala, Honduras, El Salvador, Nicaragua, Costa Rica, and Panama. In colonial times, this area was known as the Capitanía General de Guatemala. From 1823-1838, all these countries belonged to the Provincias Unidas de Centroamérica, but later became independent nations. The Panama Canal, which connects the Atlantic with the Pacific Ocean, goes through the Isthmus of Panama in the south of the region.

Guatemala

Guatemala is to the south of Mexico. The capital is Ciudad de Guatemala and the currency is the quetzal. The Maya inhabited the area in Pre-Colombian times. In 1523, Pedro de Alvarado began the Spanish conquest of the territory and quickly created a colony. Then the Capitanía General de Guatemala was formed, which had jurisdiction over all of Central America. In 1821 the states in the captaincy general declared their independence from Spain, and during the period from 1821 to 1838, Guatemala and the other Central American republics were part of the Provincias Unidas de Centroamérica. In 1839, Guatemala officially became its own country. Agriculture is the most important sector of the economy of Guatemala, especially coffee, sugar cane, and bananas.

El Salvador

El Salvador is the smallest country in Central America. It is to the south of Guatemala and the west of Honduras. The currency is the Salvadoran colón. In pre-Colombian times, it was inhabited by the Mayans, specifically the Pipils. In 1524, Pedro de Alvarado conquered the territory and founded San Salvador, today's capital. In 1824, it incorporated with the Provincias Unidas de Centroamérica and, in 1841, it declared its independence as a nation. El Salvador suffered a civil war between leftist guerillas and right-wing military from 1977 to 1979. A presidential regime was established in 1983. Coffee is the main agricultural product of El Salvador.

Honduras

Honduras is a country in Central America between Guatemala, El Salvador, and Nicaragua. The capital is Tegucigalpa, and the currency is the lempira. In Pre-Colombian times, it was inhabited by the Mayans. By 1524, Cortés and Alvarado were founding settlements in the region. In 1824, it incorporated into the Provincias Unidas de Centroamérica. In 1838, it seceded and became independent, although its neigbors have frequently interfered in its political affairs. Bananas are the main export of modern Honduras. Coffee, corn, and tobacco are also exported.

Nicaragua

Nicaragua is to the southwest of Honduras and El Salvador. It borders with Costa Rica in the south. The capital is Managua and its currency is the córdoba. In Pre-Colombian times, it was inhabited by many Native American groups, including the Nahuas. In 1522, Gil González De Ávila discovered the territory. In 1824, it integrated with the Provincias Unidas de Centroamérica and in 1838, it declared its independence, the first state to do so. In the nineteenth century, the USA was interested in creating a canal in Nicaragua. This interest led to a long history of US intervention in Nicaraguan politics. Agriculture is the most important part of its economy. It exports cotton, coffee, sugar, and bananas.

Costa Rica

Costa Rica is located between Nicaragua and Panama in Central America. The capital is San José, and the currency is the Costa Rican colón. In Pre-Colombian times, it was the contact area between the Mesoamerican cultures of the south of Central America and those in the north of South America. The Spaniards did not establish a permanent settlement in what is today Costa Rica until 1563. In 1823, Costa Rica was incorporated to the Provincias Unidas de Centroamérica and in 1848, it declared its independence. Costa Rica has been one of the most stable and democratic countries in Latin America. The economy of Costa Rica is based mainly in agriculture and fishing. Coffee, bananas, pineapple, and cocoa are exported.

Panama

Panama is to the south of the countries of Central America and to the north of Colombia. The capital is Ciudad de Panamá, and the currency is the balboa. In Pre-Colombian times, it was inhabited by the Chocó, the Chibcha, and the Caribe. In 1501, Panama was discovered by Rodrigo de Bastidas y Colón, and Vasco Nuñez de Balboa established the first colony in 1510. In 1513 he used the isthmus to sail to the Pacific. The territory was incorporated to the Viceroyalty of Peru and Nueva Granada. In 1821, it became part of Colombia. Because of its interest in creating the Panama Canal, the United States was a key player in Panamanian independence from Colombia, achieved in 1903. The USA settled the Hay-Bunau-Varilla treaty with the new Panamanian republic, which gave the USA jurisdiction over the zone where the canal was to be built. The Panama Canal is a strategic holding both economically and militarily. After unrest in the 1970s, the USA agreed to gradually hand over control of the canal to Panama.

South America

South America, known in Spanish as Suramerica or Sudamerica, begins in Colombia and includes Venezuela, Ecuador, Guyana, Suriname, Brazil, Peru, Bolivia, Paraguay, Uruguay, Chile, and Argentina. Some well-known geographical features are the Amazon River, the longest in the world (in Peru, Brazil, Bolivia, Colombia, and Ecuador) and the mountain range of the Andes, which runs from the north of the continent to the south.

Colombia

Colombia is in South America, south of the Isthmus of Panama, and is the country where South America begins. It borders with Venezuela and the Atlantic Ocean on the east, the Pacific Ocean on the northeast, Ecuador and Peru on the southwest, and Brazil on the southeast. The Andes run through the country. The capital is Bogotá, and the currency is the Colombian peso. In Pre-Colombian times, the Chibchas, the Muiscas, and the Quechuas inhabited the area. In 1501, Rodrigo de Bastidas explored the region. Between 1524 and 1534, the Spaniards colonized the area and called it Nueva Granada. In 1821, after many battles and changes in government, Colombia, together with Ecuador and Venezuela, was organized under the name República de la Gran Colombia. In 1830, after the secession of Ecuador and Venezuela as independent nations, the territory that is today Colombia also became its own republic. It was known as Nueva Granada until 1863, when its name changed to the United States of Colombia. In the last half of the 20th century, Colombia has seen much violence from both leftist and rightist guerilla groups (FARC being the most well-known). The drug trade allowed these groups to find funding more easily. The Colombian economy is chiefly agricultural. Most important exports are coffee, corn, rice, sugar, cotton, and bananas. Oil is also a leading import, as are illegal drugs such as cocaine.

Ecuador

Ecuador is in South America, to the south of Colombia and to the north of Peru. The Pacific Ocean is to its west. The capital of the country is Quito, and the currency is the US dollar. In Pre-Colombian times, several Native American tribes inhabited the area but were conquered by the Incas. The center of the Incan empire was in what is today the city of Quito. In 1527, Ecuador was discovered by the Spaniards, and in 1533 it was conquered by Sebastián de Benalcázar. In 1563, the Audiencia of Quito was founded, but in the 17th century the area was incorporated to the Viceroyalty of Nueva Granada. After several battles and changes in government during the 18th and 19th century, it declared its independence from Spain. The economy of Ecuador is based on agriculture and service. The country is the world's largest exporter of bananas. Oil and its products are also important for the economy of Ecuador.

Venezuela

Venezuela is in South America, north of Brazil and east of Colombia. Guyana is to its east and the Caribbean Sea and the Atlantic Ocean are to its north. The capital is Caracas, and the currency is the bolivar. The Arawaks and the Caribs inhabited the area in Pre-Colombian times. Venezuela was discovered in the expeditions of Alonso de Ojeda and Amerigo Vespucci. Caracas was founded in 1567, and the area became important due to its exports of cocoa. It was part of the Viceroyalty of Nueva Granada, and the Audiencia de Caracas was formed in 1786. In 1811 it declared its independence. Simón Bólivar, the South American liberator was born in Venezuela. Venezuela has some of the worlds' largest oil reserves, a fact which has driven much of the politics in Venezuela. In the 21st century, Venezuelan president Hugo Chavez attracted much attention with his attempts toward socialism and nationalism. The economy of Venezuela primarily exports oil and its products.

Uruguay

Uruguay is in South America between Argentina and Brazil, in the area of the Río de la Plata. The capital is Montevideo, and the currency is the Uruguayan peso. In Pre-Colombian times, several groups of Native Americans inhabited the area, most notably the Charrúa, who rebelled against the Spaniards who wanted to conquer the region. In 1516, Juan Díaz de Solís discovered the Río de la Plata, and shortly after the area we know today as Uruguay was explored. Sebastián Gaboto founded the first settlement in 1527, but it was destroyed by the indigenous peoples. In 1680, the Portuguese founded a colony that was given to the Spaniards in 1777. Montevideo was occupied by the British in 1806 and beseiged by Brazilian troops in the 1840s. After fighting against the Spaniards and the Portuguese and different changes in government, Uruguay declared independence in 1825. Uruguay's economy is primarily agricultural and pastoral.

Argentina

Argentina is in South America to the south of Bolivia, Paraguay, Uruguay, and part of Brazil. Chile is to its west. The capital is Buenos Aires, and the currency is the peso. Several Native American groups inhabited the large territory in Pre-Colombian times. In 1516, Juan Díaz de Solís discovered the Río de la Plata, and in 1536 Pedro de Mendoza founded Buenos Aires. The region was not very important to Nueva España until 1776 when Spain established the Viceroyalty of the Río de la Plata. Argentina stayed under the dominance of Spain until 1816 when it declared its independence. In the second half of the 20th century, Argentina's politics were dominated by Juan Perón, a popular dictator, and groups who opposed him. Argentina is still haunted by the "disapperances" of dissenters that occurred in the '70s and '80s under the military rule that deposed the Perones. The economy of Argentina is based on livestock, grains and oil.

Bolivia

Bolivia is in South America to the south of Brazil and Peru, to the east of Chile, and to the north of Argentina and Paraguay. It is interesting to note that the country does not have access to the sea. The constitutional capital is Sucre, but the administrative capital and seat of the government is La Paz. It has declared Spanish, Quechua, and Guaraní, Aymara, and 33 other indigenous languages official languages. In Pre-Colombian times, the Pukina and the Aymara inhabited the area but were under the Inca Empire. In 1530, Bolivia was discovered by Gonzalo and Hernando Pizarro while they were exploring what is now Peru. Bolivia was important during the colonial period because of its silver mines in Cerro Rico in Potosí. Bolivia was part of the Alto Peru until 1776 when it was incorporated to the Viceroyalty of the Río de la Plata. In 1825, Simón Bolívar declared the independence of Bolivia. A large majority of Bolivians are of indigenous heritage but have not traditionally had political or economic power. In recent years, this has begun to change, most notably with the election of Evo Morales as president. Bolivia has rich national resources, including tin, silver, and natural gas, but most of the economy can be described as subsistence. Coca is one of the major crops.

Paraguay

Paraguay is in South America to the south of Bolivia and to the east of Argentina. The river Paraguay divides the country into east and west. It is interesting to note that the country does not have access to the sea. Paraguay has two official languages: Spanish and Guaraní. The capital is Asunción, and the currency is the guaraní. In Pre-Colombian times, the Guaraní inhabited the area. Aleixo García led several trips to explore the region, and in 1536, Pedro de Mendoza began colonization. Between 1735 and 1756 the Guaraní rebelled against the Spaniards. In 1776, the area was incorporated to the Viceroyalty of the Río de la Plata. Paraguay fought against Spain and against Argentina, and, in 1811, declared its independence. Paraguay has had many strong leaders in its history as an independent nation.

PERU

Peru is in South America to the south of Colombia and Ecuador, the west of Brazil and Bolivia, and to the north of Chile. The Pacific Ocean is at its west. The Andes run through the country. The capital is Lima, and the currency is the sol. The official languages are Spanish and Quechua, Aymara, and other indigenous languages in the regions where they are spoken. In Pre-Colombian times, the region was home to the earliest known American civilization, dating to c3200 B.C. Many developed cultures lived in the region, but by the 1300s, it was the Inca who had conquered a great deal of South America. Machu Picchu, a great Incan fortress city, is a famous ruin. In 1532, Francisco Pizarro landed in Peru and he conquered the region in the following years. In 1542, Lima became the base for Spanish rule in South America. In 1780, the Inca Túpac Amaru rebelled against the Spaniards. In 1821, José de San Martín took control of the country and declared its independence. The economy of Peru is based in agriculture.

CHILE

Chile is in South America to the south of Peru, the southeast of Bolivia, and the west of Argentina. The Andes run through the country. The Atacama Desert is in the north. The capital is Santiago, and the currency is the Chilean peso. In Pre-Colombian times, the Incas and the Araucanians inhabited the area. In 1536, Diego de Almagro explored the territory. In the 1540s and 1550s, Pedro de Valdivia conquered the area. In 1778, it became its own colonial division rather than being connected to the viceroyalty of Peru. After long fights lead by Bernardo O'Higgins and José de San Martín, in 1818, Chile declared its independence from Spain. In the 20th century, Chile grappled with leftist and rightist politics. In 1973, General Augusto Pinochet took control of the country. He was not removed from presidential office until 1990. His regime committed military violence and has faced many charges of human rights violations. The economy of Chile is based in agriculture and minerals. It is the world's largest producer of copper and has also become known for its wine. Due to the different climates in the country, tourism plays a role in the economy as well.

Pre-*Conquista* Latin American Civilizations to the 1500s

AZTECS

The Aztecs were a Native American group that inhabited what is now central Mexico. Before the arrival of Cortés, the Aztecs were the most powerful group in Mesoamerica. The best-known Aztec leaders were Moctezuma I and Moctezuma II. The capital of the empire was Tenochtitlán and their language was Náhuatl. The Aztecs had a very developed and centralized society. Their religious system is well-known. Members of their pantheon were Quetzalcoatl, the god of life, Tezcatlipoca, the god of the sorcerers and the young warriors, Huitzilpochtli, the god of war and the sun, Tlaloc, god of the rain, and Coatlicue, the mother goddess. Like many Mesoamerican peoples, the Aztecs used animal and human sacrifices to honor their gods.

MAYA

The Maya were one of the three most important Native American groups of the Pre-Colombian world. They inhabited what today is the Yucatán in Mexico, Guatemala, Honduras, and Belize. The Maya culture was one the most advanced cultures in the Pre-Colombian world. The Maya were intellectuals, and they had an arithmetic system, a calendar, and hieroglyphic writing. The Popol Vuh is a Mayan literary work. The best known historic Mayan sites are Palenque, Copán, Tikal, Uxmal, and Chichen Itza. The Mayan practiced human sacrifices to appease their gods: Itzamná, the supreme god, Kinich Ahau, the sun, and Chac, the rain. Their language was Mayan.

Incas

The Incas were the Native Americans that inhabited the region that is now Ecuador, Peru, Bolivia, Argentina, and Chile. The Incas had a very advanced culture; its social structure was based in ayllu, or clans. The culture was formed around communal agriculture. The Incas extended their empire over other weaker or less advanced neighboring tribes. They enforced tyrannical policies and used violence to control their subjects. The most famous Inca sites are Machu Pichu, Cuzco, and Pisac. Their main gods were Inti, the sun, and Viracocha, the supreme god. They left impressive feats of architecture and engineering throughout their empire. Their languages included Quechua and Aymara, which is still spoken in some parts of Peru, Bolivia, and Ecuador. The Incas practiced human sacrifices at particular points in time (for example, crises, important times in agriculture)

Popol Vuh (16th century)

The Popol Vuh, also known as El libro del consejo, was written by an anonymous Native American who, it is believed, was instructed by the Spaniards. The Popol Vuh was written in the Mayan-Quiché language and later translated to Spanish. There is a lot of controversy regarding who wrote and who translated the book. In the book, the author compiles the Mayan myths that explain the creation of the world, the history of the Mayans, and some Mayans traditions. It is considered a very important source about the Mayans of the Pre-Colombian period.

Conquista and Colonial Periods in Latin America: 1500s-1750

Conquistadores

Several European men are famous (or infamous) as *conquistadores*, or conquerors, in Latin America - those who explored and took over portions of North, Central, and South America on behalf of their country in Europe. Below are the most well-known of the conquistadores.

Cristóbal Colón (1451-1506)

A navigator originally from Genoa, Italy, Colón (or Columbus, as he is known in English), sailed to the New World four times as a representative of the Spanish Crown (Ferdinand II and Isabella I). His original goal was to find a route to the East. He is credited with visiting and/or colonizing the Caribbean islands of Bahamas, Haiti, Cuba, the Antilles, and the eastern coasts of Central and South America and is considered the first of the discoverers of America.

Hernán Cortés (1485-1547)

Cortés first sailed to Cuba and Hispaniola (modern Haiti and the Dominican Republic) and the Spanish colonies already established there. From Cuba he went on expedition to the mainland of North America. He is most well-known for his role there in toppling the Aztec empire and colonizing most of modern-day Mexico for Spain. He did this by allying with the Tlaxcaltecs, enemies of the Aztecs and is also known for his harsh treatment of the Aztecs and other indigenous peoples.

Francisco Pizarro (1471-1541)

Pizarro had taken part in several expeditions in South America, using modern-day Panama as a launching point. It was only on his third attempt that he successfully conquered Peru and the seat of the Inca empire there, establishing a Spanish colony in the region.

Relationships Between Indigenous Cultures/Peoples and Europeans

While each region or colony had its own unique governance, some consistent themes arise in examining the relationship between the indigenous cultures of Latin America and the European colonizers. European diseases, which had not yet been encountered by the indigenous populations, caused significant mortality during and after the conquests. The conquests were armed conflicts and therefore many atrocities were visited on the indigenous peoples by the Europeans. Much indigenous agriculture went on unhindered, especially in rural areas - the colonial powers were most interested in governing and exploiting natural resources and ruling city centers. This led to a divide that is still felt today in Latin America between the European ruling class in the urban centers and the rural indigenous farmers. When compared to the English colonial powers in North America, the Spanish were more open to having romantic and marital relationships with the indigenous population, which created a complex hierarchical system of ethnicity. Ultimately, while the indigenous peoples were not systematically separated and/or killed as in the United States, they were still economically and culturally marginalized by the Europeans.

SYNCRETISM

The Catholic church was highly involved in the colonization of Latin America. While many indigenous people ultimately began to practice Catholicism, a good deal of syncretism marks the religion of Latin America. Indigenous religious practices and festivals were mixed or integrated with Catholic practices and festivals, creating unique religious traditions in regions of Latin America. One prime example of this is *Día de los muertos* in Mexico – the Catholic practice of All Saints Day blended with indigenous traditions for honoring ancestors to become a new and uniquely Mexican celebration. The same syncretism is also evident in various art forms of the region.

SOR JUANA INÉS DE LA CRUZ (1651-1695)

Sor Juana Inés de la Cruz is known as one of the most important Latin American authors of lyric poetry. She lived in Mexico and wrote poetry, theater plays, and prose. Her works deal with many themes – love, philosophy, gender, religion, beauty, and more. She was a nun, and she used the opportunity to live an intellectual life that otherwise might not have been afforded a woman in her era in Mexico. She is an important representative of the baroque ear, and some of her best known works are *Respuesta a Sor Filotea de la Cruz* (prose), *Primer sueño* (poetry), and *El divino Narciso* (theater).

Movements and Modernism in Latin America: 1750-1900

TIMELINE OF INDEPENDENCE MOVEMENTS

In two bursts of activity, Spain's colonies in the New World asserted, fought for, and won their independence. This was triggered by a variety of factors. The creole population (individuals born in Latin America to European parents) were disenchanted with being ruled from afar. Happenings in the Napoleanic Wars gave the colonies a taste of freedom of trade, and they wanted more of this. The Enlightenment ideals that had already spurred several revolutions found voices in Spain's colonies as well. Following is a brief summary timeline of the Latin American independence movements. Not noted are the multiple starts and stops of the movements - the failed attempts prior to these successful independence movements:

- **1808-1810**: Juntas and loyalists struggle over power in the capitals of Mexico, Uruguay, Chile, Venezuela, Colombia, Bolivia, Argentina, and Ecuador.
- **1810**: Mexico calls for independence and armed resistance begins
- **1810-1817**: Revolutionary troops led by José de San Martín combined with other regional forces to win military victories against Spanish troops in the southern region of South America

- **1813-1822**: Under the command of Simón Bólivar, another revolutionary army fought for control of the northern region of South America
- **1821**: Mexico achieves independence and solidifies self-rule
- **1822**: Bólivar and San Martín meet in Ecuador and decide to join forces
- **1822**: The colonies in Central America join the new Mexican empire
- **1823**: Central America breaks off from Mexico and forms its own federation
- **1824**: The last major battle for South American independence is fought in Ayacucho
- **1826**: Loyalist resistance in South America is completely defeated
- **1826-1850**: Individual nations begin to form in Central and South America.
- **1898**: Cuba and Puerto Rico win their independence from Spain in the Spanish-American War after several unsuccessful attempts at revolution.

Miguel Hidalgo y Costilla (1753-1811)

Miguel Hidalgo y Costilla, better known as Miguel Hidalgo, was a Mexican priest and patriot. He is known as the father of the country, as the initiator of the Mexican independence movement, and as "Father Hidalgo". On September 16, 1810, he gave a battle cry in Dolores Hidalgo, Guanajuato, known as "the cry of Dolores" that started the Mexican war of independence from Spain. He is an important figure in Mexican history, because he also ended slavery and fought for the rights of the indigenous peoples. He succeeded in establishing a national government but soon after, the Royalists executed him.

José de San Martín (1778-1850)

José de San Martín was an Argentinian general, known as the liberator of Argentina and Chile. He fought with the Spaniards against the French in Spain's war of independence, but later he fought against the Spaniards for the independence of Latin American countries. With the help of the Chilean General Bernardo de O'Higgins, he organized the army of the Andes. San Martín unified several independence movements and helped Argentina, Chile, and Peru gain their independence. He is also known as the protector of Peru.

Simón Bolívar (1783-1830)

Simón Bolívar is known as the liberator of Venezuela. He also helped Ecuador, Peru and the Alto Peru (today's Bolivia) to obtain their independence. It is said he was the most important man of the independence wars in South America. He had a vision of a united Spanish America that he was unable to bring to fruition. Besides being a general, he was an educated man and a writer. He had studied with Andrés Bello and Simón Rodríguez, who taught him the ideas of freedom. He wrote several works, including *Memoria dirigida a los ciudadanos de Nueva Granada por un caraqueño* (1812) and *Carta a Jamaica* (1815). He also wrote the constitution for the Republic of Bolivia.

Domingo Faustino Sarmiento (1811-1888)

Domingo Faustino Sarmiento was an Argentinian writer. He was also president of Argentina from 1868 to 1874. He was also interested in education and worked as a pedagogue. One of his main interests was education. In 1845, he wrote his novel *Facundo, o Civilización i barbarie*. Other works by Sarmiento include *De la educación popular, Las ciento y una, conflictos y armonías de las razas de América, Mi defensa, and Recuerdos de provincia.*

José Martí (1853-1895)

José Martí was a Cuban writer and politician. He was a hero of the Cuban independence movement. Because of his status in the movement, he was exiled from Cuba more than once. He died fighting against the Spaniards with Cuban revolutionaries. The main themes of his works are freedom and liberalism. Martí's poetry can be considered where modernism began in Latin American poetry. Some of his well-known works of poetry are *Ismaelillo, Versos libres,* and *Versos sencillos.* He also wrote newspaper articles and essays such as his "Nuestra América".

Rubén Darío (1867-1916)

Rubén Darío was a writer from Nicaragua, and is a major figure in modernism. He is best known for his poetry, in which he displayed an emphasis in form and beauty. In his poetry, he used traditional forms (such as the sonnet) but inside those forms employed rhythm and word choice to transform them. He served as a diplomat and a journalist as well, and in his prose dealt with social and political issues of his day. His most popular works are *Prosas profanas, Cantos de vida y esperanza,* and *Canto errante.* Among his prose, the best known work is *Azul.*

José Enrique Rodó (1871-1917)

José Enrique Rodó was a Uruguayan essayist and philosopher. He is known as the best modernist prose writer. His primary message was a warning about the North American influence in Latin America. He wanted the Latin American youth to reject materialism and to embrace their culture. His best known work is *Ariel,* which has been taken as the intellectual guide for people from his generation.

Horacio Quiroga (1878-1937)

Horacio Quiroga was a Uruguayan writer, best known for his short stories. He lived most of his life in Argentina, and he also wrote poetry. Horacio Quiroga was influenced by Edgar Allan Poe, and his stories have elements of horror, American nature, and the supernatural. His stories in particular had great impact on later Latin American writers such as Borges and Cortázar. His main poetry work is *Arrecifes de coral.* His stories include *El crimen del otro, Historia de un amor turbio, Cuentos de amor, de locura y de muerte, Cuentos de la selva, Anaconda,* and *Los desterrados.* He also wrote a short novel, *Pasado amor.*

Latin American Revolutions and Post-Modernism: ~1900-1960

General Themes in 20th-Century Latin American Politics

The 20th century in Latin American politics was tumultuous. While each country has had its own political journey, some common themes and patterns emerge in the struggles of the region.

Oligarchy and Marxism

Even after the independence movements of the 19th century, many countries in Latin America were marked by an oligarchical structure of governance politically, economically, and culturally. The elite class (primarily of European descent) held an outsized amount of power and capital. To counter the oligarchy common in the countries of the region, Marxism presented itself as an appealing structure. Broadly speaking, many of the 20th-century conflicts in Latin America have had at their root the contrasting political, economic, and social views of the traditional oligarchy and of left-leaning reformers.

Entering the World Economic Market

Prior to independence, the trade and natural resources of the colonies in Latin America were controlled by Spain. After independence, the nations had to navigate international trade on their own, as well as decide how to control and exploit their own natural resources rather than letting the USA or Europe do so. Once again, the opposing viewpoints of the oligarchy and Marxism presented two different visions for economic development.

Military Regimes and Dictatorships

From the beginning of the revolutionary movements, the military leaders were heavily involved in the formation and ruling of the countries of Latin America. This legacy lived on in the 20th century, and the military often involved themselves in overthrowing a government viewed as too authoritarian or too leftist. However, these military regimes often violated human rights and devolved into dictatorships. Some of the well-known Latin American military dictators of the last century include members of the Somoza family (ruled 1936-1979) in Nicaragua, Augusto Pinochet (ruled 1973-1990) in Chile, Rafael Trujillo (ruled 1930-1961) in the Dominican Republic, and Fidel Castro (ruled 1959-2008) in Cuba.

Urbanization

Urbanization has brought great change and new challenges to Latin America in the 20th century. As more individuals moved from subsistence farming in rural areas to the urban centers, issues such as housing, poverty, and infrastructure came to the surface. Additionally, urbanization increased the contact between indigenous cultures/languages and the "dominant" culture/language. This increased contact has both highlighted the discrimination present in Latin America and allowed for some demarginalization of indigenous people groups.

Indigenous Rights

Because of the increased contact between indigenous communities and the urban culture, indigenous rights has been a key issue in Latin American politics in the 20th century. Indigenous languages such as Náhuatl and Quechua have been granted official language status in some countries. There has been a push against the idea that the more European you look, the more status you can have, a cultural ideal since the colonization of the region. At the beginning of the 21st century, individuals of indigenous descent reached the highest political offices of their countries for the first time (for example, Evo Morales of Bolivia and Alejandro Toledo of Peru).

Key Political Events of the 20th Century

Mexican Revolution (1910-1920)

Also known as the Mexican Civil War, the Mexican Revolution was prompted by discontent with the 31-year rule of Porfirio Díaz. The landed elites sought to oust him through an election in 1910; when the election proved to be rigged against them, they rose up in arms. Francisco Madero was chosen as the leader of the new government in 1911, but the revolution spread to the middle and laboring classes, and Madero was met with disenchantment from his fellow elites on the right and from the new, poorer revolutionaries on the left. A counter-revolutionary regime, led by General Victoriano Huerta, came into power after assassinating Madero in 1913 and was ousted in 1914. At this point, an all-out civil war began between the Constitutionalists and the revolutionaries, who were led by famous fighters Pancho Villa and Emiliano Zapata. The armed conflict lasted until 1919 and shifted from a two-sided fight to a power struggle between multiple factions. A constitution was written in 1917 and began to be enforced in 1920. The death toll of the Civil War was high – some estimates set it at 10% of the population at the time. The war had a lasting impact on Mexican society, as the government formed afterward provided a shift toward social justice and liberal economics.

Deposition of Perón in Argentina (1955)

Juan Perón had an outsized influence on the politics of Argentina for a good part of the 20th century. Elected in 1946 with the support of the working classes, he improved living conditions in Argentina but restricted constitutional liberties. As Argentina's economy began to struggle in the 1950s, Peron began to rule in a more authoritarian style, lost the support of the workers, and was ultimately ousted by the military in 1955. He lived in exile in Spain, while the government that took over was unsuccessful in dealing with Argentina's economic difficulties. In 1972 he was allowed back in the country, and successfully ran for president again in 1973. He died in 1974, and the military coup that seized power from his wife subjected the country to years of dictatorial rule.

Cuban Revolution (1953-1959)

Fulgencio Batista, the military dictator of Cuba, incited the population to anger with his links to organized crime and to American industry in Cuba. Fidel Castro, sympathetic to communist politics attempted to have Batista removed by the Cuban courts and lost his case. He then organized an armed revolt in 1953. Both communist and anti-communist guerillas fought against Batista's forces at first, ultimately uniting to fight together. The United States withdrew their support for Batista in 1957-1958. In 1959, the Cuban revolutionary forces took over major cities and the capital, Havana and began to rule. The Castro government enacted many positive social reforms such as investing in infrastructure and education and pushing back against racial discrimination. However, the government also engaged in repression of anti-communist sentiment, resulting in political and religious persecution. Castro was also interested in "exporting" revolution to other countries in Latin America and aligned himself with the USSR. This created fear of leftist ideas among the ruling elite and/or the military in many neighboring countries and shaped USA policy in Latin America for decades.

Jorge Luis Borges (1899-1986)

Jorge Luis Borges is one of the best-known writers in the Spanish language. He was born in Argentina but lived in Europe for some time. Besides writing poetry, essays, and stories, he was a professor of English literature at the Universidad de Buenos Aires. Borges was a leader in a literary movement called ultraism, which sought to break from the structures of the past (unlike modernism). His works are fantastic and deal with metaphysical problems. His most famous works of poetry are *Fervor de Buenos Aires, Luna de enfrente,* and *Cuaderno de San Martín*. Some of his best-known short stories and collections are *Historia universal de la infamia*, "El jardín de los senderos que se bifurcan", *Ficciones, El Aleph*, and *Historia de la eternidad.*

Pablo Neruda (1904-1973)

Pablo Neruda was a Chilean poet with Marxist convictions. He is known as one of the most important poets of the 20th century. Neruda served as a diplomat for Chile in many parts of the world. He was friends with some of the Spanish poets from the Generation of '27. In his work, he identified with the victims of wars, social injustice, and tyranny which he witnessed around the world and in his own home country. In 1971, Neruda won the Nobel Prize for Literature for his poetry, which includes *Crepusculario, Veinte poemas de amor y una canción desesperada, España en el corazón, Residencia en la tierra, Canto general, Odas elementales*, and *Cantos ceremoniales.*

Juan Rulfo (1918-1986)

Juan Rulfo was a Mexican writer who wrote a novel and many short stories. He is considered the most profound of the Mexican prose writers of the 40s. Rulfo is known as one of the creators of magic realism, a mingling of the very ordinary with fantasy and myth. He created historic stories based on ignorant, poor, and desolated country people. His works deal with social injustice, hard life, pain, and suffering. The magic aspects of his works include the fantastic and the supernatural, such as the use of ghosts as characters in his works. Although Rulfo wrote only two pieces, a collection of stories, *El llano en llamas*, and a novel, *Pedro Páramo*, he won several prizes.

Diego Rivera (1886-1957)

Diego Rivera was a Mexican painter. He is one of the most famous muralists in the world and the most famous of the three main Mexican muralists: Rivera, Orozco, and Siqueiros. He was influenced by the Italian Renaissance but also by the Russian communist movement. After the Mexican revolution, he painted several murals in Mexico City. Many of his pieces include the revalorization of indigenous Mexican roots. They also include symbols and historical figures from the colonial period. His major works (*La creación, La leyenda de Quetzalcoatl, Historia de México: de la conquista al futuro, Sueño de una tarde dominical en la Alameda Central, La historia de la cardiología*) are in Mexico City in the Palacio de Bellas Artes, the Escuela Preparatoria Nacional, the Universidad Iberoamericana, and the Palacio Nacional. Other works can be found in New York and Detroit. He was married to the painter Frida Kahlo.

José Clemente Orozco (1883-1949)

José Clemente Orozco was a Mexican painter. Together with Rivera and Siqueiros, Orozco is one of the three Mexican muralists whose work revitalized modern Mexican art. He painted murals after the Mexican Revolution, and his work shows different aspects of the human condition. Besides the revolution, he focused on Pre-Colombian culture. He was less political than Rivera, but political issues still influenced his work. In his murals, messages of social justice for the working class and for Native Americans are found. Orozco's works can be found in Mexico City, Guadalajara, Veracruz, and New York. Among his best-known pieces are *Omnisciencia, Luchas proletarias, La justicia, Riquezas nacionales, Buena vida*, and *La independencia nacional.*

David Alfaro Siqueiros (1896-1974)

David Alfaro Siqueiros was a Mexican painter contemporary with Orozco and Rivera. He painted murals in Mexico after the Mexican Revolution. His murals and other works are more realistic than those of Rivera and Orozco, but they show also aspects of Pre-Colombian culture and its relationship with colonial culture in Mexico. He was very influenced by and involved in politics and his works have Marxist messages. All his works are in Mexico City. Among his best known pieces are *Nueva democracia, Víctimas de la guerra, Víctimas del fascismo, El tormento de Cuauhtémoc, El entierro del obrero sacrificado, Los elementos, Los mitos*, and *El llamado de la libertad.*

Frida Kahlo (1907-1954)

Frida Kahlo was a 20th-century Mexican painter. She was born and died in Mexico City. She contracted polio as a child, and throughout her life she suffered because of this and other health issues, some of them caused by a bus accident when she was a teenager. After the accident, she stopped the medical studies she was pursuing and started her career as a painter. She married Mexican painter Diego Rivera. In her work, she used bright colors and simple and primitive forms deeply rooted in Mexican and Amerindian culture. Her paintings were also influenced by

Surrealism. She is known mainly for her self-portraits and other depictions of the feminine form. Julie Taymor directed the movie *Frida* in which Salma Hayek played the role of the artist.

The "Boom" and "Post-Boom" in Latin American Literature: 1960-1980s

Boom

The Boom refers to a group of Latin American writers in the 1960s-1970s whose works reached European audiences to a greater extent than in previous generations. The works produced during the Boom are modernist in style, sometimes employing multiple voices. The writers used both urban and rural settings and educated and colloquial language. They were not afraid to deal with political and social turmoil, and mixed history and fantasy in addressing the themes confronting Latin American society in their time.

Ernesto Sábato (1911-2011)

Ernesto Sábato was an Argentine writer and literary critic. He studied physics in his country and then attended the Sorbonne University in Paris and worked at the Curie Institute and later at MIT. After World War II he started to write and to be politically involved in the events of his country. He also started to paint. He translated some scientific books and wrote numerous essays and articles on literature, science, metaphysics, and politics. He is internationally recognized for his novels *El túnel, Sobre héroes y tumbas*, and *Abaddón el exterminador*. After the military regime of the 1970s and 1980s had lost its power, Sábato was tapped to conduct the investigation into the human rights violations they committed. His second son Mario, a film director and screenwriter, directed the movie *El poder de la tinieblas*, which is based on the section *Informe sobre ciegos* from *Sobre héroes y tumbas*.

Octavio Paz (1914-1998)

Octavio Paz was a Mexican poet and essaysist. He won the Nobel Prize for Literature in 1990. He can be classified neither as an idealist nor as a symbolist because his style of writing was very unique. The concepts he most often dealt with in his works are loneliness and existential restlessness. His most important poetry works are *Libertad bajo palabra, Piedra de sol, Salamandra, Ladera este, Topoemas, Prueba del nueve, Arbol adentro,* and *Obra poética*. He also wrote essays, the most famous being *El laberinto de la soledad, El arco y la lira, Corriente alterna,* and *Sor Juana Inés de la Cruz o las trampas de la fe.*

Julio Cortázar (1914-1984)

Julio Cortázar was a very important Argentinian author who wrote stories, essays, and novels. He lived a great deal of his life in France. He had great influence in the narrative art. His work deals with reality, fantasy, and the absurd. He was a surrealist and was committed to Latin American Marxist politics His most famous works are *Rayuela, Final del juego, Bestiario, Las armas secretas, Todos los fuegos el fuego, Alguien que anda por ahí, Los premios*, and *Nicaragua tan violentamente dulce.*

Gabriel García Márquez (1928-2014)

Gabriel García Márquez was a Colombian who is recognized as one of the greatest narrative writers of the 20th century. In 1982, García Márquez won the Nobel Prize for Literature. The magic realism in his works examines the relationships between space and time and also exposes Colombian life and the relationship between the social and the political in everyday life. His best-known works are *Cien años de soledad* and *El amor en el tiempo de cólera*. Some of his other novels include *La hojarasca, El coronel no tiene quien le escriba,* , *El general en su laberinto*, and *Del amor y otros demonios.*

Carlos Fuentes (1928-2012)

Carlos Fuentes was a Mexican writer and diplomat. In his novels, he explores Mexican culture and looks for a way to preserve it. His novels include *La region más transparente, Las buenas conciencias, Cambio de piel, La muerte de Artemio Cruz, Aura, Zona sagrada, Terra nostra, Cumpleaños, La cabeza de hidra, Gringo viejo, Cristóbal Nonato*, and *La frontera de cristal*. They are based in the historical and explore real themes, but do so as works of fiction, often employing magic realism. Fuentes also wrote non-fiction, essays, and short stories.

Mario Vargas Llosa (1936–2025)

Mario Vargas Llosa is a Peruvian novelist and politician. His work falls into the genre of realism. In his works, he examines the vulgarity of the human nature, not only externally but also internally. His topics are usually political in nature. In 1990 he was a presidential candidate for Peru. In 2010, he received the Nobel Prize for Literature. His best-known works are: *Los jefes, la ciudad y los perros, Conversación en la cathedral; Pantaleón y las visitadoras, Lituma en los Andes, La guerra del fin del mundo, Historia de Mayta, El hablador*, and *¿Quién mató a Palomo Montero*?

Isabel Allende (1942--)

Isabel Allende is a writer born in Peru. Shortly after, she moved to Chile with her family, and she considers herself Chilean. Allende has primarily lived outside of Chile since the coup in 1973. In her works, Allende mixes the fantastic with the real. Her works could be classified as of the magic realism genre and are greatly influenced by García Márquez. Her most celebrated piece is *La casa de los espíritus*, in which she follows a Chilean family for four generations. In the novel, Allende examines sociopolitical issues in Chile in the postcolonial period. Other works from Allende are *De amor de la sombra, Eva Luna, Cuentos de Eva Luna, El plan infinito, Paula, Hija de la fortuna, La ciudad de las bestias*, and *Inés del alma mía*. She continues to write novels today.

Fernando Botero (1932--)

Fernando Botero is a painter born in Medellín, Colombia. He was trained as a matador while in high school and later on lived for some time in Spain and France. Botero is one of the most celebrated Latin American artists of the century. In his figurative paintings, he uses exaggerated and disproportionate volumes, especially to depict the human figure, adding humorous details to show criticism and irony. His figures are easily recognized, and his particular, unmistakable style is sometimes referred to as Boterismo. He continues to exhibit regularly and lives and works in New York and Paris.

Latin American Cultural Practices and Perspectives

Diversity

While it is convenient to talk about Latin America as one region, it is important to note that what we call Latin America is not monolithic or homogeneous in cultural practices and perspectives. Each region and/or country has its own heritage which includes European and indigenous influences and unique social and political history and structure.

Religion

The Catholic Church played a large role in the colonization of Latin America by Spain. Because of this legacy, the church is culturally entrenched and yet often vilified, especially during the political turmoil of the last century. Latin American Catholicism is marked by syncretism and, in the last 50 years, liberation theology with its emphasis on anti-imperialism and care for the poor. A majority of individuals in the region still identify as Catholic, although protestant Pentecostalism has spread rapidly in Latin America in recent decades as well.

Family and Lifestyle

While Latin America has undergone significant urbanization, there are still many distinctions between rural and urban life, with urban lifestyles very similar to those around the world and rural lifestyles more similar to the culture in previous generations. Traditional family values (strong father, caregiving mother, close extended family) are still common in Latin American countries, though there is a rise in single parenthood and in opportunities outside the home for women. Community is valued, and celebrations are an important part of family and community life.

Festivals and Traditions

Día de los muertos is perhaps the most well-known Latin American festival. Many Latin American festivals revolve around Catholic feasts or holy days, but similarly to *Día de los muertos*, involve a good deal of syncretism and therefore reflect local history and tradition as well. *Semana santa* (Holy week), *Las posadas* (on Christmas Eve) and *Carnaval* (Mardi Gras) are some examples of these celebrations. Many of the regions have local saints that they celebrate (*La Virgen de Guadalupe, La Virgen de la Candelaria*, etc.). It is also traditional for a girl to have a lavish party on her 15th birthday, called a *quinceañera*.

Language

While Spanish is spoken throughout Latin America, several indigenous languages are still spoken as well. Quechua has over 6 million speakers in the Andean region, and other prominent languages include Mayan, Guaraní, Nahuatl, and Aymara. These languages have gained official recognition in the last decades and are being used (often for the first time in centuries) in publication and education.

Listening, Reading, Writing, Speaking

General Test-Taking Strategies

Knowing Beforehand the Structure of the Test

Familiarize yourself with the structure of test. It is important to know the different sections of the tests; if it is timed as whole or by sections; what is the format required for the answers (multiple choice, one-sentence answers, one-paragraph answers, a combination of them). For the writing sections, will the test require a minimum and/or a maximum number of words? Also, learn whether the test will be done on a computer, on paper, or a combination of both. If computerized, make sure your typing skills are up to the task, both in speed and in accuracy. You may be allowed to access a practice test ahead of time through your test's website that will let you see the user interface that will be provided for recording your speaking, inserting Spanish symbols, and completing other test-specific tasks.

Importance of Timing During Tests

The test you take will be timed. It may allocate a certain amount of time for the whole test and let you decide how much time you will spend in each section. Or it may be more structured and will assign specific time for each section. In both cases, you have to perform a series of tasks (reading, writing, listening, answering multiple-choice or essay questions, etc.) in the time you have been given. It is very important you know how much time you have and how to best use it. Organize yourself: give yourself time to think, to draft, and to review. Do not rush but do not spend too much time on a certain point either. If you see you are running out of time, do not panic; your performance will be better if you stay calm.

Identifying Patterns and Purposes

Asking some questions about the information presented in a written or oral piece and paying attention to specific elements will help you identify what type of text you have in front of you. These questions and elements will also help you when you are being asked to write a specific type of text or speak for a certain purpose. Some of the more common options are listed below.

- What happened? → narration
- What does it look, sound, smell, or taste like? → description
- It includes examples or reasons. → illustration/support
- It is like, or different from, something else. → comparison and contrast
- It happened because… → cause and effect
- What is it? → definition
- It states opinions. → position
- How to do it. → process analysis

Listening

Listening Comprehension

During the test, you will listen to a text or conversation. You will have to answer a series of multiple-choice questions and/or write a piece based on what you heard.

Listening and Taking Notes

Listen carefully through the passage to grasp and understand its content. Take notes as you listen. Find main and secondary ideas as well as supporting information and examples. What was the purpose of the speech or conversation? Who was the audience? If two points of view were presented, how did they differ? Look out for style and tone. Is it a formal discourse? Does it sound friendly? Does it use simple language? All these elements are clues that you can use to infer information not specifically said in the text but somehow included in the passage. The better you understand the text, the more accurate your answers will be.

Context, Tone, and Intonation

For the listening comprehension section, it is important to pay attention to the general context of the narration, description, conversation, or statement. Understanding context is extremely helpful to infer the meaning of words you might not know. It also helps to identify the appropriate meaning for those words that have more than one (*cara*: expensive or face; *frente*: front or forehead). The tone used in an oral piece (happy, serious, ironic, formal) will be another tool to assess the situation. Intonation will help you determine the tense (*hablo* → present and *habló* → past) and if a sentence is an affirmative or a question. Emphasis on particular words will give you clues about what information is important (*mi **lápiz** es azul*/my pencil...not my pen; *mi lápiz es **azul***/it is blue...not red).

Using and Answering the Questions

In most tasks you will be allowed to see or hear the question(s) ahead of time. These questions can be very helpful in forming your understanding of the passage. For example, if a question asks "*¿Qué quiere hacer la mujer mañana?*", you can anticipate that you will hear a man and a woman talking about plans for tomorrow, and that you will need to learn the woman's point of view. Focus your note-taking and listening on the information the question requires.

Reading

Reading Comprehension Passages

During the test, you will be given passages to read. You will have to answer a series of multiple-choice questions and/or write a piece based on that text. Read carefully through the passage to grasp and understand its content.

Ideas and Examples

Find main and secondary ideas as well as supporting information and examples. You may choose to underline short phrases that communicate these or write one- to three-word summaries in the margins. Pay attention to any sequence of events presented as well as to cause-and-effect relationships.

Audience and Tone

Determine who the audience is, as well as the style and tone of the text. Is it written in a formal or a familiar style? Is it polite, authoritarian, or ironic? Is it written in simple or scholarly language? This will give a more accurate indication of the purpose of the material. These elements are cues that you can use to infer information not specifically written in the text but somehow included in the passage that will help you better understand the text.

Style and Purpose

When reading a text, it is important to determine the style of the piece. In the informative style, the author presents the information and the data in an objective way. He/she is trying to educate or give something to the audience. On the other hand, in the persuasive style, the writer is trying to convince the reader of his/her ideas. He/she presents the information from his/her own point of view. In a piece written in the persuasive style, it is important to be able to separate the actual facts from the opinions of the author.

Multiple-Choice Questions After Reading a Passage

Carefully read/listen to the passage a first time as described above. Read the questions and answer the ones you are sure about. Make notes about the possible answers to those questions you are in doubt or do not know. Do not spend too much time on any particular question. Read/listen to the passage again, concentrating on finding the missing answers. Go through the questions again and answer them. In most cases, two readings will be enough to complete all questions. If not, reread/listen to the passage and go over the missing answers one more time. Read/listen to the passage one final time. Revise and do a final check on your answers.

One main way that your understanding of the passage will be tested is by the use of synonyms. For example, if the passage states "*La familia Picasso se vio obligada a abandonar Málaga, debido a la poca estabilidad económica de la que disfrutaba.*", a question may ask "¿Por qué se mudó la familia Picasso? You will need to identify that in this context, "***se mudaron***" is synonymous with "***abandonar***". The correct answer choice will rephrase "*la poca estabilidad económica de la que disfrutaba,*" perhaps by saying something like "*no tenían suficiente dinero*".

Written Response Questions After Reading a Passage

You may be asked to respond in writing after reading a passage. After identifying what your task is, there are some key considerations that will help you maximize your score.

1. What grammar structures does the writing prompt seek to elicit? For example, if it asks you to summarize what happened in the passage, you will use the past tenses (preterite and imperfect). If it asks you to state your opinion about the topic of the passage, you will use the subjunctive. If it asks you to describe what will happen as a result of the information in the passage, you will use the future.
2. Make use of the vocabulary provided in the passage. For example, you are given a passage on students going to college a year early. You read it, and then as you begin to write, you cannot remember the Spanish word for "early". Go back to the passage and find the Spanish word or phrase that told you the idea of "early".
3. Do not copy large chunks of the passage. For example, if the passage says "*La universidad mejor para ti depende en tus metas educacionales y profesionales.*" If you are asked to give your opinion about what university a student should choose, do not copy this entire sentence. Instead, use the vocabulary provided but in a different format as elicted by the prompt; "*Es importante que un estudiante considere sus metas educacionales y profesionales.*"

Summarizing a Written Piece

You may be asked to summarize a written or oral piece. In doing so, you are being asked to state the same ideas as developed in the piece but in a much more concise form. The amount of information you include in a summary depends on the length allowed for it. Go through the text and find the main ideas. State them as briefly as possible. If you were allotted a small amount of words, the main ideas will be all you can include in the summary. If you still have room, go through the text again and find secondary ideas. Pick up the important ones and include them in the summary, also as briefly and clearly as possible. Make sure you are true to the text. Do not include details and do not add new ideas or your own opinions.

Speaking

Speaking Tasks

The test will include speaking tasks. You will have some time to prepare before your speaking is recorded. During the preparation, make sure that:

- you accurately respond to the content, audience, style, and format requirements
- you present your ideas in an organized, logical manner
- your speech is coherent and has unity (flows smoothly)
- you use the right words (vocabulary) and grammar

When you deliver your speaking task, make sure that:

- you speak clearly
- you speak neither too fast nor to slow
- you pay close attention to pronunciation
- you quickly correct errors

Simulated Conversation Section

You may be asked to simulate a conversation in Spanish. You will be given an outline of the conversation. The outline will not give you the exact words that you will hear but just a general idea of what you can expect. You will have a certain time to prepare and deliver your part of the conversation after each line. Listen carefully to the first line of the conversation. Look for the main topic, who the other person is, and what information he/she is asking you for. Pay attention to formal versus informal or familiar words and expressions. Pay attention also to regional cues, educational level of the language, and tone used by the other person. All these elements will help you choose the appropriate content, style, and tone you will use in your answers.

Oral Discourse

You will be asked to speak for a more extended period of time to complete a speech task. Some examples of these tasks include giving instructions or asking for information, describing a personal experience, and expressing and defending your opinion or position on a topic. You will have some time to prepare your response.

Read/listen carefully to the prompt. During your preparation time, write down your main points and vocabulary or examples that will add detail to your instructions/story or that will support your point of view. Organize your arguments in a clear, logical manner. For example, if you are asked to tell about a time you overcame a difficulty, your notes may look like this:

Competencia de atletismo (primera en la universidad)

- *me lastimé la pierna en enero*
- *no podía correr para un mes*
- *tuve que nadar, hacer ejercicios para mantenerme en forma*
- *la competencia en marzo*
- *tenía miedo de ser la última persona*
- *corrí 12 veces por la pista*

- *después de 8 veces, era la primera*
- *gané*

If you are asked to give your opinion on school uniforms, your notes may look like this:

Creo que las uniformes escolares son buenas

- *Ocultan diferencias entre los estudiantes*
    - *Ricos/pobres*
    - *Tipos de cuerpos*
- *Ayudan a los estudiantes enfocarse*
    - *Todos mismos – no distracciones*
    - *Mas profesionales – escuela es algo importante*
- *Muchas reglas no son necesarias*
- *Los estudiantes son un grupo, parte de un "equipo"*
- *Por el otro lado: estudiantes no pueden expresarse con la ropa*
    - *Tienen otras oportunidades...clases de arte, tiempo afuera de la escuela, cuando son mayores*

You may also find it helpful to write down connective words and phrases to use. When delivering your speech, avoid using an aggressive tone or getting emotional. Speak clearly and not too fast but not too slow either. Pay special attention to your pronunciation.

How to Practice for Speaking Tasks

Practice telling stories or sharing your point of view on a topic out loud in Spanish. Do so in the car while driving, in the shower, at home, or wherever you are comfortable talking aloud to yourself. By forcing yourself to speak out loud, you will notice vocabulary that you need to review and tenses that you struggle to use quickly and accurately. Use these gaps to focus your studying and further practice.

Writing

Components of the Writing Part of the Test

The writing part of the test will include a variety of styles and requirements: letters, memos, or e-mails; narrative, descriptive, analytic, or opinion texts; formal or informal forms of address. In all cases, your ideas should be organized and neatly stated. You will be timed; make sure that you understand how much time you have to complete the task(s). In some sections, you will have a given amount of time to complete one writing task. In other sections, you may have a given amount of time to complete more than one writing task. Divide your time wisely between the tasks rather than spending too much time on the first.

Elements to Consider When Writing a Piece

When writing, there are certain basic elements that should be taken into consideration. They apply to all writing assignments in all languages. Among them:

- Match answer to assignment (purpose, content, style, and length)
- Consider your audience
- Develop an outline
- Organize the body of the piece (by space, time, emphasis, or other clustering concept)

- Start with an introduction
- End with a conclusion
- Check for unity and coherence
- Proofread for grammar, spelling, and punctuation

Matching Answer to Assignment

After reading the prompt, identify the subject – make sure you will write about what is required. If the subject is too broad or general to be addressed in the length assigned, focus on a specific part of the subject, narrowing it to a topic or set of points that can be covered with the number of words required. Make sure you understand the purpose of your written response – is it to describe, inform, persuade, or analyze? Identify the grammatical structure(s) and vocabulary that you will need in order to answer the prompt well.

Knowing Your Audience

Knowing who you are writing for is a very important element for any type of writing assignment. In general, your audience will be defined or implied in the instructions. All good written pieces match the information and the way it is presented to the designated audience. Too much, too detailed, or too specific information may not be appropriate for a general audience. Too general or too little information will not suit a knowledgeable audience. The format and style you use to present the information should also match the audience. Informal, personal sentences are fitting for an e-mail to a friend or family member. A formal tone is required for a letter to a future employer. If you cannot identify your audience from the instructions, consider it as the general public with no in-depth knowledge of your particular subject.

Writing Process

The writing process consists of three basic stages: development, drafting, and revision. During the development, you will gather information about your topic. You will then select the most relevant information and organize it in an outline. In the drafting stage, you will write your ideas based on the information collected during development, explaining and connecting them. During the revision, you will go through your text, rethinking and rewriting to improve the overall structure and content, editing for clarity and flow, and proofreading for grammar, spelling, and punctuation.

Outline

The outline is one of the most useful tools to build a clear, well-organized piece. It basically lists your ideas in the order they will be covered. It will guide you through your writing and will show the relative importance of each element. It is particularly useful to shape the body of your piece. Make a section for each main idea. Check the order of the sections. Do they follow the order you want (chronological, spatial, from general to specific)? Are all of them relevant? Are there any gaps or overlaps? Under each section, add the secondary ideas and then, the supporting information and examples. Apply the same questions to the secondary ideas and to supporting material. Reorganize as needed. Once your outline is ready, follow its structure to draft your essay.

Introduction

All writing assignments should begin with an introduction. The topic will be described in the test's instructions, but it has to be presented at the beginning of your text. You cannot assume the reader knows the topic, and you cannot start your piece as a continuation of the instructions. You should also include a brief outline of the main points. The introduction should be simple, clear, and concise. Do not use *el propósito de este escrito es* (the purpose of this essay is), *estoy escribiendo acerca de* (I am writing about), or similar expressions. The length of the introduction will depend on the total number of words required for the particular assignment. Most of the times, one or two sentences are enough. In other cases, a longer paragraph is more appropriate.

Conclusion

All writing assignments should end with a conclusion. The conclusion will wrap up your piece. It is telling the reader you have finished. It should briefly summarize the main points and might include results or a suggested course of action. Do not restate your introduction and do not include new ideas. The length of the conclusion will depend on the total number of words required for the particular assignment. Most of the time, one or two sentences are enough. In other cases, a longer paragraph is more appropriate.

Importance of Unity and Coherence

Unity and coherence are the two elements that will make a written or oral piece flow smoothly. When checking for unity, see if all parts of the piece support the main idea. All examples and details should be relevant to the central idea. All sections of your piece should relate to each other. If a piece is coherent, the reader/listener will be able to see relations and easily go from one thought to another one. Organize your material in a logical manner. Check for gaps and abrupt transitions and add connective words or phrases to guide the reader along your thinking path. For a list of helpful connective words and phrases, see Module 5.

Revision and Editing

It is very important that you have time to revise and edit your written assignments. In this last step, you will be able to correct any mistakes, omissions, or other errors that you overlooked while writing. When revising and editing check that:

- The subject of your piece matches your assignment
- You have answered all questions and included everything that was requested
- You have followed the instructions regarding format
- You have used the appropriate style and tone for your audience
- You have used the right vocabulary and clear and readable language
- Your piece is well-organized
- There are appropriate transitions between paragraphs
- Your grammar is correct
- There are no misspelled words
- You have used the correct punctuation

Missing a Particular Word When Writing or Speaking

Many times, you will be writing or speaking and you realize you do not know or do not remember a particular word. Do not panic or try stubbornly to get the word, just go around it. For nouns (*percha*/hanger), describe what the object looks like (*un triángulo con un gancho*/a triangle with a hook), what it is made of (*alambre*/wire, *madera*/wood, *o plastic*/or plastic) what it is used for (*para colgar la ropa*/to hang clothes), or where you can find it (*en el armario*/in the closet). For adjectives, use opposites (*ella no es tímida*/she is not shy=she is outgoing). For verbs, use the results of the action. Convey your message with the proper spelling or pronunciation and in a grammatically correct way.

Types of Writing Tasks

Writing Memos

A memo (short for memorandum) is usually a short, concise written piece used at work to inform, instruct, or remind about a particular subject. Memos do not have to be very formal, but they do not tend to be too informal either. They must be very clear. The heading of a memo should start with the date, the recipient, and the sender. Include a Subject line at the beginning stating, in a few words, the topic of the memo (see example of heading below). Use short paragraphs and simple sentences. Include lists and use specific vocabulary. Avoid the passive voice and unnecessary details. Memos do not include a salutation and signature at the bottom.

MEMORANDUM

July 13, 2012

To: Paul Johnson

From: Lisa Smith

SUBJECT: Personnel changes

Writing E-Mails and Letters

Emails and letters communicate in writing for personal and for business purposes. In both letters and emails the format and style will depend on the relationship between the sender and the recipient. Family members and friends will use a very informal, colloquial language with each other. E-mails or letters sent to a company asking for a job will be formal and structured. Read your assignment carefully, and determine how the sender and recipient are related. Use the degree of formality that matches that connection. Whether formal or informal, organize your thoughts and present them in a clear, logical manner. Start with an appropriate salutation and end with a signature.

Writing Descriptions

A description answers the question, "What does it look (smell, sound, taste, or feel) like?" A description can be subjective or objective, depending on whether you use your emotions and personal bias. A description can be organized relative to space, as from right to left or from top to bottom; from the whole to the parts, as when you describe the general shape of a face and then the eyes, mouth, nose, etc.; or for emphasis, where you start with the most important or relevant traits and then go into other features.

Describing a Process

When you explain how to perform a task or how something works, you are describing a process. The first step would be to analyze and fully understand the process. Once familiar with the process you can describe it in a chronological or in spatial way. The method you choose will depend on your subject. Chronologically, you will explain the different steps as they occurred in time, first to last. Spatially, you will organize the information relatively to its physical position (from left to right, for example). Clarity is very important in describing a process – make sure that you provide any needed context for the steps you include in your description.

Narrations

A narration answers the question, "What happened?" The subject is developed as a story or a sequence of events. The events can be real or fictional. A narration is commonly organized in chronological order. Narrations are usually written in the first or third person. Since you will be writing about situations that might occur at different times, make sure you use the right tenses for all verbs and that they reflect the different points in time associated with each action.

Comparison and Contrast Pieces

Comparison and contrast pieces describe similarities and differences among ideas, people, or things. The introduction should state the subjects and a general description of what features you will compare. For the body, the two most commonly used ways to develop comparisons and contrasts are subject-by-subject and point-by-point. In subject-by-subject, each subject is discussed separately, fully describing one and then the other. When using this method, keep the order of the elements you compare in the same order for both subjects. In the point-by-point method, the two subjects are discussed at the same time, each element covered for both subject side by side. Examples are usually very useful to clarify ideas in this kind of piece. Finish the piece with your conclusion.

Cause and Effect Pieces

Cause-and-effect or cause-and-consequence pieces answer the question "Why?" You will analyze and present why something happened or what is likely to happen in the future. The prompt may ask you to focus on the causes (Why did this happen?) or the effects (What happened because of...?). It is very important that you keep your ideas well-organized. Do not mix causes and effects. To avoid confusions and misinterpretations, keep each cause or effect and its supporting information in the same sentence or paragraph. Cohesion words are useful for this type of piece: **since, because, consequently, as a result, therefore, for this reason, because of, due to**, and **so**. See the list of cohesion words and phrases in Module 5 for a variety of ways to communicate these ideas.

Opinion or Position Piece

You may be asked to develop a piece based on your own personal opinions about a certain subject. In the introduction, you should start by briefly stating your point of view. The body of the piece should describe your opinion in detail, explaining and justifying it, and refuting any objections. The body should also include examples and material from other sources to support your opinion. Do an outline to make sure your arguments are organized in a clear, logical manner. Avoid using an aggressive tone and attacking other perspectives. Finish the piece restating your opinion and adding possible future actions, if applicable.

Writing Tasks: An Example

Below is a prompt similar to those you may see on your test. Following the prompt are examples of how to follow the writing process to successfully complete the task.

Algunas personas creen que las clases en las artes (música, teatro, arte visual, etc.) son un gasto de recursos y que es más importante que los estudiantes reciban mucha instrucción en las ciencias, las matemáticas, y la tecnología. ¿Está usted de acuerdo con esta posición? Apoye su posición con ejemplos específicos. Escriba un mínimo de 120 palabras.

Purpose: share my position on whether or not arts classes are a waste of time in 120 + words.

Audience: general

Vocab and grammar: subjunctive: *es mi opinion que, creo que, si*, Future: what will happen if...

My position: *Proveer clases en las artes no es un gasto de recursos sino una inversión en el futuro de nuestros estudiantes y de nuestra sociedad.*

Specific examples/points brainstorming:

- *los estudiantes tienen el derecho de ser* (exposed? Don't know Spanish word. *Tener la oportunidad a experimentar?) a muchos tipos de actividades y empleos. No es bueno que elijamos por ellos*
- *La sociedad no tendrá películas, música ni libros si no permitimos que los niños aprendan las artes. Estas cosas enriquecen las vidas de todos.*
- *Muchas carreras requieren una mezcla de habilidad artística y científica/tecnológica (arquitectura, diseño gráfico)*

Outline:

- Intro w/my position
- *Derechos de los estudiantes*
  - *Tener la posibilidad de experimentar diversos tipos de actividades y empleos*
  - *Tener la oportunidad a elegir para si mismo lo que le gusta*
- *Carreras que requieren artes y ciencias*
  - *Arquitectura*
  - *Diseño gráfico*
- *Lo que gana/pierda la sociedad*
  - *Artes populares (películas, libros, música)*
  - *Arte "alta" - gran obras*
- Conclusión: *Estudiar las artes es importante al desarrollo personal de los estudiantes, abre las puertas a muchas carreras, y enriquece nuestras vidas con lo que provee.*

GACE Practice Test

Want to take this practice test in an online interactive format?
Check out the online resources page, which includes interactive practice questions and much more: **mometrix.com/resources719/gacespanish**

Listening

Refer to the following for questions 1–6:

-Disculpe...

-Hola! ¿Necesita Ud. algo?

-Si, me mudé a este vecindario recientemente y no sé cómo llegar a la oficina de correos.

-Bueno, no es difícil. De aquí, hay que seguir en la avenida de San Martín por 6 cuadras. Va a pasar un parque y una iglesia y luego un centro comercial. Cuando llega al semáforo, va a doblar a la izquierda en la avenida Noreste. Después de cruzar la plaza Manzanita, nada más hay que doblar a la derecha en la calle Mayor y el correo estará a su izquierda.

-A ver: la avenida de San Martin, a la izquierda en la avenida Noreste y luego a la derecha en la calle Mayor. ¡Gracias! ¿Y sabe Ud. a qué hora cierra?

-Creo que cierra a las 5.

-Ah, sí. ¿Y puedo recoger la llave para mi buzón allí?

-No sé. Pero me parecería que sí.

-Bueno, gracias otra vez

-A la orden. ¡Y bienvenidos!

Practice Audio: Listening Sample
Visit mometrix.com/academy and enter Code: 100368

1. Esta conversación tuvo lugar entre:

a. Un hombre y su hijo
b. Dos amigos
c. Dos vecinos
d. Un profesor y un estudiante

2. Que propósito tiene el primer hablador?

a. Buscar información
b. Introducirse
c. Compartir su punto de vista
d. Quejar

3. Según el segundo hablador, ¿a qué hora cierra la oficina de correos?

a. a las seis
b. a las dos
c. muy pronto
d. a las cinco

4. ¿Cuál de los siguientes adjetivos describe mejor el intercambio?

a. cariñoso
b. cortés
c. extenso
d. tenso

5. En el contexto, ¿cuál de las siguientes es un sinónimo para la expresión -*a la orden*- que se usó?

a. de nada
b. organizado
c. a la vez
d. mucho gusto

6. ¿Qué forma gramática usó el segundo hablador para describir los pasos para llegar al correo?

a. El imperativo
b. El se impersonal
c. El futuro próximo
d. Los infinitivos como mandatos

Refer to the following for questions 7–12:

Quiero compartir con ustedes cuatro pasos simples para asegurar la seguridad alimentaria en su hogar.

1. Limpiar

- Lávese las manos con agua tibia y jabón por lo menos durante 20 segundos. Hágalo antes y después de tocar algún alimento.
- Lave las planchas para cortar, los platos, tenedores, cucharas, cuchillos y los mesones de la cocina con agua caliente y jabón.
- Enjuague las frutas y las verduras.

2. Separar (Mantener aparte)

Mantenga los alimentos crudos separados por tipo. Los gérmenes pueden pasar de un alimento a otro.

- Mantenga la carne, pollo, pescado, mariscos y huevos separados de otros alimentos. Hágalo en el carrito de la compra, en las bolsas y en la refrigeradora.
- No vuelva a utilizar los adobos que utilizó para marinar alimentos crudos, a menos que los hierva primero.
- Utilice una plancha o un plato especial para cortar solamente alimentos crudos.

3. Cocinar

Los alimentos tienen que calentarse y mantenerse calientes, porque el calor mata los gérmenes.

- Cocine a temperaturas seguras: - Carne de res, cerdo, cordero 160 °F- Pescado 145 °F- Carnes molidas de res, cerdo, cordero 160 °F- y de pavo, pollo, pato 165 °F
- Utilice un termómetro especial para alimentos que le permita asegurarse que el alimento no está crudo. No siempre es posible saberlo solamente con mirarlo

4. Refrigerar

- Ponga los alimentos en la refrigeradora o el congelador dentro de las dos horas siguientes a la cocción o la compra. Si la temperatura exterior es de 90 grados o más, no deje pasar más de una hora sin refrigerar los alimentos.
- Nunca descongele los alimentos sacándolos de la refrigeradora. Para hacerlo:- Déjelos en la refrigeradora- Sumérjalos en agua fría- Colóquelos en el horno de microondas
- Para marinar los alimentos manténgalos en la refrigeradora.

Si siguen estos pasos, guardará a su familia de muchas enfermedades causadas por los alimentos.

https://www.fda.gov/media/120101/download

Practice Audio: Listening Sample
Visit mometrix.com/academy and enter Code: 100323

7. ¿Qué es el propósito de este pasaje?

a. Debatir
b. Educar
c. Persuadir
d. Entretener

8. Según el pasaje, ¿cuál de las siguientes NO es un paso importante para evitar enfermedades causadas por los alimentos?

a. Refrigerar
b. Limpiar
c. Esperar
d. Cocinar

9. Según el pasaje, ¿cómo se debe tratar la carne cruda?

a. Lavarla con agua tibia
b. Cocinarla hasta que alcance cierto temperatura
c. Guardarla en una bolsa
d. No marinarla

10. Cuando le aconseja al escuchador que "separe", ¿qué intención tiene el hablador?

a. La separación ritual de comidas para propósitos religiosos
b. La separación del trabajo de la cocina y el resto de la casa
c. La separación de las comidas frías y las comidas calientes
d. La separación de diferentes tipos de comidas que llevan diferentes gérmenes

11. En el contexto, ¿qué es un antónimo para la palabra "crudo"?

a. educado
b. refinado
c. cocido
d. duro

12. ¿En cuál manera se expresa que el pasaje se puede considerar una lista?

a. El uso de números ordinales
b. El uso repetitivo de una forma verbal
c. El uso de frases de cohesión
d. El uso de oraciones muy cortas

Refer to the following for questions 13–18:

Como padre, usted tiene un interés especial en la educación de su hijo. Al involucrarse cada vez más en la misma, puede usar en su casa algunos de los siguientes consejos:

Aliente a su hijo a leer.

Entre todo lo que puede hacer para ayudar a su hijo a triunfar en la escuela, esto es lo más importante. Lea con su hijo desde la infancia, y encárguese de que cuente con mucho material de lectura en la casa.

Hable con su hijo.

El hablar y escuchar son componentes importantes del éxito de los niños en la escuela. Al contar con muchas oportunidades para usar y oír el lenguaje hablado, los niños tienen una gran ventaja, adquieren la capacidad lingüística necesaria para obtener buenos resultados en la escuela.

Controle la tarea escolar, y la cantidad de tiempo que los niños pasan viendo la televisión, jugando a los videojuegos, y usando el Internet.

Ayude a su hijo a organizarse y establezca un lugar tranquilo en el hogar para estudiar. Limite la cantidad de tiempo que su hijo pasa mirando la televisión, navegando el Internet, y jugando con los videojuegos. Ayude a su hijo a aprender a usar el Internet de manera apropiada y eficaz.

Promueva la responsabilidad y el trabajo independiente en su hijo.

Aclare para su hijo que tiene que asumir responsabilidad por sus acciones tanto en la casa como en la escuela.

Promueva el aprendizaje activo.

Escuche las ideas de su hijo y reaccione a ellas. El aprendizaje activo también puede ocurrir cuando su hijo practica los deportes, actúa en una obra teatral de la escuela, toca un instrumento musical, o visita los museos y las librerías.

Practice Audio: Listening Sample
Visit mometrix.com/academy and enter Code: 100324

https://www2.ed.gov/espanol/parents/academic/escuela/brochure.pdf

13. ¿A quiénes se dirige este pasaje?

a. Padres
b. Maestros
c. Oficiales del gobierno
d. Estudiantes

14. Según el pasaje, ¿qué es la cosa más importante que los padres pueden hacer para ayudar a sus hijos experimentar éxito en la escuela?

a. Limitar las horas que gastan navegando el Internet
b. Llevarlos a actividades fuera de la escuela y la casa
c. Leer con ellos
d. Conversar con ellos

15. Según el pasaje, ¿por qué es importante hablar con sus hijos?

a. Para saber que están pensando
b. Para fomentar una relación cariñosa
c. Para enseñarles lo que ustedes ya lo aprendieron
d. Para darles muchas oportunidades escuchar y hablar

16. ¿Cuál de las siguientes carece de apoyo en el pasaje?

a. Leer aun con infantes lleva beneficios para ellos
b. Es importante usar el idioma de la escuela en casa con sus hijos de edad escolar
c. Hay que ensenar a los niños como usar el Internet en una manera provechosa
d. Los niños pueden aprender tanto fuera de la escuela como en la escuela

17. ¿Cuál conclusión representa mejor las ideas presentadas en este pasaje?

a. Los hijos reciben beneficio cuando sus padres se involucran en su aprendizaje
b. Los padres pueden apoyar mejor a sus hijos si ellos mismo recibieron una educación.
c. Los niños no deben usar el Internet sin la supervisión de los adultos
d. Es importante que los jóvenes se involucran en actividades extracurriculares.

18. ¿Cuál de las siguientes palabras o frases se usa como sinónimos en el pasaje?

a. ventajas, acciones
b. triunfar, obtener buenos resultados
c. encárguese, promueva
d. aprendizaje, lenguaje

Refer to the following for questions 19–24:

Lo siguiente es un mensaje de Las Abuelas de Plaza de Mayo, un grupo de mujeres cuyos hijos e hijas "desaparecieron" durante la dictadura militar en Argentina entre los años 1976-1983.

No te quedes con la duda.

Porque hay historias truncas...
Porque hay historias silenciadas...
Porque hay historias plagadas de mentiras...

Porque hay Abuelas sin nietos, que tejen desde hace 23 anos...
Porque entre nosotros existen jóvenes con la identidad robada...

Y, fundamentalmente porque esto nos define como sociedad.

Mientras haya una sola persona en estas condiciones, se pone en duda la identidad de todos.

Han pasado 23 años desde que un grupo de Abuelas se reunió por primera vez para buscar a nuestros nietos: niños desaparecidos o nacidos en cautiverio, víctimas del terrorismo de Estado.

Cumplir 23 años es una buena excusa para que sigamos abriendo las puertas de nuestra casa, para que todos aquellos que no conozcan a estas Abuelas se arrimen y respiren su amor, su cotidianeidad, su realidad.

Cumplir 23 años es una buena oportunidad para celebrar con los amigos el camino recorrido.

Cumplir 23 años es un momento ideal para demostrarnos que nada es en vano, que debemos seguir encontrándonos...que ese es el verdadero sentido de la vida.

Una sociedad necesita definir su identidad.

Construirla es un compromiso de todo.

Podemos dudar de muchas cosas, pero no debe quedar ningún hombre con la duda de si es bueno o malo decirle a un joven quienes fueron sus padres y abuelos biológicos.

Practice Audio: Listening Sample
Visit mometrix.com/academy and enter Code: 100325

https://commons.wikimedia.org/wiki/File:Mensuario_Abuelas_de_Plaza_de_Mayo,_diciembre_de_2000.jpg

19. Según su conocimiento cultural, ¿cuál de las siguientes representa el fondo de este anuncio?

a. La primera elección de Juan Perón en Argentina
b. El exilio de Juan Perón de Argentina
c. La junta militar que sucedió a Juan Perón en Argentina
d. La presidencia de Raúl Alfonsín en Argentina

20. En este pasaje, ¿a qué refiere "la duda"?

a. No saber que ocurrió a los hijos desaparecidos
b. No saber quién es su familia biológica
c. No saber lo que el gobierno hará
d. No saber si encontrarán a su familia biológica.

21. ¿Qué es el propósito de este anuncio?

a. Informar
b. Entretener
c. Presentar dos puntos de vista
d. Persuadir

22. ¿El grupo que publicó este pasaje estarían de acuerdo con cuál de las siguientes?

a. Lo que ocurrió a sus hijos y nietos afecta a todo el país, no solo a ellas.
b. Nunca van a encontrar a todos sus nietos.
c. El gobierno tiene que tomar responsabilidad para sus acciones
d. Los nietos adoptados han sufrido mucho.

23. ¿Cuál es el mejor sinónimo para la palabra *desaparecidos* en el contexto de este pasaje?

a. perdidos
b. ocultados
c. secuestrados
d. ausentes

24. ¿Cuál de los siguientes recursos literarias usa el anuncio?

a. la aliteración
b. la onomatopeya
c. la repetición
d. el símil

Refer to the following for questions 25–30:

Transcript:

Cada persona reacciona de manera diferente ante situaciones estresantes como la pandemia de COVID-19. Este puede ser un momento de emociones fuertes tanto para los adultos como para los niños. Puede que Ud. se sienta ansioso, enojado, triste, o abrumado.

Encuentre formas de reducir el estrés por Ud. y por sus seres queridos

Infórmese sobre los signos comunes del estrés como cambios en los patrones de sueño o de alimentación. Dificultad para concentrarse. Empeoramiento de los problemas de salud crónicos y aumento en el consumo de alcohol, tabaco, u otras drogas.

De tanto en tanto, no preste atención a las noticias, incluidos los medios sociales. Cuide su cuerpo. Respire profundamente. Haga ejercicios de estiramiento o medite. Trate de comer alimentos saludables y comidas bien balanceadas. Hacer ejercicio con regularidad, dormir lo suficiente y evitar el alcohol y las drogas. Dedique tiempo para relajarse. Trate de hacer otras actividades que disfrute. Conéctese con otras personas por medio de mensajes de texto o correo electrónico. Comparta sus preocupaciones y lo que siente con personas de confianza.

Si Ud. o una persona conocida tienen afecciones de salud mental preexistentes, continúen con el tratamiento y estén atentos a los síntomas nuevos y a los que empeoran. Comuníquese con un proveedor de atención medica si tiene alguna preocupación o si el estrés interfiere en sus actividades diarias por varios días seguidos. Si Ud. o un ser querido se siente abrumado por emociones como tristeza, de presión, o ansiedad, busque apoyo llamando a 1-800-985-5990 o envíe un mensaje de texto al 66746 que diga "Háblanos. Obtenga más información sobre el COVID-19 en cdc.gov/coronavirus-es y coronavirus.gov

Practice Audio: Listening Sample
Visit mometrix.com/academy and enter Code: 100343

25. ¿Quién publicó este mensaje?

a. una agencia del gobierno
b. un grupo religioso
c. una oficina medical
d. una organización escolar

26. ¿Cuál de las siguientes carece de apoyo en el pasaje?

a. La situación actual puede aumentar los niveles de estrés.
b. Los niños no sufren de estrés como los adultos.
c. Un individuo puede bajar su nivel de estrés.
d. Hay recursos para los que sufren el estrés.

27. Según el pasaje, ¿cuál de las siguientes puede reducir el estrés?

a. Pasar tiempo leyendo las noticias
b. Comer su comida favorita
c. Guardar silencio
d. Hacer ejercicios

28. ¿Cuál de las siguientes sería buen título para este mensaje?

a. Como reconocer y reducir el estrés
b. El estrés y la ansiedad: problemas grandes para la sociedad
c. Como ayudar a gente con afecciones de salud mental
d. Hablemos de COVID-19

29. Según el mensaje, ¿cuál de las siguientes NO es un signo común del estrés?

a. Un cambio en cuándo o cuánto uno come
b. No poder enfocarse
c. Pasar tiempo mandando mensajes de texto
d. Síntomas físicas

30. Basándose en el contexto del mensaje, ¿qué quiere decir la frase "seres queridos"?

a. Actividades que disfruta
b. Personas a quienes le ama
c. Cosas que le ayuda a relajar
d. Oportunidades raras

Reading Comprehension

Refer to the following for questions 1–8:

Excerpt from Vuelva Usted Mañana (Mariano José De Larra, 1833)

Intro: Monsieur Sans-délai vino de Paris a Madrid para resolver un asunto familiar. Pidió la ayuda del narrador.

-Mirad -le dije-, monsieur Sans-délai -que así se llamaba-; vos venís decidido a pasar quince días, y a solventar en ellos vuestros asuntos.

-Ciertamente -me contestó-. Quince días, y es mucho. Mañana por la mañana buscamos un genealogista para mis asuntos de familia; por la tarde revuelve sus libros, busca mis ascendientes, y por la noche ya sé quién soy. En cuanto a mis reclamaciones, pasado mañana las presento fundadas en los datos que aquél me dé, legalizadas en debida forma; y como será una cosa clara y de justicia innegable (pues sólo en este caso haré valer mis derechos), al tercer día se juzga el caso y soy dueño de lo mío. En cuanto a mis especulaciones, en que pienso invertir mis caudales, al cuarto día ya habré presentado mis proposiciones. Serán buenas o malas, y admitidas o desechadas en el acto, y son cinco días; en el sexto, séptimo y octavo, veo lo que hay que ver en Madrid; descanso el noveno; el décimo tomo mi asiento en la diligencia, si no me conviene estar más tiempo aquí, y me vuelvo a mi casa; aún me sobran de los quince cinco días.

Al llegar aquí monsieur Sans-délai traté de reprimir una carcajada que me andaba retozando ya hacía rato en el cuerpo, y si mi educación logró sofocar mi inoportuna jovialidad, no fue bastante a impedir que se asomase a mis labios una suave sonrisa de asombro y de lástima que sus planes ejecutivos me sacaban al rostro mal de mi grado.

-Permitidme, monsieur Sans-délai -le dije entre socarrón y formal-, permitidme que os convide a comer para el día en que llevéis quince meses de estancia en Madrid.

-¿Cómo?

-Dentro de quince meses estáis aquí todavía.

-¿Os burláis?

-No por cierto.

-¿No me podré marchar cuando quiera? ¡Cierto que la idea es graciosa!

-Sabed que no estáis en vuestro país activo y trabajador.

-¡Oh!, los españoles que han viajado por el extranjero han adquirido la costumbre de hablar mal siempre de su país por hacerse superiores a sus compatriotas.

-Os aseguro que en los quince días con que contáis, no habréis podido hablar siquiera a una sola de las personas cuya cooperación necesitáis.

-¡Hipérboles! Yo les comunicaré a todos mi actividad.

-Todos os comunicarán su inercia.

Conocí que no estaba el señor de Sans-délai muy dispuesto a dejarse convencer sino por la experiencia, y callé por entonces, bien seguro de que no tardarían mucho los hechos en hablar por mí.

Amaneció el día siguiente, y salimos entrambos a buscar un genealogista, lo cual sólo se pudo hacer preguntando de amigo en amigo y de conocido en conocido: encontrámosle por fin, y el buen señor, aturdido de ver nuestra precipitación, declaró francamente que necesitaba tomarse algún tiempo; instósele, y por mucho favor nos dijo definitivamente que nos diéramos una vuelta por allí dentro de unos días. Sonreíme y marchámonos. Pasaron tres días; fuimos.

-Vuelva usted mañana -nos respondió la criada-, porque el señor no se ha levantado todavía.

-Vuelva usted mañana -nos dijo al siguiente día-, porque el amo acaba de salir.

-Vuelva usted mañana -nos respondió al otro-, porque el amo está durmiendo la siesta.

-Vuelva usted mañana -nos respondió el lunes siguiente-, porque hoy ha ido a los toros.

-¿Qué día, a qué hora se ve a un español? Vímosle por fin, y «Vuelva usted mañana -nos dijo-, porque se me ha olvidado. Vuelva usted mañana, porque no está en limpio».

A los quince días ya estuvo...

1. ¿Qué sección en la narración muestra mejor el simbolismo del nombre *monsieur Sans-délai*?

a. ...aún me sobran de los quince cinco días.
b. Dentro de quince meses estáis aquí todavía.
c. -Vuelva usted mañana -nos respondió el lunes siguiente-...
d. A los quince días ya estuvo...

2. ¿Qué planes tiene Sans-délai después de resolver sus asuntos en España?

a. Regresar inmediatamente a casa
b. Visitar los sitios turísticos en Madrid
c. Tomar una siesta
d. Cenar con el narrador

3. Infiriendo del texto, ¿qué es el asunto que Sans-délai tiene que resolver?

a. Ha sido acusado de cometer un crimen y necesita restituir su buen nombre
b. Quiere encontrar un miembro de su familia que nunca ha conocido
c. Realiza una investigación porque está escribiendo un resumen de la vida cotidiana en España
d. Cree que ha recibido una herencia y tiene ganas de reclamarla

4. En el contexto, ¿cuál de las siguientes es el mejor sinónimo para la palabra *carcajada*?

a. tos
b. risa
c. grita
d. murmullo

5. Según el texto, ¿por qué no creyó al narrador Sans-délai?

a. Porque el narrador no presentó bien su punto de vista
b. Porque Sans-délai amaba la cultura de España
c. Porque Sans-délai prefería experimentar cosas para sí mismo
d. Porque Sans-délai salió y volvió por la mañana.

6. ¿Cuál de las siguientes *NO* se expresa como una razón que Sans-délai tiene que volver otro día a la oficina de genealogista?

a. El genealogista necesitaba más tiempo para considerar el asunto
b. El genealogista estaba tomando una siesta
c. La recepcionista ya salió
d. El genealogista fue a ver el toreo

7. Which of the following represents a grammatical form that is no longer typically used in Spanish?

a. vos venís
b. permitidme
c. nos diéramos
d. Sonreíme

8. ¿Qué sería buen resumen de la vista de la cultura española que presenta este texto?

a. La cultura española es exigente y apresurada
b. La cultura española se caracteriza por descortesía
c. La cultura española carece de una apropiada diligencia
d. La cultura española mantiene vínculos familiares fuertes

Refer to the following for questions 9–16:

La Reserva Nacional Tambopata

La Reserva Nacional Tambopata (RNTMB) está ubicada al sur del río Madre de Dios en los distritos de Tambopata e Inambari de la provincia de Tambopata, departamento de Madre de Dios; y su extensión es de 274 690.00 hectáreas. La presencia de este importante espacio natural protegido busca conservar la flora, la fauna y los procesos ecológicos de una muestra de la selva húmeda tropical. Así también, la RNT genera procesos de conservación que aseguran el uso sostenible de los recursos naturales y del paisaje.

La cuenca del río Tambopata presenta uno de los mayores índices de diversidad biológica en el mundo. La RNT se ubica en la zona media y baja de esta cuenca, vecina a la ciudad de Puerto Maldonado. Entre sus ecosistemas más comunes se encuentran los aguajales, los pantanos, los pacales y los bosques ribereños, cuyas características físicas permiten a los pobladores locales el aprovechamiento de los recursos naturales.

Se ubica además de manera contigua al Parque Nacional Bahuaja Sonene que la rodea íntegramente por el sur, formando con este una unidad de protección de alta importancia para el país. La conectividad existente con las áreas naturales protegidas del departamento (la Reserva Comunal Amarakaeri y los parques nacionales Alto Purús y Manu) y los de la vecina Bolivia, sustenta la existencia del propuesto corredor biológico Vilcabamba - Amboró.

La RNTMB alberga hábitats principalmente acuáticos que son usados como paraderos de más de 40 especies de aves migratorias transcontinentales. En la reserva nacional se protege importantes especies consideradas en vías de extinción y le ofrece al turismo un destino privilegiado para la observación de la diversidad de flora y fauna silvestre.

En la zona de amortiguamiento se encuentran las comunidades nativas de Palma Real, Sonene e Infierno pertenecientes al grupo etnolingüístico Ese' Eja; y la comunidad nativa Kotsimba del grupo etnolingüístico Puquirieri.

La temperatura media anual es de 26º C, fluctuando entre los 10º y 38º C. Las temperaturas bajas están condicionadas por vientos antárticos fríos que llegan a través de los Andes e ingresan a la cuenca del Amazonas. La presencia de vientos fríos se da con mayor intensidad en los meses de junio y julio. Las lluvias se presentan en los meses de diciembre a marzo.

9. ¿Qué es el propósito de este texto?

a. Convencerles a los lectores que visiten a un parque nacional
b. Informarles a los lectores acerca de un parque nacional
c. Persuadirles a los lectores que apoyen a un parque nacional
d. Proveer detalles logísticos a lectores que planean una visita a un parque nacional

10. Según el texto, ¿cuál es la razón más saliente para la existencia de la Reserva Nacional Tambopata?

a. Para que el mundo pueda visitar y ver la biodiversidad
b. Para asegurar la supervivencia de unos grupos indígenas
c. Para proteger a una multitud de plantas y animales
d. Para averiguar que la gente no entre en este ecosistema muy frágil

11. ¿A qué se refiere la frase *los aguajales, los pantanos, los pacales y los bosques ribereños?*

a. A una variedad de especies protegidos
b. A una variedad de hábitats específicos
c. A una variedad de naciones indígenas
d. A una variedad de condiciones de clima

12. En el contexto, ¿cuál sería el mejor sinónimo para la palabra *contigua*?

a. adyacente
b. reunida
c. junto
d. riña

13. Según el texto, ¿cuál grupo indígena habla un idioma distinto de los otros grupos que viven en la Reserva?

a. Palma Real
b. Sonene
c. Infierno
d. Kotsimba

14. ¿Cuál frase del texto apoyaría el sentimiento que la reserva provee una rara oportunidad a la gente del mundo?

a. La cuenca del río Tambopata presenta uno de los mayores índices de diversidad biológica en el mundo.
b. ...permiten a los pobladores locales el aprovechamiento de los recursos naturales.
c. ... le ofrece al turismo un destino privilegiado para la observación de la diversidad de flora y fauna silvestre.
d. En la zona de amortiguamiento se encuentran las comunidades nativas...

15. Basándose en el texto y en su conocimiento cultural, ¿dónde se ubica esta Reserva?

a. En Cuba
b. En México
c. En Venezuela
d. En Perú

16. ¿Cuál de las siguientes es un hecho que este pasaje implica?

a. La historia del colonialismo en Latinoamérica está llena de explotación de recursos naturales
b. Los ecosistemas de Latinoamérica cuentan con una extraordinaria cantidad de diversidad por causa de las formaciones geográficas en la región.
c. Las comunidades nativas faltan de un conocimiento de cómo preservar y usar los recursos naturales.
d. Las aves migratorias transcontinentales pasan el invierno en la Reserva.

Refer to the following for questions 17–23:

Fiestas Religiosas Y Ritos Políticos En Chile Colonial

La vida cotidiana en el período colonial estaba profundamente marcada por las fiestas y ritos religiosos y civiles que se sucedían a lo largo del año, los que reforzaban el sistema de creencias, organizaban a la población en torno a grupos identitarios y contribuían a reforzar la ideología oficial de la sociedad colonial.

La gran cantidad de fiestas religiosas, que en total llegaban a más de 90 al año, conformaban un nutrido calendario que llenaba la vida cotidiana de las personas y dominaba la vida social. En las fiestas religiosas cada uno de los grupos que conformaban la sociedad colonial cumplía un papel en el espectáculo público, ya sea a través de las ceremonias oficiales, cuya dirección estaba reservada a la elite, o a través del sistema de cofradías, las que identificaban visiblemente a cada uno de los sectores sociales y hacían presente su posición en el conjunto de la sociedad.

Las celebraciones públicas por el acceso al trono de un nuevo monarca, el nacimiento de un heredero real o la recepción de las autoridades coloniales llegadas a Chile formaban un segundo conjunto de fiestas, caracterizadas por el despliegue de un aparatoso ritual cívico-religioso orientado a legitimar tanto a las autoridades como a las elites locales, a la vez que reforzaban los soportes ideológicos de la monarquía. Las noticias eran anunciadas a los súbditos de las colonias americanas a través de reales cédulas, las que en muchas ocasiones llegaban con uno o más años de retraso, y en ellas se ordenaba realizar las ceremonias y demostraciones de alegría y fidelidad correspondientes. Dentro de este grupo de celebraciones, las Juras Reales tuvieron una especial importancia, puesto que eran el momento en el cual la comunidad local reafirmaba sus vínculos de fidelidad con la lejana monarquía española.

La organización y coste de las fiestas, tanto civiles como religiosas, eran responsabilidad de los Cabildos, los que destinaban gran parte de su presupuesto anual a ellas. Las festividades públicas se caracterizaban por el gran despliegue de elementos escénicos, tales como el paseo público del estandarte real, la creación de escenografías realizadas para la ocasión, procesiones, ceremonias, torneos, banquetes, obras de teatro, corridas de toro y todo tipo de regocijos populares.

El modelo que seguían las fiestas y celebraciones públicas era el de la metrópolis española y, de una manera más cercana, la corte virreinal de Lima. Sin embargo, la pobreza del país, acentuada por permanentes catástrofes, guerras y terremotos hizo que las fiestas públicas tuvieran un grado mayor de austeridad que en el caso peruano. De todas maneras, las permanentes dificultades económicas no fueron obstáculo para que los Cabildos y las demás autoridades civiles asumieran su responsabilidad de organizar y financiar el espectáculo festivo.

Tras la Independencia, las festividades reales fueron reemplazadas por otras de corte republicano y nacional. Así, se instituyó la fecha del 18 de septiembre como la principal celebración pública de Chile, en homenaje al día en que se estableció la Primera Junta de Gobierno.

http://www.memoriachilena.gob.cl/602/w3-article-626.html

17. ¿Cuál de las siguientes NO es un tipo de festival mencionado en el pasaje?

a. festivales religiosas
b. festivales reales
c. festivales de artes
d. festivales civiles

18. ¿Cuál de las siguientes resuma mejor este pasaje?

a. Las fiestas en Chile colonial representaban y mantenían las fuerzas sociales que gobernaban el país.
b. Las fiestas en Chile colonial eran diversas y daban voz a cada individuo en la sociedad.
c. Las fiestas en Chile colonial proveían una oportunidad borrar las divisiones sociales que existían.
d. Las fiestas en Chile colonial no eran muy organizadas, pero eran muy divertidas.

19. En el contexto, ¿cuál de las siguientes podría reemplazar la frase *cumplía un papel*?

a. hacia la tarea
b. leía una obra
c. completaba
d. participaba

20. Según el pasaje, ¿cuál era el intento de los festivales civiles?

a. Entretener a la comunidad
b. Fortalecer el poder del gobierno local y real
c. Recaudar fondos para las autoridades civiles
d. Fomentar el patriotismo

21. ¿Cuál de las siguientes NO era parte de las fiestas?

a. terremotos
b. torneos
c. teatro
d. toreo

22. ¿Por qué menciona el pasaje a Perú?

a. Para contrastar la importancia dado a las tradiciones indígenas en las dos colonias
b. Para mostrar que las fiestas formaban parte de la vida cotidiana en muchas colonias latinoamericanas
c. Para comparar el estado financiero de las dos colonias
d. Para demonstrar diferentes maneras en que las colonias se relacionaban a la corona española.

23. Según el pasaje, ¿cuál tipo de fiesta ya no se celebra en Chile?

a. La de Las Juras Reales, porque ya no hay monarquía en Chile
b. La de las cofradías, porque la religión ya no tiene dominancia en la sociedad
c. La de el 18 de septiembre, porque el gobierno fue reemplazado
d. La de los toros, porque ahora se considere inhumano.

Refer to the following for questions 24–30:

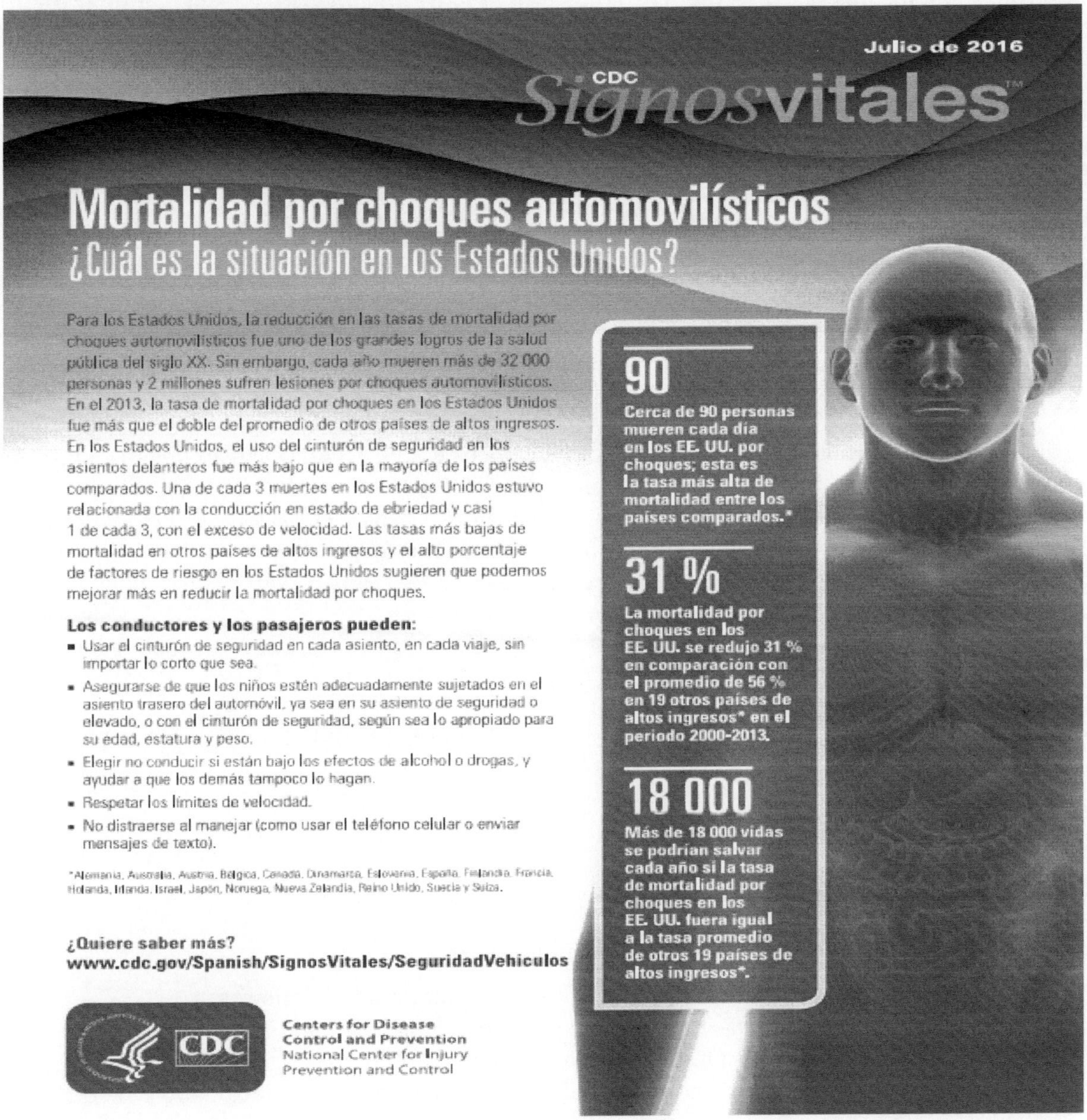

Julio de 2016

CDC Signosvitales™

Mortalidad por choques automovilísticos
¿Cuál es la situación en los Estados Unidos?

Para los Estados Unidos, la reducción en las tasas de mortalidad por choques automovilísticos fue uno de los grandes logros de la salud pública del siglo XX. Sin embargo, cada año mueren más de 32 000 personas y 2 millones sufren lesiones por choques automovilísticos. En el 2013, la tasa de mortalidad por choques en los Estados Unidos fue más que el doble del promedio de otros países de altos ingresos. En los Estados Unidos, el uso del cinturón de seguridad en los asientos delanteros fue más bajo que en la mayoría de los países comparados. Una de cada 3 muertes en los Estados Unidos estuvo relacionada con la conducción en estado de ebriedad y casi 1 de cada 3, con el exceso de velocidad. Las tasas más bajas de mortalidad en otros países de altos ingresos y el alto porcentaje de factores de riesgo en los Estados Unidos sugieren que podemos mejorar más en reducir la mortalidad por choques.

Los conductores y los pasajeros pueden:

- Usar el cinturón de seguridad en cada asiento, en cada viaje, sin importar lo corto que sea.
- Asegurarse de que los niños estén adecuadamente sujetados en el asiento trasero del automóvil, ya sea en su asiento de seguridad o elevado, o con el cinturón de seguridad, según sea lo apropiado para su edad, estatura y peso.
- Elegir no conducir si están bajo los efectos de alcohol o drogas, y ayudar a que los demás tampoco lo hagan.
- Respetar los límites de velocidad.
- No distraerse al manejar (como usar el teléfono celular o enviar mensajes de texto).

*Alemania, Australia, Austria, Bélgica, Canadá, Dinamarca, Eslovenia, España, Finlandia, Francia, Holanda, Irlanda, Israel, Japón, Noruega, Nueva Zelandia, Reino Unido, Suecia y Suiza.

¿Quiere saber más?
www.cdc.gov/Spanish/SignosVitales/SeguridadVehiculos

90
Cerca de 90 personas mueren cada día en los EE. UU. por choques; esta es la tasa más alta de mortalidad entre los países comparados.*

31 %
La mortalidad por choques en los EE. UU. se redujo 31 % en comparación con el promedio de 56 % en 19 otros países de altos ingresos* en el periodo 2000-2013.

18 000
Más de 18 000 vidas se podrían salvar cada año si la tasa de mortalidad por choques en los EE. UU. fuera igual a la tasa promedio de otros 19 países de altos ingresos*.

CDC
Centers for Disease Control and Prevention
National Center for Injury Prevention and Control

https://www.cdc.gov/spanish/signosvitales/seguridadvehiculos/index.html

24. Según este folleto, ¿qué es el significado del número 32.000?

a. Representa las vidas que se podría salvar cada año en los Estados Unidos si la gente usara los cinturones de seguridad
b. Representa los casos de conducir en estado de ebriedad cada año en los Estados Unidos
c. Representa las vidas perdidas cada año en choques de carro en los Estados Unidos
d. Representa los niños lastimados en choques de carro en los Estados Unidos cada año

25. ¿Cuáles son los dos factores mencionados que llevan consigo gran riesgo de morir en un choque de carro?

a. No llevar un cinturón de seguridad y distraerse
b. Distraerse y conducir bajo los efectos de alcohol o drogas
c. Conducir demasiado rápidamente y conducir bajo los efectos de alcohol o drogas
d. Conducir con niños en el carro y no llevar un cinturón de seguridad

26. En el contexto, ¿qué es el mejor sinónimo para la frase *altos ingresos*?

a. economías avanzadas
b. muchas entradas
c. gran número de ciudadanos
d. estados unidos

27. Según el folleto, ¿cuál de las estadísticas siguientes serían correctas?

a. La tasa de mortalidad de choques automovilísticos es .3% en otros países de altos ingresos; en los Estados Unidos, la tasa de mortalidad es .7%.
b. Otros países de altos ingresos han reducido la mortalidad de choques automovilísticos por 31%; los Estados Unidos ha reducido la mortalidad por 56%.
c. Uno de cada 3 personas en un choque de carro en los Estados Unidos muere; en otros países de altos ingresos, uno de cada 19 muere.
d. En otros países de altos ingresos, 90% de la genta usa cinturones de seguridad delanteros; en los Estados Unidos, 67% los usan.

28. Según el folleto, ¿cuál de las siguientes NO es un factor que hay que considerar para sujetar a un niño seguramente en un carro?

a. La edad del niño
b. La distancia del viaje
c. El peso de niño
d. La posición del asiento en el carro

29. ¿Por qué se menciona el folleto una lista de países?

a. Porque quiere mostrar que muchos países tienen dificultades similares
b. Porque quiere proveer más información para apoyar su argumento
c. Porque quiere que los Estados Unidos adopte leyes similares a estos países
d. Porque quiere demonstrar la dificultad de reducir la mortalidad relacionado a choques automovilísticos

30. ¿Cuál frase del texto representa mejor la tesis de la tabla con tres estadísticas a la derecha del folleto?

a. ...uno de los grandes logros de la salud público del siglo XX
b. ...sugieren que podemos mejorar más en reducir la mortalidad por choques
c. ...la tasa de mortalidad por choques en los Estados Unidos fue más que doble del promedio de otros países
d. ...ayudar a que los demás tampoco lo hagan

Cultural Knowledge and History

1. ¿*Álgebra, aldea,* y *alfombra* son ejemplos de cuál de las siguentes?

a. La morfología de la lengua Latín con sus abundantes afijos
b. La hegemonia linguística que el reino de Ferdinando e Isabella trajo a España
c. La influencia perdurable de la lengua y la cultura Arabe en España
d. La belleza de una variedad de recursos poéticos en español

2. ¿Cuáles de las siguentes escritores *NO* se considere parte del *Siglo de Oro*?

a. Gustavo Adolfo Bécquer
b. Garcilaso de la Vega
c. Miguel de Cervantes Saavedra
d. Lope Félix de Vega y Carpio

3.

https://commons.wikimedia.org/wiki/El_Tres_de_Mayo_(Goya)

¿ Cuál de las siguientes demuestra esta obra artística?

a. Un cambio en el arte español del realismo a las representaciones estilizadas de los acontecimientos históricos.
b. La influencia fuerte de la familia real que ejerció sobre los artistas espanoles en el siglo XVIII
c. El apoyo artístico para la orden social conservador del siglo XVIII
d. La autonomía del artista en escoger estilo y sujeto

4.

https://commons.wikimedia.org/wiki/File:Juan_Gris_-_Violon_et_guitare_-_Google_Art_Project.jpg

¿ Cuál de las siguentes demuestra esta obra artística?

a. el cubismo matemático de Juan Gris
b. el surrealismo de Salvador Dalí
c. el cubismo revolucionario de Pablo Picasso
d. la representación abstracta de Joan Miró

Refer to the following for questions 5–6:

Empieza el llanto
de la guitarra.
Se rompen las copas
de la madrugada.
Empieza el llanto
de la guitarra.
Es inútil callarla.
Es imposible
callarla.

5. Según sus conocimientos culturales, ¿con cuál región autónoma de España se puede relacionar este poema?

a. Galicia
b. Andalucía
c. Cataluña
d. Valencia

6. ¿En cuál época de poesía español se sitúa este poema?

a. el Siglo de Oro
b. el Neoclasicismo
c. la Generación de '98
d. la Generación de '27

7. ¿La Guerra Civil de España se describe mejor con cuál de las siguientes?

a. Un conflicto geográfico entre el sur rural y el norte urbano
b. Un conflicto religioso entre el ateísmo y la iglesia católica
c. Un conflicto político entre las vistas conservadores e izquierdistas del gobierno
d. Un conflicto étnico entre la minoridad euskera y la mayoridad castellano

8. Aunque solo una minoridad de los ciudadanos españoles practica una religión frecuentemente, ¿la gran mayoría de la población español se identifica como parte de cuál tradición religiosa?

a. el protestantismo
b. el catolicismo
c. el judaísmo
d. el islam

9.

HORARIO RESTAURANTE:
De 13:30 a 15:30 horas - De 20:30 a 23:00 horas
RESTAURANTE EL JARDÍN - PROESA. CIF A47005228 . Pza. San Miguel, 10.47003 VALLADOLID. R47.1142

https://www.hotelolid.com/events/menu-de-temporada/

Según sus conocimientos culturales, ¿a cuál practica cultural refiere esta imagen?

a. la siesta
b. la corrida
c. el ceceo
d. las tapas

10.

https://commons.wikimedia.org/wiki/File:Matador_bullfight.JPG

Según sus conocimientos culturales, ¿a cuál practica cultural refiere esta imagen?

a. el café con leche
b. un beso en la mejilla
c. la corrida de toros
d. las fallas

11. ¿Qué tiene en común Cristóbal Colón, Hernán Cortés, y Francisco Pizarro?

a. Representan la vanguardia del arte español en el siglo XVI.
b. Sus ensayos y su poesía frecuentemente tratan del tema de revolución.
c. Dirigieron los movimientos de independencia contra la regla española en Latinoamérica.
d. Exploraron y conquistaron porciones de Latinoamérica para la Corona española.

12.

https://commons.wikimedia.org/wiki/File:Busto_quetzalc%C3%B3atl_en_Teotihuac%C3%A1n.jpg

Según sus conocimientos culturales, ¿qué representa esta imagen?

a. Un antiguo deidad Azteca
b. Un semidios tradicional Maya
c. La lucha de la gente indígena en Latinoamérica
d. Un ejemplo de la ingeniería Inca

13. Cuando se compare con otras culturas precolombinas, ¿cómo se puede describir la civilización inca?

a. Conocida por emplear sacrificio humano para venerar a sus deidades
b. Caracterizada por la agricultura, la ingeniería, y una estructura social estricta
c. Principalmente una unión informal de tribus más pequeños
d. Intelectuales que dejaron un sistema de matemáticas, un calendario, y obras literarias

14. La Maya vivieron primeramente en cual región de los Américas?

a. el norte de México
b. Centroamérica
c. Las Islas del Caribe
d. Sudamérica

15. ¿Cuál de las siguientes describe mejor el papel de la iglesia católica en la colonización de Latinoamérica?

a. La iglesia católica honró las derechas y las costumbres de la gente indígena.
b. La iglesia católica tuvo como objetivo la conversión de la gente indígena al cristianismo.
c. La iglesia católica no se metió en el gobierno en las colonias latinoamericanas.
d. La iglesia católica esperó hasta que la regla colonial fue establecida firmemente antes de entrar la región.

Writing–Response to a Personal Letter

1. Instructions: Read the following email and write a fitting response. You will need to budget your time so that you can plan, write, and revise your response in the time allotted. Your response should be at least 60 words in length and must be in Spanish.

Imagine que usted es profesor(a) de español en un colegio. Ha recibido este correo electrónico de la madre de uno de sus estudiantes. Escriba su respuesta, proveyendo la información que pide.

Asunto: La calificación de Antonio
De: Mariana de la Luz
Fecha: 17 de octubre, 2020

Hola, Sr(a),

Anoche estaba viendo las notas de mi hijo Antonio en Canvas y me di cuenta de que él está sacando malas notas en tres de sus clases, incluyendo la suya. Como es un patrón, supongo que la culpa es con Antonio. Estoy mandando mensajes a Ud. y a sus otros profesores para adivinar tres cosas. En su opinión, ¿cuáles son las razones por las malas calificaciones de Antonio en su clase? ¿Hay algo que él puede hacer para recuperar la tarea que no entregó? En el futuro, ¿qué puede hacer Antonio para mejorar las calificaciones?

Gracias por su atención.

Mariana de la Luz

Writing–Opinion/Position Essay

2. Instructions: Read the topic question provided. Choose a point of view and write your response. Make sure that your essay provides supporting details/examples for your position. You will need to budget your time so that you can plan, write, and revise your response in the time allotted. Your response should be at least 120 words in length and must be in Spanish.

Muchas universidades usen la etnicidad de un candidato como parte de las decisiones de admisiones, una práctica llamada acción afirmativa. ¿Está usted de acuerdo con esta práctica?

Defienda su posición con ejemplos específicos.

Writing–Respond to a Passage

3. Instructions: Read the article provided. After reading the passage, you will answer a prompt based on the passage. Make sure that your essay provides supporting details/examples for your position found in the article. You will need to budget your time so that you can plan, write, and revise your response in the time allotted. Your response should be at least 120 words in length and must be in Spanish.

Reading selection:

Hay gran debate en el mundo educativo acerca de las tareas. ¿Son necesarias? ¿Beneficiosas? ¿Cuáles estudiantes reciben más beneficios? ¿Qué es la meta de las tareas en casa? Pero las preguntas no son sólo relacionadas a la educación...hay que pensar en la salud física y mental de los estudiantes, las otras responsabilidades de sus padres, y más.

Por muchos años hasta hoy en día, la posición oficial ha sido que 10 minutos de tarea para cada grado es suficiente – entonces un estudiante del segundo grado haría 20 minutos de tarea cada día y un estudiante en su último año de colegio haría 2 horas. Estos números tiene su fondo en investigaciones que muestran un vínculo entre tareas completadas y logros académicos - el vínculo fue más fuerte para estudiantes mayores. También considere el desarrollo mental de niños – un estudiante de 7 años no se puede enfocarse como un estudiante de 17 años.

Pero ahora unos expertos dicen que no es el tiempo que importa sino el contenido de las tareas. Las tareas deben tener un propósito claro que los estudiantes y los padres entienden. Tienen que ser conectadas al aprendizaje en clase. Además de estas consideraciones educativas, hay que preguntar si las tareas promuevan una actitud positiva hacia el aprendizaje y una vista balanceada de las necesidades de los niños. Por ejemplo, unas escuelas primarias han reemplazado tareas tradicionales con recomendaciones para las familias que los niños jueguen afuera, lean, coman cena con la familia, y duerman. Esta posición reconoce que es posible que las familias necesiten orientación para usar mejor su tiempo con los niños, pero gastar todo el tiempo sentado y haciendo problemas matemáticos no es en el mejor interés de los padres ni los hijos.

Los proponentes de tareas dicen que los estudiantes se benefician de oportunidades para reforzar el aprendizaje del día. Unos estudiantes necesitan más tiempo con la materia, y este tiempo no se encuentra durante el día escolar, se encuentra en casa. Las tareas ayudan a los estudiantes desarrollar su ética laboral y autocontrol. Y en un día donde hay gran competición para las admisiones universitarias, nadie quiere que sus estudiantes se queden atrás.

Los detractores de tareas dicen que gastar tanto tiempo en actividades académicas ignora las otras áreas de aprendizaje que son importantes para los niños – desarrollo físico (jugar afuera, participar en deportes organizados), desarrollo social (pasar tiempo con amigos, tener tiempo libre para conectar con su familia), y desarrollo emocional (investigar el mundo, perseguir un pasatiempo). Especialmente para familias con menos recursos, tener mucho que hay que completar fuera de la escuela puede poner estrés en los padres que trabajan horas no alineadas con el día escolar, o las familias que carecen de un lugar callado y seguro con todos los recursos disponibles para hacer la tarea. Dicen que lo mejor sería apoyar a los padres en apoyar el desarrollo de sus niños, no en mandar tareas cada noche.

Entonces, el debate no termina, pero hay muchas ideas en cómo podemos mejorar las tareas que los estudiantes reciben.

Writing task: Basándose en el artículo arriba, escriba un ensayo en que se resuma las razones por y contra las tareas. En sus propias palabras, dé por lo menos tres razones para cada punto de vista.

Speaking–Respond to a Passage

4. Instructions: You will be asked to complete a speaking task based on the article used in the writing section. Read the speaking task, then take 1 minute to look over the article again. You will then have 2 minutes to prepare your response and 2 minutes to record your response.

Speaking task: Imagina que usted es director de una escuela primaria. Está hablando en la primera reunión de la asociación de padres y maestros. Explique la postura de su escuela hacia la tarea y dé apoyo para sus decisiones basándose en el artículo debajo.

Reading selection:

Hay gran debate en el mundo educativo acera de las tareas. ¿Son necesarias? ¿Beneficiosas? ¿Cuáles estudiantes reciben más beneficios? ¿Qué es la meta de las tareas en casa? Pero las preguntas no son solo relacionadas a la educación...hay que pensar en la salud física y mental de los estudiantes, las otras responsabilidades de sus padres, y más.

Por muchos años hasta hoy en día, la posición oficial ha sido que 10 minutos de tarea para cada grado es suficiente – entonces un estudiante del segundo grado haría 20 minutos de tarea cada día y un estudiante en su último año de colegio haría 2 horas. Estos números tiene su fondo en investigaciones que muestran un vínculo entre tareas completadas y logros académicos - el vínculo fue más fuerte para estudiantes mayores. También considere el desarrollo mental de niños – un estudiante de 7 años no se puede enfocarse como un estudiante de 17 años.

Pero ahora unos expertos dicen que no es el tiempo que importa sino el contenido de las tareas. Las tareas deben tener un propósito claro que los estudiantes y los padres entienden. Tienen que ser conectadas al aprendizaje en clase. Además de estas consideraciones educativas, hay que preguntar si las tareas promuevan una actitud positiva hacia el aprendizaje y una vista balanceada de las necesidades de los niños. Por ejemplo, unas escuelas primarias han reemplazado tareas tradicionales con recomendaciones para las familias que los niños jueguen afuera, lean, coman cena con la familia, y duerman. Esta posición reconoce que es posible que las familias necesiten orientación para usar mejor su tiempo con los niños, pero gastar todo el tiempo sentado y haciendo problemas matemáticos no es en el mejor interés de los padres ni los hijos.

Los proponentes de tareas dicen que los estudiantes se benefician de oportunidades para reforzar el aprendizaje del día. Unos estudiantes necesitan más tiempo con la materia, y este tiempo no se encuentra durante el día escolar, se encuentra en casa. Las tareas ayudan a los estudiantes desarrollar su ética laboral y autocontrol. Y en un día donde hay gran competición para las admisiones universitarias, nadie quiere que sus estudiantes se queden atrás.

Los detractores de tareas dicen que gastar tanto tiempo en actividades académicas ignora las otras áreas de aprendizaje que son importantes para los niños – desarrollo físico (jugar afuera, participar en deportes organizados), desarrollo social (pasar tiempo con amigos, tener tiempo libre para conectar con su familia), y desarrollo emocional (investigar el mundo, perseguir un pasatiempo). Especialmente para familias con menos recursos, tener mucho que hay que completar fuera de la escuela puede poner estrés en los padres que trabajan horas no alineadas con el día escolar, o las familias que carecen de un lugar callado y seguro con todos los recursos disponibles para hacer la tarea. Dicen que lo mejor sería apoyar a los padres en apoyar el desarrollo de sus niños, no en mandar tareas cada noche.

Entonces, el debate no termina, pero hay muchas ideas en cómo podemos mejorar las tareas que los estudiantes reciben.

Speaking–Oral Presentation

5. Instructions: You will be asked to give your opinion on a topic. You will be given 15 seconds to review the prompt, then 2 minutes to prepare your response. You will then have 2 minutes to record your response.

Speaking task: Las escuelas en muchas partes del mundo experimentaron un cambio rápido al aprendizaje a distancia por causa de la pandemia global. Explique y defiende su opinión acerca del aprendizaje a la distancia.

Speaking–Conversation Topic

6. Instructions: You will take part in a conversation using the following template. Once the conversation begins, you will hear the interlocutor speak following the left side of the template. When they finish, you will hear a tone and then you will have 25 seconds to respond appropriately. Use the right side of the template as your guide.

Amigo: Le saluda y le hace una pregunta.	Usted: Salude y responda a la pregunta.
Amigo: Responde y hace otra pregunta	Usted: Responda a la pregunta.
Amigo: Le hace una pregunta.	Usted: Responda a la pregunta.
Amigo: Responde y hace otra pregunta	Usted: Responda a la pregunta
Amigo: Continúa la conversación	Usted: Responda y despídase

Amigo: !Hola! Estoy muy emocionado venir para visitarte este fin de semana. Pero estoy haciendo mi maleta y tengo unas preguntas para ti. ¿Qué tiempo hará este fin de semana?

(You have 25 seconds to record your response)

Amigo: Bueno, gracias. Me ayuda saber si debo traer mi abrigo. ¿Qué haremos el viernes por la noche?

(You have 25 seconds to record your response)

Amigo: Mmmm – parece muy divertido. Y cuando vamos al concierto el sábado, ¿qué vas a llevar?

(You have 25 seconds to record your response)

Amigo: Ah, sí. Me llevaré algo similar. ¿Y como vamos a llegar al concierto?

(You have 25 seconds to record your response)

Amigo: ¿Hay algo especial que debo saber o traer? No sé si me olvido de algo. ¡Y no puedo esperar hasta el viernes!

(You have 25 seconds to respond and say goodbye)

Answer Key and Explanations

Listening

1. C: The speakers do not know each other prior to this conversation, and both use the formal register with each other.

2. A: The first speaker is asking for directions

3. D: He states that he believes the office closes at 5

4. B: The conversation was polite but short and formal.

5. A: *A la orden* in this context is another way to express the idea "You're welcome".

6. C: He gave directions by saying "va a doblar…va a pasar.".

7. B: The speaker is seeking to educate the listeners on food safety

8. C: The speaker mentioned four steps: *Limpiar, separar, cocinar*, and *refrigerar*

9. B: The speaker shared safe cooking temperatures for various types of meats

10. D: The speaker urged the listeners to keep raw meats and eggs separate from other foods

11. C: In the context of this passage, *crudo* is used as a term that could be translated "raw".

12. B: The speaker used formal commands in almost every piece of advice listed.

13. A: This passage contains advice for parents on how to support their children's academic efforts.

14. C: The passage states that supporting reading is the most important thing parents can do for their child's scholastic success.

15. D: The passage states that children derive academic benefit from lots of practice hearing and speaking language.

16. B: The passage does not specify that parents should speak with their children in the language used at school. It merely advocates talking with your children.

17. A: This statement is the main point of the passage

18. B: *Triunfar* is used to describe a student's success in school.

19. C: It was under the military junta that the grandmothers' children "disappeared".

20. A: While choice B does have something true, that the grandmothers don't want anyone to doubt what their true identity is and seek to find their biological grandchildren, the main idea of the story deals with national uncertainty and the disappearance of their children during the dictatorship. This is what "la duda" or the doubt mentioned in the title is all about.

21. D: The announcement is intended to persuade adoptive families to talk with their children about the truth about their past.

22. A: The passage states in several ways that this is a matter that affects everyone in their country, for example "*Mientras haya una sola persona en estas condiciones, se pone en duda la identidad de todos.*"

23. C: *Desaparecidos* is used to refer to the young people arrested and killed by the government, and to their own babies born in captivity who never reappeared. It is a phrase frequently used to describe the victims of the Argentinian government in this situation.

24. C: The announcement opens with a repetition of the phrase "*Porque hay...*"

25. A: This is a public service announcement produced by a governmental agency.

26. B: The speaker states that children as well as adults can experience stress.

27. D: The passage lists exercising as one way to reduce stress.

28. A: The purpose of the message is to help the listener identify and deal with feelings of stress.

29. C: This was a suggestion for staying in touch with others.

30. B: This phrase is used to refer to individuals who you care about.

Reading Comprehension

1. A: He has plans to finish up all his business in less than 15 days and does not anticipate running into any delays.

2. B: The text reads "*y son cinco días; en el sexto, séptimo y octavo, veo lo que hay que ver en Madrid...*"

3. D: The text mentions the need to prove his ancestry, make his claims to a judge, and leave with what belongs to him, all steps for claiming an inheritance.

4. B: *carcajada* refers to a strong laugh. It is also summarized in the paragraph as *mi inoportuna jovialidad*

5. C: The text says, *no estaba el señor de Sans-délai muy dispuesto a dejarse convencer sino por la experiencia*

6. C: The receptionist explains that the genealogist has gone out, not vice-versa

7. D: *Vos* (A) and *vosotros* forms (B) are still used in some Spanish-speaking countries. *Nos diéramos* (C) is the imperfect subjunctive form of *darse*. However, adding object and reflexive pronouns on the end of preterite verb forms is no longer considered correct.

8. C: The text portrays Spanish culture as slow and even lazy, as it is impossible for Sans-délai to accomplish anything. The narrator even predicts that he will be in Spain for at least 15 months to try to claim his inheritance.

9. B: This text provides general information about a national park.

10. C: The text repeatedly mentions protecting flora, fauna, and a variety of ecosystems.

11. B: The text explains that this is a list of *sus ecosistemas más comunes.*

12. A: The text states that the reserve is surrounded to the south by national park.

13. D: The paragraph divides the native communities into two ethnolinguistic groups and only Kotsimba (D) belongs to the second group.

14. C: A does not include benefits to humans, while B and D mention only local or native communities.

15. D: The final paragraph states that the cold season is in June and July. Peru is the only answer choice below the equator where June and July would be winter. The text also mentions that Bolivia is this country's neighbor.

16. B: The passage mentions the rainforest, large rivers, and the Andes mountain range as features that effect the ecosystems present in the reserve.

17. C: While the passage states that arts were employed in celebrations, they were not the reason for the celebrations.

18. A: The passage focuses on the strong links between the festivals and the social and religious orders of the day.

19. D: *cumplir un papel* could be translated "play a part" in English in this context.

20. B: The passage states that the civil festivals were... *orientado a legitimar tanto a las autoridades como a las elites locales, a la vez que reforzaban los soportes ideológicos de la monarquía.*

21. A: Earthquakes are listed as a reason the country suffered from poverty.

22. C: The paragraph describes Chile's financial woes and how their celebrations were therefore more austere than those in Peru.

23. A: This festival celebrated the ties to the Spanish monarchy and, according the last paragraph, was replaced by a celebration of the formation of an independent Chilean government.

24. C: The text states *...cada año mueren mas que 32.000 personas...*

25. C: While most of these factors are mentioned as suggestions for driving safely, the text states that 2 out of 3 accident mortalities are due to excessive speed or driving under the influence.

26. A: An English translation for this phrase would be "high income".

27. A: The text states *En el 2013, la tasa de mortalidad por choques en los Estados Unidos fue más que doble el promedio de otros países de altos ingresos.* The article presents the statistics in B in the reverse – other countries have reduced mortality more.

28. B: The text states *...en cada viaje, sin importar lo corto que sea.*

29. B: This list represents the other 19 high-income countries to which the pamphlet repeatedly refers.

30. B: The table is presenting statistics in order to argue that the USA can do more to reduce mortality due to car accidents, since other similar countries have done better.

Cultural Knowledge and History

1. C: Many words that begin with *al-* in Spanish have their roots in Arabic. Arabic-speaking Muslims, sometimes known as the Moors, ruled portions of Spain for approximately 700 years.

2. A: Bécquer lived from 1836-1870 and is considered a Romantic-Modern poet. The *Siglo de Oro* refers to the flourishing of the arts in Spain under the reign of the Hapsburgs in the 1500s and 1600s.

3. D: Francisco Goya is the creator of this work. He was known for his move away from flattery in portraiture toward realism and for his use of art as social commentary. He suggested that this work, *el 3 de mayo 1808*, be commissioned by the provisional Spanish government to commemorate the popular uprising against the Napoleanic takeover of the Spanish monarchy.

4. A: This is an example of cubism by Juan Gris, whose cubist paintings were considered more mathematical than those of Picasso. A square and/or triangular grid is often visible in Gris' works, whereas Picasso's Cubist works are more free-form.

5. B: Guitar music and the work of Federico Garcia Lorca, who wrote this poem, are associated with the south of Spain and particularly Andalusia.

6. D: This poem, written by Federico Garcia Lorca, with its neo-folkloric nature, belongs in the Generation of '27. Its reliance on folkloric rhythms and themes does not represent classical (A) or neoclassical poetry (B). The Generation of '98 (C) was known for seeking a united representation of Spain rather than representing its diverse regions and ethnic traditions.

7. C: The Spanish Civil War was a complex conflict with coalitions of varying viewpoints on each side. However, the primary division between the two sides was their political leaning, whether conservative or leftist.

8. B: Catholicism has a long history of being the predominant religion in Spain, and up to 70% of the population still identifies as Catholic, although a much smaller number practice the religion.

9. A: In parts of Spain, a siesta, or afternoon nap, is still practiced. Many shops and restaurants close in the mid-afternoon and then reopen in the early evening.

10. C: The running of the bulls and bull fights have been a cultural practice in Spain for many years. Its popularity is in decline, as it is viewed as inhumane by many.

11. D: Cristóbal Colón, Hernán Cortés, y Francisco Pizarro are the most well-known of the "*conquistadores*", men who explored portions of the Americas and claimed them, often by force, for Spain.

12. A: This is an image of Quetzalcoatl, a well-known Aztec god, also known as the feathered serpent.

13. B: The Inca culture is known for its engineering and agriculture as well as its social order. While they used human sacrifice at times, other pre-Colombian cultures practiced this more frequently. The Mayans are the culture best known for their contributions to math and literature.

14. B: The Maya inhabited the Yucatan in modern-day Mexico, as well as portions of what is today Guatemala, Honduras, and Belize.

15. B: While the Catholic church by no means restricted themselves to religious activity in Latin America, their primary purpose and activity revolved around the conversion of the indigenous peoples to Christianity.

Writing–Response to a Personal Letter

1. ***Sample response:***

Asunto: Re: La calificación de Antonio
De: Sara Ramos
Fecha: 18 de octubre, 2020

Buenos días, Sra. de la Luz,

Gracias por ponerse en contacto conmigo para discutir la calificación de Antonio. Me alegraría charlar acerca de lo que Antonio puede hacer para experimentar más éxito en mi clase. Ud. preguntó mi opinión acerca de las razones para su nota. No puedo hablar para sus otros profesores, pero en mi clase, Antonio gasta mucho tiempo visitando con amigos y como consecuencia no cumple su tarea. Entonces la lleva a casa para completarla y nunca la entrega. Se puede resolver este problema en el futuro en dos maneras. Primero, él debe usar su tiempo en clase con más cuidado. Yo le puse en un asiento nuevo más lejos de sus amigos en la semana pasada, pero a fin de cuentas es su responsabilidad escoger a enfocarse en la tarea no importa donde se siente. Pero, si después de trabajar para todo el periodo de clase, el necesita más tiempo para completar la tarea, llevarla a casa no es un problema. Es posible que podamos ayudarle organizar mejor la carpeta para que sepa qué tarea tiene y para que no la pierda. Entonces puede encontrar su tarea, completarla, y entregarla sin problemas.

Usted también preguntó si hay algo que Antonio puede hacer para recuperar la tarea que no entregó. La política del colegio es que Antonio tiene hasta que el fin del periodo de calificación, que en este caso termina el 23 de octubre, para entregar tarea tarde. Yo tengo horas de tutoría el lunes y el jueves antes y después de la escuela y sugiero que el venga para completar lo que falta. No tenemos mucho tiempo, pero estoy seguro de que, con su mejor esfuerzo, Antonio puede hacerlo.

Otra vez quiero decirle gracias para empezar esta conversación. Si desde su punto de vista hay algo más que yo pueda hacer para apoyar a Antonio, favor de avisarme.

Sinceramente,

Sara Ramos

Criteria:

Fully addresses and completes the task – the requested information is provided in the appropriate format
Directly relates to the topic; topic well developed. All or almost all supporting details or examples are appropriate and effective – the letter contains the appropriate level of detail to answer the prompt letter thoroughly.

Response is well organized and generally coherent

- Demonstrates a mid-high or high degree of control of a variety of structures; a few grammatical errors occur with no evident patterns
- Varied vocabulary appropriate for the content and used with precision
- Very few errors in conventions of the written language (orthography: spelling, accent marks, and punctuation; sentence structure)
- Register is appropriate (accurate social and/or cultural references included)

Writing–Opinion/Position Essay

2. *Sample response:*

Aunque no sea una posición popular, yo no estoy de acuerdo con la práctica de acción afirmativa en las universidades. Acción afirmativa tiene la meta de arreglar un sistema que discrimina contra algunos individuos, pero en realidad causa tantos problemas como arregla. En vez de este sistema, sugiero que nos enfoquemos en las raíces de la desigualdad donde empiezan.

En las decisiones de admisión universitaria, hay que reconocer que el proceso entero es un proceso de discriminación. La pregunta es, ¿cuáles factores representan buena razón admitir a un estudiante y no a otro estudiante? Yo enseñé en un colegio con muchas estudiantes cuyas familias inmigraron de Asia, y para estos estudiantes fue muy difícil lograr admisión a sus universidades preferidos porque como grupo, los estudiantes asiano-americanos son muy exitosos académicamente. Sus amigos de origen latinoamericano o africano, aun hasta sus amigos de origen europeo tenían calificaciones y marcas peores, pero fueron admitidos a más universidades. Entiendo que la historia muestra que ciertos grupos han sufrido por la discriminación, pero incluso en estos grupos son individuos de países en Asia. En este caso, parece que la acción afirmativa no solo quiere resolver la discriminación histórica pero también la desigualdad de resultados actual. Decidir usar el mérito como factor en admisión hasta que un grupo muestra mucho mérito y entonces decidir penalizarles para sus logros no parece justo.

También hay la posibilidad que la acción afirmativa pone sus recipientes a desventaja. En psicología, se reconoce un fenómeno llamado "pez grande, estanque pequeño". Este fenómeno describe como una persona experimenta más éxito en una situación donde es la "pez grande" – donde se encuentra más fuerte (en los deportes) o más inteligente (en los ambientes escolares), que la mayoría de la otra gente. Pero en acción afirmativa, podemos causar que un estudiante escogido en parte por su etnicidad sea un pez pequeño en un estanque grande – se encuentra menos fuerte o menos preparado académicamente que sus compadres. Este hecho también lleva consigo la posibilidad de enforzar estereotipos para los demás, si los recipientes de acción afirmativa siempre son los "peces pequeños".

En vez de un sistema donde incluimos la etnicidad de un estudiante en las decisiones de admisión, tengo dos sugerencias. Uno es combatir los factores que sabemos que causan la desigualdad donde ocurren – en políticas del sector inmobiliario, por ejemplo. También, en vez de favorecer estudiantes por su etnicidad, podríamos usar su nivel socioeconómico como un factor en el proceso de admisiones. Esta política tendría el resultado de ayudar a los estudiantes con menos oportunidades, no importa el color de su piel o quiénes son sus padres.

Criteria:

Fully addresses and completes the task – the response clearly gives the writer's point of view as well as providing examples that support his/her point of view.

Directly relates to the topic; topic well developed. All or almost all supporting details or examples are appropriate and effective – the response does not stop with general statements but provides examples from personal experience and study.
Response is well organized and generally coherent • Demonstrates a mid-high or high degree of control of a variety of structures; a few grammatical errors occur with no evident patterns • Varied vocabulary appropriate for the content and used with precision • Very few errors in conventions of the written language (orthography: spelling, accent marks, and punctuation; sentence structure) • Register is appropriate (accurate social and/or cultural references included)

Writing–Respond to a Passage

3. ***Sample response:***

Todos tienen que hacer tareas en casa, ¿pero vale la pena? Hay muchos que dicen que sí. Para ellos, la tarea provee oportunidades importantes para los estudiantes. Cuando hacen tareas en casa, ellos están practicando las habilidades que aprendieron en la escuela. Muchos estudiantes necesitan más tiempo para fortalecer su conocimiento y las tareas les permiten trabajar en su propia manera y en su propio tiempo para reforzar su entendimiento. También, las tareas pueden ayudar a los padres saber lo que sus estudiantes aprenden en la escuela y abren la comunicación en casa acerca de la escuela. Además, es posible que los padres necesiten algo de guía para usar mejor el tiempo en casa con sus hijos. Finalmente, las tareas proveen una oportunidad para que los estudiantes aprendan el autocontrol y el ético laboral.

Pero hay otros que dicen que hay mejores maneras llegar a estas metas. Ellos dicen que especialmente en la escuela primaria, los logros alcanzados por la tarea son muy pequeños y cuestan demasiado. Según su punto de vista, el desarrollo física y emocional es tan importante que los logros académicos para los niños. Ellos sugieren no dar "tareas" tradicionales. En vez de esas, ellos sugieren una recomendación para padres e hijos que los niños jueguen afuera y pasen tiempo leyendo, hablando, y comiendo con su familia, y que se duerman a una hora buena. Así los estudiantes reciben los beneficios de conectar con sus padres, pero no tienen que sentarse y hacer trabajo escolar.

Criteria:

Fully addresses and completes the task – the response identifies at least three reasons from the article for each point of view.
Directly relates to the topic; topic well developed. All or almost all supporting details or examples are appropriate and effective. Clearly demonstrates a high degree of understanding of the content in the text – the response does not merely identify the necessary content or copy from the source text but fully integrates and reorganizes the ideas from the source text.
Response is well organized and generally coherent • Demonstrates a mid-high or high degree of control of a variety of structures; a few grammatical errors occur with no evident patterns • Varied vocabulary appropriate for the content and used with precision • Very few errors in conventions of the written language (orthography: spelling, accent marks, and punctuation; sentence structure) • Register is appropriate (accurate social and/or cultural references included)

Speaking–Respond to a Passage

4. ***Sample response:***

¡Bienvenidos! Me emociona empezar este año escolar con ustedes y con sus estudiantes. La primera cosa que quiero tratar hoy es la política de tareas aquí en la escuela primaria West.

Las investigaciones han mostrado que las tareas tradicionales, de mandar papeles con problemas matemáticas y con oraciones para copiar, no producen gran mejora académica en los estudiantes más jóvenes, como los aquí en West. Ellos todavía están aprendiendo a jugar con otros niños, a expresarse a ustedes, sus padres, y a controlarse. En la escuela tienen que controlarse mucho, ¡para 7 horas! Entonces nosotros hemos decidido no mandar tareas tradicionales a casa.

Pero, todavía queremos que ustedes sepan lo que están aprendiendo sus estudiantes y que tengan oportunidades para interactuar con sus niños en todas tópicas. Entonces, cada día, recomendamos que los estudiantes lean algo para 20 minutos. Pueden leer solos o un adulto o joven puede leer a ellos – no importa. También recomendamos que pasen una hora jugando afuera. Finalmente, cada lunes, recibirán una lista de 7 preguntas. Pueden usar estas preguntas, una cada día, para empezar conversaciones con sus niños acerca de lo que están aprendiendo en la escuela...o en el carro o a la cena o antes de dormir.

Para 5 años, ustedes han sido los primeros y los mejores maestros de sus niños. Esto no cambia. Estamos aquí para apoyar a ustedes y a sus niños en el viaje académica.

Criteria:

Criteria
Fully addresses and completes the task – the speaker plays the role requested by the prompt as well as including the requested information
Directly relates to the topic; topic well developed. All or almost all supporting details or examples are appropriate and effective. Clearly demonstrates a high degree of understanding of the content in the text – the speaker supports his/her point of view with relevant details from the text
• Demonstrates a mid-high or high degree of control of a variety of structures; a few grammatical errors occur with no evident patterns • Varied vocabulary appropriate for the content and used with precision • Well-organized, generally coherent response • Register is appropriate (accurate social and/or cultural references included) • Would demonstrate a high level of fluency • Would demonstrate very good pronunciation

Speaking–Oral Presentation

5. ***Sample answer:***

Yo entiendo que hay casos en cuando el aprendizaje a distancia fue importante para una comunidad. Pero en total, fue usado demasiado y en muchos casos tuvo mal efectos para los niños y para sus padres.

Los niños pequeños no deben pasar 8 horas por día en una computadora. Para ellos, es difícil decir que la escuela a distancia no tuvo malos efectos. Lo que ellos necesitan aprender (como leer, como interactuar con otros niños...) no se puede aprender solo en casa sentado frente de una pantalla.

Además, para esta demografía, fue necesaria que un padre se quedara en casa para estar con el niño y aun ayudarle con sus tareas. Entonces, muchas veces un padre (usualmente la madre...) tuvo que no trabajar o reducir sus horas laborales para cuidar al niño.

Los estudiantes mayores pueden usar equipo digital con menos problemas y con menos supervisión. Pero aun para este grupo, los malos efectos de no tener contacto con sus amigos y no tener la oportunidad desarrollarse socialmente fue dañino.

Y no hemos tratado de las familias que dependen a la escuela para la comida y para otros servicios sociales y médicos (como para los estudiantes con necesidades especiales). O a los niños al riesgo de abuso en sus casas. O el hecho de que las investigaciones muestran que los estudiantes aprendiendo a distancia han perdido meses de aprendizaje. No ha sido una situación buena para los estudiantes.

Criteria:

Fully addresses and completes the task – the speaker gives his/her opinion and supports it with details
Directly relates to the topic; topic well developed. All or almost all supporting details or examples are appropriate and effective– the speaker supports his/her point of view with multiple details
• Demonstrates a mid-high or high degree of control of a variety of structures; a few grammatical errors occur with no evident patterns • Varied vocabulary appropriate for the content and used with precision • Well-organized, generally coherent response • Register is appropriate (accurate social and/or cultural references included) • Would demonstrate a high level of fluency • Would demonstrate very good pronunciation

Speaking–Conversation Topic

6. Sample response:

Amigo: !Hola! Estoy muy emocionado venir para visitarte este fin de semana. Pero estoy haciendo mi maleta y tengo unas preguntas para ti. ¿Qué tiempo hará este fin de semana?

¡Hola! ¡Estoy ansiosa verte también! El tiempo para este fin de semana va a ser muy bonita – hará mucho sol, pero no mucho calor...dicen que las máximas son 75 grados y las mínimas en los 50.

Amigo: Bueno, gracias. Me ayuda saber si debo traer mi abrigo. ¿Qué haremos el viernes por la noche?

Yo pensaba ir a mi restaurante favorito...es nuevo aquí. Sirven fideos y sopas de China – ¡muy picantes y llenos de sabor! Y entonces podríamos ver una película o regresar a casa y abrir una botella de vino y charlar.

Amigo: Mmmm – parece muy divertido. Y cuando vamos al concierto el sábado, ¿qué vas a llevar?

Yo iba a llevar pantalones negros con una blusa y zapatos de tacones. Y mi chaqueta de cuero. No quiero estar incomoda, ¡pero es una ocasión especial!

Amigo: Ah, sí. Me llevaré algo similar. ¿Y cómo vamos a llegar al concierto?

Bueno, el estacionamiento es una pesadilla. ¿Qué piensas si tomamos el tren? Podríamos estacionarnos en mi pueblo y seria como media hora en tren para llegar al concierto – ¡la estación está a una cuadra de la entrada!

Amigo: ¿Hay algo especial que debo saber o traer? No sé si me olvido de algo. ¡Y no puedo esperar hasta el viernes!

Pues, el domingo voy a ir a la iglesia. Puedes venir conmigo o puedes quedarte en casa y dormir un poco más. ¡Que el viernes venga pronto! ¡Buen viaje y te veré pronto!

Criteria

Responds fully to all or almost all of the parts/prompts of the conversation
Responses relate directly to the topic and include a well-developed treatment of all or almost all the elements in the thread of the conversation – each response clearly answers the question that is asked
• Demonstrates a mid-high or high degree of control of a variety of structures; a few grammatical errors occur with no evident patterns • Varied vocabulary appropriate for the content and used with precision • Well-organized, generally coherent response • Register is appropriate (accurate social and/or cultural references included) • Would demonstrate a high level of fluency • Would demonstrate very good pronunciation

How to Overcome Test Anxiety

Just the thought of taking a test is enough to make most people a little nervous. A test is an important event that can have a long-term impact on your future, so it's important to take it seriously and it's natural to feel anxious about performing well. But just because anxiety is normal, that doesn't mean that it's helpful in test taking, or that you should simply accept it as part of your life. Anxiety can have a variety of effects. These effects can be mild, like making you feel slightly nervous, or severe, like blocking your ability to focus or remember even a simple detail.

If you experience test anxiety—whether severe or mild—it's important to know how to beat it. To discover this, first you need to understand what causes test anxiety.

Causes of Test Anxiety

While we often think of anxiety as an uncontrollable emotional state, it can actually be caused by simple, practical things. One of the most common causes of test anxiety is that a person does not feel adequately prepared for their test. This feeling can be the result of many different issues such as poor study habits or lack of organization, but the most common culprit is time management. Starting to study too late, failing to organize your study time to cover all of the material, or being distracted while you study will mean that you're not well prepared for the test. This may lead to cramming the night before, which will cause you to be physically and mentally exhausted for the test. Poor time management also contributes to feelings of stress, fear, and hopelessness as you realize you are not well prepared but don't know what to do about it.

Other times, test anxiety is not related to your preparation for the test but comes from unresolved fear. This may be a past failure on a test, or poor performance on tests in general. It may come from comparing yourself to others who seem to be performing better or from the stress of living up to expectations. Anxiety may be driven by fears of the future—how failure on this test would affect your educational and career goals. These fears are often completely irrational, but they can still negatively impact your test performance.

Elements of Test Anxiety

As mentioned earlier, test anxiety is considered to be an emotional state, but it has physical and mental components as well. Sometimes you may not even realize that you are suffering from test anxiety until you notice the physical symptoms. These can include trembling hands, rapid heartbeat, sweating, nausea, and tense muscles. Extreme anxiety may lead to fainting or vomiting. Obviously, any of these symptoms can have a negative impact on testing. It is important to recognize them as soon as they begin to occur so that you can address the problem before it damages your performance.

The mental components of test anxiety include trouble focusing and inability to remember learned information. During a test, your mind is on high alert, which can help you recall information and stay focused for an extended period of time. However, anxiety interferes with your mind's natural processes, causing you to blank out, even on the questions you know well. The strain of testing during anxiety makes it difficult to stay focused, especially on a test that may take several hours. Extreme anxiety can take a huge mental toll, making it difficult not only to recall test information but even to understand the test questions or pull your thoughts together.

Effects of Test Anxiety

Test anxiety is like a disease—if left untreated, it will get progressively worse. Anxiety leads to poor performance, and this reinforces the feelings of fear and failure, which in turn lead to poor performances on subsequent tests. It can grow from a mild nervousness to a crippling condition. If allowed to progress, test anxiety can have a big impact on your schooling, and consequently on your future.

Test anxiety can spread to other parts of your life. Anxiety on tests can become anxiety in any stressful situation, and blanking on a test can turn into panicking in a job situation. But fortunately, you don't have to let anxiety rule your testing and determine your grades. There are a number of relatively simple steps you can take to move past anxiety and function normally on a test and in the rest of life.

Physical Steps for Beating Test Anxiety

While test anxiety is a serious problem, the good news is that it can be overcome. It doesn't have to control your ability to think and remember information. While it may take time, you can begin taking steps today to beat anxiety.

Just as your first hint that you may be struggling with anxiety comes from the physical symptoms, the first step to treating it is also physical. Rest is crucial for having a clear, strong mind. If you are tired, it is much easier to give in to anxiety. But if you establish good sleep habits, your body and mind will be ready to perform optimally, without the strain of exhaustion. Additionally, sleeping well helps you to retain information better, so you're more likely to recall the answers when you see the test questions.

Getting good sleep means more than going to bed on time. It's important to allow your brain time to relax. Take study breaks from time to time so it doesn't get overworked, and don't study right before bed. Take time to rest your mind before trying to rest your body, or you may find it difficult to fall asleep.

Along with sleep, other aspects of physical health are important in preparing for a test. Good nutrition is vital for good brain function. Sugary foods and drinks may give a burst of energy but this burst is followed by a crash, both physically and emotionally. Instead, fuel your body with protein and vitamin-rich foods.

Also, drink plenty of water. Dehydration can lead to headaches and exhaustion, especially if your brain is already under stress from the rigors of the test. Particularly if your test is a long one, drink water during the breaks. And if possible, take an energy-boosting snack to eat between sections.

Along with sleep and diet, a third important part of physical health is exercise. Maintaining a steady workout schedule is helpful, but even taking 5-minute study breaks to walk can help get your blood pumping faster and clear your head. Exercise also releases endorphins, which contribute to a positive feeling and can help combat test anxiety.

When you nurture your physical health, you are also contributing to your mental health. If your body is healthy, your mind is much more likely to be healthy as well. So take time to rest, nourish your body with healthy food and water, and get moving as much as possible. Taking these physical steps will make you stronger and more able to take the mental steps necessary to overcome test anxiety.

Mental Steps for Beating Test Anxiety

Working on the mental side of test anxiety can be more challenging, but as with the physical side, there are clear steps you can take to overcome it. As mentioned earlier, test anxiety often stems from lack of preparation, so the obvious solution is to prepare for the test. Effective studying may be the most important weapon you have for beating test anxiety, but you can and should employ several other mental tools to combat fear.

First, boost your confidence by reminding yourself of past success—tests or projects that you aced. If you're putting as much effort into preparing for this test as you did for those, there's no reason you should expect to fail here. Work hard to prepare; then trust your preparation.

Second, surround yourself with encouraging people. It can be helpful to find a study group, but be sure that the people you're around will encourage a positive attitude. If you spend time with others who are anxious or cynical, this will only contribute to your own anxiety. Look for others who are motivated to study hard from a desire to succeed, not from a fear of failure.

Third, reward yourself. A test is physically and mentally tiring, even without anxiety, and it can be helpful to have something to look forward to. Plan an activity following the test, regardless of the outcome, such as going to a movie or getting ice cream.

When you are taking the test, if you find yourself beginning to feel anxious, remind yourself that you know the material. Visualize successfully completing the test. Then take a few deep, relaxing breaths and return to it. Work through the questions carefully but with confidence, knowing that you are capable of succeeding.

Developing a healthy mental approach to test taking will also aid in other areas of life. Test anxiety affects more than just the actual test—it can be damaging to your mental health and even contribute to depression. It's important to beat test anxiety before it becomes a problem for more than testing.

Study Strategy

Being prepared for the test is necessary to combat anxiety, but what does being prepared look like? You may study for hours on end and still not feel prepared. What you need is a strategy for test prep. The next few pages outline our recommended steps to help you plan out and conquer the challenge of preparation.

Step 1: Scope Out the Test

Learn everything you can about the format (multiple choice, essay, etc.) and what will be on the test. Gather any study materials, course outlines, or sample exams that may be available. Not only will this help you to prepare, but knowing what to expect can help to alleviate test anxiety.

Step 2: Map Out the Material

Look through the textbook or study guide and make note of how many chapters or sections it has. Then divide these over the time you have. For example, if a book has 15 chapters and you have five days to study, you need to cover three chapters each day. Even better, if you have the time, leave an extra day at the end for overall review after you have gone through the material in depth.

If time is limited, you may need to prioritize the material. Look through it and make note of which sections you think you already have a good grasp on, and which need review. While you are studying, skim quickly through the familiar sections and take more time on the challenging parts.

Write out your plan so you don't get lost as you go. Having a written plan also helps you feel more in control of the study, so anxiety is less likely to arise from feeling overwhelmed at the amount to cover.

Step 3: Gather Your Tools

Decide what study method works best for you. Do you prefer to highlight in the book as you study and then go back over the highlighted portions? Or do you type out notes of the important information? Or is it helpful to make flashcards that you can carry with you? Assemble the pens, index cards, highlighters, post-it notes, and any other materials you may need so you won't be distracted by getting up to find things while you study.

If you're having a hard time retaining the information or organizing your notes, experiment with different methods. For example, try color-coding by subject with colored pens, highlighters, or post-it notes. If you learn better by hearing, try recording yourself reading your notes so you can listen while in the car, working out, or simply sitting at your desk. Ask a friend to quiz you from your flashcards, or try teaching someone the material to solidify it in your mind.

Step 4: Create Your Environment

It's important to avoid distractions while you study. This includes both the obvious distractions like visitors and the subtle distractions like an uncomfortable chair (or a too-comfortable couch that makes you want to fall asleep). Set up the best study environment possible: good lighting and a comfortable work area. If background music helps you focus, you may want to turn it on, but otherwise keep the room quiet. If you are using a computer to take notes, be sure you don't have any other windows open, especially applications like social media, games, or anything else that could distract you. Silence your phone and turn off notifications. Be sure to keep water close by so you stay hydrated while you study (but avoid unhealthy drinks and snacks).

Also, take into account the best time of day to study. Are you freshest first thing in the morning? Try to set aside some time then to work through the material. Is your mind clearer in the afternoon or evening? Schedule your study session then. Another method is to study at the same time of day that you will take the test, so that your brain gets used to working on the material at that time and will be ready to focus at test time.

Step 5: Study!

Once you have done all the study preparation, it's time to settle into the actual studying. Sit down, take a few moments to settle your mind so you can focus, and begin to follow your study plan. Don't give in to distractions or let yourself procrastinate. This is your time to prepare so you'll be ready to fearlessly approach the test. Make the most of the time and stay focused.

Of course, you don't want to burn out. If you study too long you may find that you're not retaining the information very well. Take regular study breaks. For example, taking five minutes out of every hour to walk briskly, breathing deeply and swinging your arms, can help your mind stay fresh.

As you get to the end of each chapter or section, it's a good idea to do a quick review. Remind yourself of what you learned and work on any difficult parts. When you feel that you've mastered the material, move on to the next part. At the end of your study session, briefly skim through your notes again.

But while review is helpful, cramming last minute is NOT. If at all possible, work ahead so that you won't need to fit all your study into the last day. Cramming overloads your brain with more information than it can process and retain, and your tired mind may struggle to recall even previously learned information when it is overwhelmed with last-minute study. Also, the urgent nature of cramming and the stress placed on your brain contribute to anxiety. You'll be more likely to go to the test feeling unprepared and having trouble thinking clearly.

So don't cram, and don't stay up late before the test, even just to review your notes at a leisurely pace. Your brain needs rest more than it needs to go over the information again. In fact, plan to finish your studies by noon or early afternoon the day before the test. Give your brain the rest of the day to relax or focus on other things, and get a good night's sleep. Then you will be fresh for the test and better able to recall what you've studied.

Step 6: Take a Practice Test

Many courses offer sample tests, either online or in the study materials. This is an excellent resource to check whether you have mastered the material, as well as to prepare for the test format and environment.

Check the test format ahead of time: the number of questions, the type (multiple choice, free response, etc.), and the time limit. Then create a plan for working through them. For example, if you have 30 minutes to take a 60-question test, your limit is 30 seconds per question. Spend less time on the questions you know well so that you can take more time on the difficult ones.

If you have time to take several practice tests, take the first one open book, with no time limit. Work through the questions at your own pace and make sure you fully understand them. Gradually work up to taking a test under test conditions: sit at a desk with all study materials put away and set a timer. Pace yourself to make sure you finish the test with time to spare and go back to check your answers if you have time.

After each test, check your answers. On the questions you missed, be sure you understand why you missed them. Did you misread the question (tests can use tricky wording)? Did you forget the information? Or was it something you hadn't learned? Go back and study any shaky areas that the practice tests reveal.

Taking these tests not only helps with your grade, but also aids in combating test anxiety. If you're already used to the test conditions, you're less likely to worry about it, and working through tests until you're scoring well gives you a confidence boost. Go through the practice tests until you feel comfortable, and then you can go into the test knowing that you're ready for it.

Test Tips

On test day, you should be confident, knowing that you've prepared well and are ready to answer the questions. But aside from preparation, there are several test day strategies you can employ to maximize your performance.

First, as stated before, get a good night's sleep the night before the test (and for several nights before that, if possible). Go into the test with a fresh, alert mind rather than staying up late to study.

Try not to change too much about your normal routine on the day of the test. It's important to eat a nutritious breakfast, but if you normally don't eat breakfast at all, consider eating just a protein bar. If you're a coffee drinker, go ahead and have your normal coffee. Just make sure you time it so that the caffeine doesn't wear off right in the middle of your test. Avoid sugary beverages, and drink enough water to stay hydrated but not so much that you need a restroom break 10 minutes into the test. If your test isn't first thing in the morning, consider going for a walk or doing a light workout before the test to get your blood flowing.

Allow yourself enough time to get ready, and leave for the test with plenty of time to spare so you won't have the anxiety of scrambling to arrive in time. Another reason to be early is to select a good seat. It's helpful to sit away from doors and windows, which can be distracting. Find a good seat, get out your supplies, and settle your mind before the test begins.

When the test begins, start by going over the instructions carefully, even if you already know what to expect. Make sure you avoid any careless mistakes by following the directions.

Then begin working through the questions, pacing yourself as you've practiced. If you're not sure on an answer, don't spend too much time on it, and don't let it shake your confidence. Either skip it and come back later, or eliminate as many wrong answers as possible and guess among the remaining ones. Don't dwell on these questions as you continue—put them out of your mind and focus on what lies ahead.

Be sure to read all of the answer choices, even if you're sure the first one is the right answer. Sometimes you'll find a better one if you keep reading. But don't second-guess yourself if you do immediately know the answer. Your gut instinct is usually right. Don't let test anxiety rob you of the information you know.

If you have time at the end of the test (and if the test format allows), go back and review your answers. Be cautious about changing any, since your first instinct tends to be correct, but make sure you didn't misread any of the questions or accidentally mark the wrong answer choice. Look over any you skipped and make an educated guess.

At the end, leave the test feeling confident. You've done your best, so don't waste time worrying about your performance or wishing you could change anything. Instead, celebrate the successful completion of this test. And finally, use this test to learn how to deal with anxiety even better next time.

Review Video: Test Anxiety
Visit mometrix.com/academy and enter code: 100340

Important Qualification

Not all anxiety is created equal. If your test anxiety is causing major issues in your life beyond the classroom or testing center, or if you are experiencing troubling physical symptoms related to your anxiety, it may be a sign of a serious physiological or psychological condition. If this sounds like your situation, we strongly encourage you to seek professional help.

Online Resources

Due to our efforts to try to keep this book to a manageable length, we've created a link that will give you access to all of your online resources:

mometrix.com/resources719/gacespanish

It's Your Moment, Let's Celebrate It!

Share your story @mometrixtestpreparation